# LIBRARY

Gift of

## The Jane Koelges Fund

The Poetic Economies of England and Ireland,
1912–2000

# The Poetic Economies of England and Ireland, 1912–2000

Dillon Johnston
*Professor of English*
*Wake Forest University, and*
*Director*
*Wake Forest University Press*
*Winston-Salem*
*North Carolina*
*USA*

First published 2001 by
PALGRAVE
Houndmills, Basingstoke, Hampshire RG21 6XS and
175 Fifth Avenue, New York, N. Y. 10010
Companies and representatives throughout the world

PALGRAVE is the new global academic imprint of
St. Martin's Press LLC Scholarly and Reference Division and
Palgrave Publishers Ltd (formerly Macmillan Press Ltd).

ISBN 0–333–79046–4

This book is printed on paper suitable for recycling and made from fully managed and sustained forest sources.

A catalogue record for this book is available from the British Library.

Library of Congress Cataloging-in-Publication Data
Johnston, Dillon.
  The poetic economies of England and Ireland, 1912–2000 / Dillon Johnston.
    p. cm.
  Includes bibliographical references and index.
  ISBN 0–333–79046–4
  1. English poetry—20th century—History and criticism.
  2. Literature and society—England—History—20th century.
  3. Literature and society—Ireland—History—20th century.
  4. Literature publishing—England—History—20th century.
  5. Literature publishing—Ireland—History—20th century.
  6. English poetry—Irish authors—History and criticism.
  7. England—Intellectual life—20th century. 8. Ireland––Intellectual life—20th century. 9. England—Relations—Ireland.
  10. Ireland—Relations—England. I. Title.
  PR601 .J64 2001
  821'.9109358—dc21
                                                                2001021874

10   9   8   7   6   5   4   3   2   1
10   09  08  07  06  05  04  03  02  01

Printed in Great Britain by Antony Rowe Ltd, Chippenham, Wiltshire

*For Guinn Batten*
*&*
*For Mary and Jim Batten,*
*who raised her right*

# Contents

# Acknowledgments

First, I am deeply indebted to Edwin G. Wilson, my inspirational leader at Wake Forest and supporter of the Press, then my resourceful and patient partner at the Wake Forest University Press Candide Jones as well as our generous designers Richard Eckersley and Rich Hendel, and our student assistants over the years. I thank Wake Forest for Archie Grants and Reynolds Leaves, my collegues in the English Department, Jane Mead, Eric Wilson, Connie Green, but particularly Phil Kuberski, who read versions of this book in the last century, various librarians at Wake Forest's wonderful library, especially Sharon Snow in Rare Books for access to the Dolmen Archive, and literate friends on Stoots: Lee and Edith, Rick and Ken. I thank my students, especially housemates in London. I thank Seamus Heaney, Craig Raine, Jon Stallworthy, and Declan Kiberd for writing letters on my behalf; Kiberd, Dennis O'Driscoll, and Edna Longley for reading portions of this book; Nuala Ní Dhomhnaill, Eiléan Ní Chuilleanáin, and Maureen Murphy for help with the Irish language; Ray Ryan, Charmian Hearne, Tim Farmiloe, John Handford, and Eleanor Birne for help with or from Macmillan, and Paul Muldoon for advice and an advance copy of the Clarendon Lectures. I thank supporters at Washington University, especially Naomi Lebowitz, Miriam Bailin, and Fitz Smith. I am grateful to Adele Dalsimer, whose life enriched me. I thank my scattered advisors, not named above: Bill Wilson, Rand Brandes, Eileen Cahill, Tom Redshaw, David Kellogg, James Olney, Helen Emmitt, Stephen Amidon, Ian Baucom, Ciaran Carson, George Watson, Medbh McGuckian, Nigel Alderman, John Waters, Ron Schuchard, C. K. Williams, Dennis O'Driscoll, Michael Longley, Tom and Eleanor Kinsella, John Montague and Elizabeth Wassell (who laughed me out of the title *A Bearable Duty Is Borne*), Jo Miller, and my brother in the trade Peter Fallon. I thank some supreme being for my brothers, for my children wise Kathleen and acute Devin, and especially for Guinn Batten my wife to whom I dedicate this book and much more.

The author gratefully acknowledges that lines of poetry are reproduced by permission of the following individuals or publishers from the following works: R. Dardis Clarke, 21 Pleasants Street, Dublin 8 from Austin Clarke's *Collected Poems* (Lilliput Press, Wake Forest University Press); Dufour Editions, PO Box 7, Chester Springs, PA 19425 from Geoffrey Hill's *King Log* (1968); Faber & Faber Inc. from W. H. Auden's *Collected*

*Poems*, from Ted Hughes's *The Hawk in the Rain, Crow*, and *Wolfwatching*, Philip Larkin's *Collected Poems*, and Paul Muldoon's *The Annals of Chile*; The Gallery Press (Peter Fallon, editor) from Nuala Ní Dhomhnaill's *Astrakhan Cloak* (Gallery; Wake Forest University Press); Eiléan Ní Chuilleanáin's *The Brazen Serpent*; and Derek Mahon's *Collected Poems*. Seamus Heaney from 'On His Work in the English Tongue' © Seamus Heaney 2000. Jonathan Cape from Michael Longley's *The Weather in Japan*; Thomas Kinsella from 'Hen Woman' in *Collected Poems* (Oxford University Press); Paul Muldoon from his translations of Nuala Ní Dhomhnaill's *The Astrakhan Cloak*. Penguin Books Ltd from Geoffrey Hill's *Collected Poems* © Geoffrey Hill (1968, 1965); Random House, Inc. from W. H. Auden's *Collected Poems*.

I thank the special-collection librarians for correspondence, photocopying, and permission to quote from the Timothy O'Keeffe Papers, Department of Special Collections, McFarlin Library, The University of Tulsa; Special Collections, Morris Library, Southern Illinois University; Rare Books, Z. Smith Reynolds Library, Wake Forest University; Special Collections, Woodruff Library, Emory University.

Portions of this book have been revised from essays in *Gender and Sexuality in Modern Ireland*, eds Anthony Bradley and Maryann Gialanella Valiulis (Amherst: University of Massachusetts Press, 1997); *Ireland & Irish Cultural Studies*, ed. John Paul Waters; *The South Atlantic Quarterly*, 95: 1 (Winter 1996); *Irish Poetry After Joyce*, rev. edn (Syracuse, NY: Syracuse University Press, 1997); *Well Dreams: Essays on the Poetry of John Montague* (Omaha, NE: Creighton University Press, 2001).

# Preface

To the extent that poets are affiliated with the left or right bank of the Irish Sea, they inherit colonial differences which contribute to their identities, whether these identities are real or not.[1] Shaped by a colonialism that thrives on the differences it creates, English and Irish poets may be separated further by religion, original language, disposition toward their audiences, and modes of poetic discourse. However, although important and clear differences continue to divide these two traditions in the twentieth century, most Irish and English poets nevertheless have moved within the same marketplace, employing the same language, sharing many poetic models, attending each other's readings, subscribing to and publishing in the same journals, competing for the same prizes and chairs, lecturing in the same endowed forums, and submitting to some of the same editors and publishers. In certain ways, these sharings of resources and circulation of influences have constituted over most of this century a specialized regional economy in which essential goods are created at home – whether in Belfast, Dublin, or Huddersfield – and processed in and marketed from a few urban centers, rather like a colonial mercantile system. However, in the twentieth century, for the first time, poetic traffic, at least in terms of influences, has gone both ways, so that, for example, Yeats influenced especially W. H. Auden, Louis MacNeice, Vernon Watkins, Ted Hughes, Philip Larkin, and Derek Mahon, as well as other and younger poets, while Hardy influenced poets such as Edward Thomas, Auden, Patrick Kavanagh, Larkin, and Seamus Heaney. Auden, in turn, left traces on the poetry of Thomas Kinsella, Mahon, John Fuller, James Fenton, Glyn Maxwell, and Paul Muldoon, while Muldoon, in turn, has influenced Simon Armitage, Ian Duhig, Alan Jenkins, and others among the younger generation of British poets.

This mutual exchange within a poetic economy – one that emphasizes difference even as it effaces distance – only emerges in the twentieth century. In the nineteenth century, poetry in Ireland had been either still in Irish and inaccessible to the reader of English or in English and a fairly pale reflection of Romantic or Victorian poetry. As the Irish language seemed to dwindle toward extinction in the last half of that century, translations from Gaelic poetry from the eighteenth on back to the eleventh century by scholars and poets such as Standish O'Grady, Douglas

Hyde, and Augusta Gregory, infused into Irish poetry in English a new strength. Drawn from Hiberno-English diction and syntax and from subject matter, plots, and characters distinctive to Irish Gaelic literature, this resuscitation may be attributed especially to Hyde's translations, introduced in 1893, which in a recent edition of *The Love Songs of Connacht* the editor Mícháel Ó hAodha claims 'marked a turning-point in the Irish literary Revival and revealed a new source for the development of a distinctive Irish mode in verse and poetic prose' (quoted in Cronin, 135). While poetry in late Victorian and Edwardian England experienced no similar innovating infusion, it extended its own tradition of chiefly rural subjects and settings and elegiac and/or lyrical tones, even while it developed an urban anti-pastoral subgenre of poetry.

The relationship between poetry in England and Ireland that is the subject of this book can be said, then, to begin late in the nineteenth century. Over the four stages that this book charts – the 1910s, 1930s, 1960s, and 1990s – the relation between Irish poetry in English and its sources grows increasingly complex, as questions of origin, identity, and authenticity become more complicated and sophisticated. Although the twilight note and coloring in Yeats's early verse derives in part from the translations of Hyde, O'Grady, and Gregory, it also draws sufficiently on Pre-Raphaelite conventions to make it familiar, if somewhat exotic, to English Victorian readers. As the twentieth century of Irish poetry progresses – from the Hyde-influenced English of 1912, when this book opens, to the Gaelic-tinctured poetry of Austin Clarke in the 1930s, to Kinsella's skillful translation of the *Tain* and its influences and the use of a palpable Hiberno-English by Heaney and other poets in the 1960s, to the strong interrelation of Irish poetry in the two languages within this past decade – Irish poetry in English draws closer and closer to certain distinctive, ultimately untranslatable features of poetry in Irish.

Although the number of native Irish speakers shrank severely in the Victorian era, the cause of this demise, often attributed solely to the famine, also lies in the slow dampening of Irish spirit by the penal laws and by a profound sense in the Irish of economic inferiority. As the Irish language dwindled and withdrew to the isolated fringes, most Irish writers picked up English as the mother tongue, but at arm's length and with a self-consciousness about expression and audience that seems extreme in comparison to most English poets' proprietary ease with their language. The psychological consequences of a similar loss of language, in this case a shift from Romanian to French, Julia Kristeva has characterized at length:

Not to speak your mother tongue. To live in sounds, logics cut off from the nocturnal memory of the body, the bittersweet sleep of childhood. To carry within yourself a secret tomb, or like a handicapped child the language of a another time [*sic*] – treasured and useless – that fades away but never leaves you.[2]

Although Kristeva's linguistic loss may be directly comparable only to that of bilingual poets of the mid-nineteenth century, such as James Clarence Mangan, nevertheless John Montague claims, in often quoted lines from *The Rough Field*, a psychic recurrence of that earlier loss: 'To grow / a second tongue, as / harsh a humiliation; as twice to be born' (*MCP*, 37). Working self-consciously in the 'shadow' of English, the Irish poets develop multiple strategies toward their various audiences, a distinctive feature of Irish poetry which, in *Irish Poetry After Joyce*, I have called *tone*.

Questions both of *tone* and of translation attract as corollaries two other features that distinguish Irish and English poetry. First, toward the twentieth century's close both English and Irish societies grew increasingly multicultural: Britain absorbed immigrants who are mostly former colonists from India, Pakistan, the Caribbean, and South Africa, whereas Ireland is learning to accommodate refugees from Bosnia, Africa, and other distressed zones in a spirit of restitution toward those who have accommodated the Irish diaspora over the centuries. Nevertheless, compared to Europe both English and Irish societies remain relatively insular, and their poetry often registers the fact of geographical and psychological enclosure in its images of verticality, its tendency to spelunk or dig down – as into Auden's limestone caves or Heaney's bog – or to ascend. Relative to American poetry, for instance, neither poetry can 'slice a big sun at evening . . .' as Heaney says in 'Bogland.'

However, compared to English poets, modern Irish poets – whether speaking as Montague's water-carrier, Heaney's Undine, or Kinsella's Amergin – seem more compelled to return to the midden, to resettle land that has been 'camped on before,' to free Yeats's fountain and tap into a global aquifer (and thereby become more modernist as I will argue in Chapter 2) in contrast to Arnold's, and English culture's, seabound river. When we read accounts in London papers of some event in Ireland that relates to the 'mainland,' by which is meant 'Britain,' we recognize how relative advantages – the larger island, a tenfold greater population, the more global economy – can render their island a continent, within which the English poet is content to remain. On the other hand, English poetry often achieves an opposite verticality by ascending heights to achieve

Wordsworth's sublime epiphany on Mount Snowdon or the isolation of Hardy on the 'Wessex Heights' or a Miltonic overview that draws providential history or the shires of England into a meaningful integrity or unity. This perspective is pervasive enough in English poetry for Auden to extend it playfully, assuming an airman's dwarfing perspective or approaching 'frontiers,' not the wide open spaces of American literature but dangerous borders between gender identities, nation states, or states of mind. If the Irish poet assumes the shovel or sounding rod with his responsibility to disclose and translate his culture, the English poet can ascend mountains and cast the empirical eye over dominions to approach a transcendence that, nearly always, remains grounded in a practical or materialist outlook.

Perhaps through this same empirical legacy and a reaction against modernism, modern English poetry has resisted obscurity and placed a high premium on clarity. In the autumn of 1986, during a reading in the former site of the Poetry Society in Earl's Court, a red-faced auditor rose to demand of – was it? – Jon Silkin: how dare he resort to elitist obscurity in his poetry which had seemed to me bracingly clear. On the other hand, even when Irish poetry seems clear – as it almost always does in the work of such poets as Mahon, Longley, Durcan, Boland, or Murphy – it often contains keys that open different levels of access and thereby often divides the audience between those uninitiated into Irish myth or folklore and the inheritors of such traditions. For example, to understand Paul Muldoon's poems such as 'Aisling' or 'Immram,' we would have to know or learn how eighteenth-century personifications of Ireland and ancient voyage literature are oblique keys to narratives set in thoroughly postmodern society. Cloaked references to Gaelic culture or Irish history have increased in recent Irish poetry, but two kinds of unstated or suppressed references have operated in Irish poetry, story, and song since the shift into English: first, those omissions introduced to frustrate a colonial auditor and convey secrets to a primary audience, and, second, those omissions introduced into a song or story when the fuller context is lost over time or simply dropped because in a place as small as Ireland everyone knows the plot. This unstated context for the narrative song – the original occasion for the poem, the fuller narrative – Hugh Shields identifies as the traditional *údar*, the authority for the song, saying, 'Those who listen to songs know that certain things occurred which were the occasion of the songs, even if they do not know what things they were' (83). Perhaps enumerating general distinctions between poetry from England and Ireland becomes interesting only when, highly qualified, such generalizations illuminate individual poems. We acknowledge, uncomfortably, that in all societies stereotypes are sometimes fulfilled, and some of the binary distinctions of English and Irish, offered by Matthew Arnold well over a century ago, still hold in some cases, probably because both colonizer and colonist define themselves in contrast to the other. Without accepting the English charge of being *superstitious*, levelled against Catholics after the Reformation, poets in Ireland, including some Protestant poets, leave the door open to the infinite. Poets in England, on the other hand, more often will follow Hardy in reporting on the fact of spiritual longing without slipping on, what T. E. Hulme called, 'spilt religion.'

Still shaped by colonial history, the Irish poet, whether Protestant or Catholic, knows that dismissals of superstition or idolatry, on the one hand, or of materialism or literalism on the other, are closely related to poetic and linguistic questions concerning representation, metaphor and metonomy or even metamorphosis, and duplicity or sincerity in language. Although English poets may have been less self-conscious concerning the relation of religion and poetic language, the English poet Ted Hughes has recognized in his post-Reformation society a drive toward mastery: spirit over matter, mind over body, man over nature, man over woman. In 1970 he offered this Weberian critique of English Protestantism: 'The subtly apotheosized misogyny of Reformed Christianity is proportionate to the fanatic rejection of Nature, and the result has been to exile man from Mother Nature – both inner and outer nature' (*HWP*, 129). We know that Geoffrey Hill would second Hughes in this critique, but I'm tempted to say that most other English poets would follow Hardy in questioning – explicitly or ironically or even regretfully – representation of both immanence and transcendence as expressions of superstition.

In observing the relationship between English and Irish poetry over four different decades, this book will return to these distinguishing characteristics of Irish and English culture: degrees and kinds of translation, tone, spatial orientation, levels of secrecy, and the relation of body and spirit, but the focus of the study will be on individual poets and their poems within specific decades. The success of this study may be measured by the extent to which poems, especially familiar poems by major poets, can be viewed afresh when they are studied as circulating within a dynamic poetic economy.

The book opens in 1912 with a meeting in Dorchester between Thomas Hardy and representatives of the Royal Literary Society, William Butler Yeats and Henry Newbolt, three figures who will be involved fundamentally – through the institutions of publishing and literary societies, as well as through their own writing – with the alliance of poetry and culture throughout the century. This chapter advances through 1916, when the consequences of horrendous battles on the Belgian and French fronts and of the 1916 Rising in Dublin will have a profound effect on English and Irish cultures and on their poetry. The second chapter revisits the idea of culture, considers the exchange of metaphors representing culture, and recognizes the relative centrality of poetry to culture. The third chapter studies exchanges across boundaries of Irish and English poetry in the 1930s as illustrated by the famous 'tundish' passage in Joyce's *A Portrait of the Artist As A Young Man* when in the presence of a representative Englishman Stephen muses on language – its origins, its duplicity, its metaphorical dimension, and its levels of concealment and disclosure. On the basis of Joyce's paradigm, we can see that Auden's 'language of indirection,' enforced on him by his illegal, homosexual status, shares certain evasive strategies with the colonial writer's awareness of multiple audiences and the dangers of openness. By taking an extended look at publishing in the 1960s, both in Dublin and London, Chapter 4 returns to the relationship of poetry to culture before considering the association of poets with their readers. Perhaps in reaction to the anti-nuclear and anti-Vietnam movements in London, Philip Larkin and the Movement adherents of Hardy's poetry express, often wittily, their repressed sense of loss and decline. In Ireland, the rekindling of the Troubles closes off the path of political nationalism and leaves Irish poets to progress either into a neutral ground or toward a linguistically refracted cultural nationalism. Rather than ameliorating the differences between English and Irish poetry, the 1990s sees these distinctions sharpen, with the best of English poets recently dead or shrinking into satirical roles and with Irish poets winning a disproportionate number of prizes, including Heaney's Nobel Prize, Muldoon's and Heaney's ascension into the Chair of Poetry at Oxford, and Kinsella's selection for the first European Poetry Prize. The ascent of Irish poetry over the century and the relative decline of English poetry, which springs from the mysterious distribution of genius, can nevertheless be elucidated by the facts of poetry production and exchange within the economy of English and Irish poetry.

Before launching into a study of such a poetic economy, I should offer a word about my method of advancing and about certain assumptions and questions that impel this book. If we begin with the question 'What is the good of poetry?' then we can acknowledge that attempts to answer that question in this book usually concern social value and the concept of *culture*. Answers to that question might begin with a second question concerning what we would be willing to exchange for poetry.

We might speculate on the amount of money invested in individual books of poetry which, of course, might vary widely from title to title. A book for which the purchaser pays, say, £8 might have already been underwritten by charitable or governmental institutions. To arrive at the book's actual value, we would have to factor into the actual cost of the book subsidies to the publisher, underwriting of individual titles as through the Poetry Book Society's choice, which guarantees a certain number of books sold, grants to the poet or forms of employment that give him or her time to write, airing of the books in public – at readings or on radio or television – in exchange for a fee, lucrative prizes, and the selling of poetic remains (manuscripts, letters, and journals whose value accrues from the poems) for as high as six figures in sterling. We would then recognize that the value of the book increases geometrically and that this surcharge, the price beyond the £8, is borne by society at large in the often unspoken name of culture rather than directly by individual readers.

Although we might support such subsidies and value poetry's contribution to culture, ultimately the value of poetry arises from the relationship between individual readers and single poems that, paradoxically, lift us out of our individual condition through symbolic exchange: the language and verbal constructions readers share with the poet. Although we may attempt to evaluate this relationship generally, this abstraction may seem remote from the individual relationship to the literary text on which this value is based. Acknowledging this gap in our understanding, we then can only consider all aspects of a poetic economy – including such diverse aspects as the exchange between bookseller and readers, the influence of one poet on another, the making of a canon – as enlargements of or digressions from the exchange between a reader and a poem.

# List of Abbreviations

*ACP*  Auden, W. H. *Collected Poems*, ed. Edward Mendelson. London: Faber & Faber, 1976.

*ACPW*  *The Complete Prose Works of Matthew Arnold*, ed. R. H. Super. Vols III, V and IX. Ann Arbor: University of Michigan Press, 1962.

*AF&A*  Auden, W. H. *Forewords and Afterwords*. Selected by Edward Mendelson. New York: Vintage Books, 1989.

*CSP*  Clarke, Austin. *Selected Poems*, ed. Hugh Maxton. Dublin: Lilliput Press; Winston-Salem, NC: Wake Forest University Press, 1991.

*AEA*  Auden, W. H. *The English Auden: Poems, Essays, and Dramatic Writings, 1927–1939*, ed. Edward Mendelson. London: Faber & Faber, 1977.

*ESP*  Eliot, T. S. *Selected Prose of T. S. Eliot*, ed. Frank Kermode. New York: Harcourt, Brace, Jovanovich, 1975.

*HCP*  Hardy, Thomas. *The Complete Poems of Thomas Hardy*, ed. James Gibson. New Wessex Edition. London: Macmillan (now Palgrave), 1976.

*HEL*  Hardy, Florence Emily. *The Early Life of Thomas Hardy, 1840–1891*. London: Macmillan (now Palgrave), 1928.

*HL*  *The Collected Letters of Thomas Hardy*, eds Richard Little Purdy and Michael Millgate, vol. III, 1902–08, Oxford: Clarendon Press, 1982; vol. IV, 1909–1913, Oxford: Clarendon Press, 1984. (Cited as *HL* III or IV.)

*HLY*  Hardy, Florence Emily. *The Later Years of Thomas Hardy, 1892–1928*. London: Macmillan (now Palgrave), 1930.

*HN&CP*  Hill, Geoffrey. *New & Collected Poems*. Boston: Houghton, Mifflin, 1994.

*HWP*  Hughes, Ted. *Winter Pollen: Occasional Prose*, ed. William Scammell. London: Faber & Faber; New York: Farrar, Straus, Giroux, 1992.

*KCP*  Kinsella, Thomas. *Collected Poems, 1956–1994*. Oxford: Oxford University Press, 1996.

*LCP*  Larkin, Philip. *Collected Poems*, ed. with introduction by Anthony Thwaite. London: Faber & Faber/Marvell Press, 1988.

*LFC*  Leavis, F. R. *For Continuity*. Freeport, NY: Books for Libraries Press, 1968; 1933.

McCP    MacNeice, Louis. *The Collected Poems of Louis MacNeice*, ed. E. R. Dodds. London: Faber & Faber, 1966.

MCP     Montague, John. *Collected Poems*. Oldcastle: Gallery Press; Winston-Salem, NC: Wake Forest University Press, 1995.

MP      MacNeice, Louis. *Modern Poetry*. New York: Haskell House, 1969; 1938.

RW      Larkin, Philip. *Required Writing: Miscellaneous Pieces 1955–82*. London: Faber & Faber, 1983.

WC&C    Williams, Raymond. *The Country and the City*. New York: Oxford University Press, 1973.

YCL     Yeats, W. B. *Collected Letters of W. B. Yeats. Vol. III*, eds John Kelly and Ronald Schuchard. Oxford: Clarendon Press, 1994.

YCP     ——. *W. B. Yeats: The Poems*, ed. Richard J. Finneran. New York: Macmillan Publishing Co., 1983.

YE&I    ——. *Essays and Introductions*. New York: Macmillan (now Palgrave), 1961.

YL      ——. *The Letters of W. B. Yeats*, ed. Allan Wade. New York: Macmillan (now Palgrave), 1961.

YUP, 1  ——. *Uncollected Prose*, 1: First Reviews and Articles, 1886–1896, collected and edited by John P. Frayne. New York: Columbia University Press, 1970.

YUP, 2  ——. *Uncollected Prose*, 2: Reviews, Articles and other Miscellaneous Prose, 1897–1939, collected and edited by John P. Frayne and Colton Johnson. New York: Columbia University Press, 1976.

# 1
# Yeats, Hardy, and Poetic Exchange

## 1912: a June meeting in Dorchester

Those summer days in the few years leading up to August of 1914, made idyllic in British memory, are evoked by Philip Larkin in 'MCMXIV':

> And the countryside not caring:
> The place-names all hazed over
> With flowering grasses, and fields
> Shadowing Domesday lines
> Under wheat's restless silence;
>
> (*LCP*, 127)

Within such a setting on 2 June 1912 – summery if not summer – the Irish writer W. B. Yeats and the popular English poet Henry Newbolt met with Thomas Hardy on his 72nd birthday at Max Gate, his home on the edge of Dorchester, to award the aged novelist and emerging poet the gold medal of the Royal Society of Literature.

Without serious historical significance, this meeting accrues meaning nevertheless for the participants, as they approach critical crossroads in their lives, but also for this study, as these three writers come to play crucial roles in the poetic economy between Britain, or more specifically England, and Ireland. In travelling by train from London's Paddington Station to Dorchester, Yeats was fulfilling the sort of extra-mural role within the British literary establishment that usually would be ignored by his Irish biographers. In the spring of 1910, Yeats had been named as one of the 30 founding members of the English Academy of Letters, called the Academic Committee, under the aegis of the Royal Society of

1

Literature. In August he would be notified by the British Prime Minister's office that he had been awarded an annual pension of £150 which he accepted with the understanding that he remain 'free to join an Irish insurrection,' pointing out to his English friend Ethel Mannin, two decades later, that the pension came as much from Irish taxpayers as from English (*YL*, 873). Although Yeats, who had rebuffed an informal offer of the pension in the previous year, had cleared his own conscience about his political independence, this hardly weighed with Irish nationalists such as Arthur Griffith who began referring to Ireland's greatest poet as 'Pensioner Yeats.'[1]

While Yeats participated in a select jury to determine prizewinners, backing John Masefield, in one case, as the only 'man considerable enough by energy and imagination,' he envisioned the Academic Committee primarily as a lobby on behalf of artistic freedom against any form of censorship. In this cause he found, in one instance at least, Hardy his ally. Yeats attempted to galvanize the Committee, first, to oppose the suppression of a story by T. Sturge Moore, threatened by the Vigilance Committee,[2] and, later, to oppose the passage of an emerging bill, initiated by the editor of the *Spectator*, calling for more vigilance from the Home Office in suppression of what was described as 'demoralizing literature' (*YL*, 565). These causes deeply concerned not only Yeats's freedom as a writer but also his future in Ireland. In a letter to Edmund Gosse, dated 15 February 1912, Yeats points out that the arguments on behalf of this bill endorsing censorship were quoted in Ireland as if they 'represented all worthy English opinion.' The bill gave support in Ireland, Yeats asserted, to

> a violent agitation to prevent the sale of English Sunday newspapers. The pretended object is to prevent the people being demoralised by reports of divorce cases, the real object is to keep out socialistic papers... and all opinions disagreeable to the parish priest... Recent articles have been calling out quite openly for mob violence to enforce the boycott; once extend this to books and the small Irish country town will be plunged a little deeper in ignorance even than it is. (*YL*, 565–6)

Despite Yeats's growing antipathy to the Catholic Church in the 1910s and to the Catholic commercial class in Ireland, whom he saw as enemies to his art, Yeats's characteristic political opposition to England was unwavering. His political commitment to Ireland conflicted with his love for English literature and his respect for the literacy of British readers. As he wrote near the end of his life:

No people hate as we do in whom that past is always alive. . . . Then I remind myself that . . . I owe my soul to Shakespeare, to Spenser and to Blake, perhaps to William Morris, and to the English language in which I think, speak, and write. . . . My hatred tortures me with love, my love with hate. . . .                                                                      (*YE&I*, 519)

Such radical ambivalence may have been intensified by the amount of time Yeats spent in England, his English life being, in Roy Foster's phrasing, 'a parallel but invisible existence (like that of Swedenborg's ghosts) into which he could slip with ease' (433). Although we might picture Yeats's life in relation to dramatic Irish moments (forcing Maud Gonne from harm's way in the anti-Jubilee demonstrations of 1897 or facing down the rioters against the *Playboy* at the Abbey Theatre in 1907) or to his Irish homes (Merrion Square, Thoor Ballylee, Sligo), he nevertheless lived in England for a third of his life by Hugh Kenner's estimate, or half his life by Timothy Webb's more reliable guess, and he may have passed more nights in the Woburn Buildings in Bloomsbury than any other domicile. Despite his strong resistance to English coloni- alism, as Tim Webb has argued,

the inescapable irony was that economic necessity drove him to make his living as a writer in London rather than in Dublin and that he must remain dependent on English publishers, editors and reviewers until Ireland was in a position to sustain its own literature financially and intellectually.                                                              (245)

At what would be the mid-point in his career in 1912, Yeats had not yet established the publishing arrangement by which he would reach his various audiences in Ireland, Britain, and the US. As he completed individual poems, he had submitted them to various journals in London, such as the *New Statesman,* the *Nation,* and the *English Review,* to a few in the US, such as *Harper's Weekly,* and only to the occasional outlet in Ireland. Although in 1912 Yeats had not yet found a reliable American publisher for his books, his poems soon began to appear, through the intervention of Ezra Pound, in *Poetry* (Chicago). Most of his next volume – 19 of the 31 poems in *Responsibilities* (1914) – appeared to American readers at the same time as, or before, their British publication. Typically, Yeats, who could be condescending to his Irish audience, restricted Irish publication to occasional and vituperative poems: in December of 1911, he had published 'On Those Who Hated *The Playboy of the Western World*' in *The Irish Review* where one year later he also published 'At the

Abbey Theatre'; 'To A Wealthy Man...', concerning the response of 'the blind and ignorant town' to Hugh Lane's offer to Dublin of paintings, he published in January of 1913 in *The Irish Times*; and his response to the Dublin Lockout, 'September 1913,' appeared in that month, again in *The Irish Times*.

Yeats's British book publication, which has been divided among London publishers Kegan Paul, T. Fisher Unwin, Elkin Matthews, and Lawrence and Bullen, did not begin to find a single, stable home until several years after the Max Gate meeting, when Macmillan finally published *Responsibilities* with earlier poems from *The Green Helmet* in 1916. Yeats's individual poems soon could reach his international audience through various journals, and his volumes could appear first to his Irish readers initially through Maunsel and later through his sisters' fine-press Dun Emer and Cuala editions in Dublin and then to British readers through Macmillan's commercial editions in London, with eventual American publication through Macmillan's sister house in New York.

From 1902, Macmillan had also assured the continuity of Thomas Hardy's publication, from *The Dynasts* through the republication of his work in a standard Wessex edition to his last six volumes of poetry, almost his entire career as a twentieth-century poet. Hardy suffered from, and was energized by, his own form of ambivalence, between the sources of his literature in rural Dorsetshire and his urban readers and reviewers, mostly in London. Hardy's anxiety about his urban audience, which was only partly relieved by his shift from writing 'degenerate' novels to poetry and short story writing, may have been a partial cause and consequence of his growing privacy and isolation at Max Gate. To his friend Edward Clodd, who was setting off for Greece, Hardy wrote in 1906, 'I, who could go anywhere, at any time of the year, go nowhere' (*Letters*, III, 197). Although his scrupulous editing of Macmillan's Wessex edition of all of his work kept him particularly home-bound in 1912, increasingly over the past decade his estrangement from his wife Emma, which kept them apart at Max Gate, also reduced his train trips to London where social events might require her accompaniment.

The mutual animosity of the Hardys, as well as his growing shyness, help account for the strange strictures he placed on the award ceremony on his 72nd birthday. Although the Royal Society had so honored only 15 writers in its ninety-year history, Hardy asked that the medal, bearing his own sculptured profile, be awarded with 'as little ceremony as possible' (*HL*, IV, 215). Newbolt and Yeats might have puzzled out the couple's degree of estrangement when the Hardys took remote ends of a long table for lunch. While Newbolt and Hardy chatted about architecture,

Yeats engaged Emma in a meal-long discussion of cats. Although Yeats was fond enough of cats to make them the frequent topic of letters and even poems, the subject probably arose from the two fine cats crouched to the left and right of Mrs Hardy's plate. (Newbolt may have been musing over Hardy's comment the previous day in a letter that diarrhea had left him prowling the house 'as weak as a cat' (Hardy, *Letters*, IV, 218).) At the meal's close, Hardy startled his guests by asking his wife to leave the three writers alone for the private awarding of the medal. Over the protests of the other three, Hardy persisted, and Emma swept out of the room with her cat-train. Then, according to Hardy (*HEL*, 152), Newbolt 'wasted on the empty room the best speech he ever made,' praising the Wessex novels, which were to begin reappearing that year in that new special edition from Macmillan. After Yeats's 'much longer and more remarkable oration' (Newbolt, *Life*, 167), Hardy, over his guests' protests against his unnecessary formality, delivered a scripted acceptance speech because 'he had already given a copy to the reporters from London . . . and he could not . . . make the falsehood theirs instead of his' (Newbolt, *Life*, 168).

Standing awkwardly like one of the 'pale unsatisfied ones,' Yeats may have inferred a subtext in Hardy's speech. The prize had come as 'a surprise to myself' (by which Hardy may have meant that 'since *Jude the Obscure* I have suffered seventeen years of vilification'). I am 'rather an old boy to receive a medal' (first, it might have come earlier; second, I understand class-terms associated with public-school award days). Any 'incentive to the cultivation and production of pure literature is of immense value' (despite my folk idioms and taboo topics, I subscribe to the current sense of *culture* as Arnold defined it: a canon of classics, chosen by current standards as the best that has been thought and said and produced and cultivated by society for its own cohesion). The enemies of 'pure literature' are the spread of literacy without discrimination, 'slipshod writing,' and 'hurried descriptive reporting in the newspapers' especially by American and women journalists (women reviewers have failed to recognize my novels' defense of women). His actual subject, which occupied the last half of his speech, is that he himself was, fundamentally and essentially, a poet, perhaps an immortal one: 'The shortest way to good prose is by the route of good verse. . . . Poetry itself cannot die. . . .'

## Hardy's relation to audience

When Yeats heard Hardy read 'I don't quite like to say so' before a paragraph-long attack on journalism, he must have realized that neither he, who shared an antipathy to journalism, nor Newbolt was being addressed. Rather, he was party to an early made-for-media event, impossible before the age of telegraph and train. As he addressed urban journal-readers, Hardy distinguished his own poetry from the media he was skillfully manipulating. As *Poems 1912–13* indicate, Hardy knew the mail-train's timetable, and of his prepared statement, he might have exclaimed in the words of his heroine, the milk-maid Tess: 'Londoners will drink it at their breakfasts to-morrow, won't they!... Strange people that we have never seen' (215).

A digression from poetry into this scene in Chapter 29 of *Tess of the d'Urbervilles* can help us recognize Hardy's vexed relationship toward history and, ultimately, toward his audience which also pervades his poetry and which identifies him as a modern, perhaps even a Modernist, poet. Initially, this scene seems both to fulfill realistic and pre-modernist fiction's function of undercutting literary romanticism and to suggest the social and economic pressures that govern Tess and Angel in their late-night ride to meet the milk-train. References to three markedly different temporal orientations in this scene – to the past of the nearby d'Urberville mansion, to the present challenge to meet market timetables, to the future entrained by Angel's proposal of marriage and Tess's promise to answer by the ride's end – are all reduced to a cash nexus.

When Tess first discloses her descent from the d'Urbervilles, Angel regrets her derivation from 'the self-seeking few who made themselves powerful at the expense of the rest.' However, he soon exposes his confused deference to rank: 'Society is hopelessly snobbish,' he says, 'and this fact of your extraction may make an appreciable difference to its acceptance of you as my wife, after I have made you the well-read woman that I mean to make you' (217). Rather than exclaiming like Eliza Doolittle 'wouldn't it be loverly,' the reader may perceive how this note of 'self-improvement' suggests Tess's future as property: 'You belong to me already,' Angel says: 'you will be invaluable as a wife to me...' (215–16).

More significantly, Tess and Angel's exigency – getting milk to market – arises from changes Hardy witnessed in Dorsetshire over the last half of the century: enclosure drastically reduced sheep farming; a migratory workforce hampered corn production; trains, which first reached Dorset when Hardy was seven, opened up markets well beyond Dorchester for milk-consumption. Dorset dairy farming grew so rapidly between 1879 and 1906 that even from that impoverished county, 5 million gallons left by train in the latter year (M. Williams, 106). When Tess exclaims that her milk-drinkers 'don't know anything of us, and where it comes from; or think how we two drove miles across the moor to-night in the rain ...' (215), her remoteness from consumption reflects the change from a regional economy to a national and even cosmopolitan economy by which the value of Hardy's idealized tableaux of communal labor – the rain-swept drive of Tess and Angel, their handsome heads against the cows' warm flanks, Talbothey's harvest table of supping laborers – cannot be evaluated by a market price.

Hardy's birthday address in 1912 may be read in light of this scene from *Tess*. In both speech and novel, he mixes ambivalently ahistorical with material causes. After his careful analysis of economic pressures on Tess's past, present, and future, he assigns the ultimate cause in this scene to 'the "appetite for joy" ... that tremendous force which sways humanity ... as the tide sways the helpless weed. ...' (218). In concluding this scene with this Darwinian quasi-myth of universal nature and the novel, postscripturally, with his invocation of the President of the Immortals, Hardy seems tempted 'to recode, to reinvent the sacred, to go back to myth,' which, according to Frederic Jameson's definition, would enlist him as a modernist (126). Jameson follows Raymond Williams in arguing that 'mercantile division and the assigning of various functions' to separate areas within one country and, eventually, to countries across the water 'create a gap in "the daily life and existential experience of the home country. ..."' 'Such spatial disjunction has as its immediate consequence the inability to grasp the way the system functions as a whole.' Jameson goes on to argue that 'it is only that new kind of art ... which reflexively perceives ... this new and historically original problem ... and lives this formal dilemma [of manifesting a gap or disjuncture] that can be called modernism in the first place' (*WC&C*, 279; *Nationalism*, 12). I would argue that particularly this characterization of Modernism as a stylistic response to a particular kind of alienation can apply helpfully to Hardy – isolated in Max Gate from his townspeople and remote from his mostly urban audience.

In 'Wessex Heights,' dated 1896 but not published until 1914, Hardy discloses this remoteness in the autobiographical tone of the later date rather than the more varied tones of the dramatic poems of the century's end. However, in recalling his ascent of 'some heights in Wessex,' the poem's speaker characterizes what Jonathan Arac reminds us is a typical overview in Victorian novels. Because of the complex social changes of which we've been speaking, 'that made it difficult for writers to achieve a total, integral, coherent view of their worlds,' according to Arac, writers of narratives such as Wordsworth, Dickens, and Carlyle often situated their narrators at great heights to achieve a vast spatial overview which offered, at least, metaphorical comprehensiveness. Arac writes, 'For a few years, the stance of overview allowed a working distance from society, from which a writer could readily return with fresh knowledge and intervene in the world' (11). He might have recognized that the overview is frequently achieved by English poets from the Dover sonnets of the Napoleonic era down to recent poetry such as Donald Davie's nationalistic poems on the Shires. Irish poetry, especially after Yeats, more rarely ascends to this unifying perspective. Yeats's 'High Talk' and 'Circus Animals' Desertion' question stiltedness or recommend descent, as, for example, Yeats's 'The Spirit Medium' will 'bend my body to the spade / Or grope with a dirty hand' to explore the buried past.

Hardy, on the other hand, takes a theoptic or lunar view of mankind in his poetry, just as in his novels he had made the hilltop overview a recurrent feature, not for comprehensiveness but to diminish the individual against the vast landscape, as in the famous opening of *The Return of the Native*. By the late Victorian era, as Arac writes, 'A growing sense of distance shadowed the writer's relation to society, making the return more difficult' (11). Hardy seeks neither 'fresh knowledge' nor social intervention in 'Wessex Heights' but an escape from his past, a past marked by the betrayal of others and his own self-betrayal. When he descends from such heights, he feels alienated: 'Down there they are dubious and askance; there nobody thinks as I,' he says in the seventh line which maintains the formal integrity of the 15-syllable line, broken more or less evenly by a mid-line caesura. The poem interrupts this pattern in the fifteenth line, which is about discontinuity, when his former self looks at his present self and wonders what 'Can have merged him into such a strange continuator as this' (*HCP*, 319). This alienation seems particularly modern, associated with 'the tall-spired town' and trains, where the self is divided – as in the fiction of Dickens or Dostoevsky or Kafka – into the guilty, haunted, and hunted self and the stalking conscience with 'weird detective ways.'

As Hillis Miller has pointed out in a very helpful reading of this poem, the speaker in 'Wessex Heights' is actually situated in neither the heights nor the lowlands but 'in some undefined place.' He says, 'This place is the locus of the poem itself, a place which exists only in the language of poetry' (345). Although written fairly close to the time of Hardy's abandonment of fiction, the poem is much less about an escape for the alienated self into poetry – 'shaped as if by a kindly hand' where 'I seem where I was before my birth, and after death may be' – than about modern humanity's futile, utopian desire to escape our social and individual divisions.

In returning to the birthday speech at Max Gate, we recognize that whatever Hardy means by his reference to 'pure literature,' he is hardly advocating a literature of escape. In that speech he suggests that, unlike ephemeral journalism, poetry 'as pure literature' cannot die, although it can be produced and cultivated under incentive (this economic term, meaning originally 'to inspire or encourage by singing,' seems symptomatic of Hardy's ambivalence). It is possible that Hardy may merely be addressing himself to the informal charter of the Academy as proposed by Edmund Gosse in a letter to Hardy dated 13 February 1910: 'the only objects paramount were to be the preservation of the purity of the language and a high standard of style' (*YL*, 549n). Yeats must also have had in mind the Academy's objective because in a letter to Sturge Moore he interprets 'purity of language' to mean 'merely [to] uphold style as opposed to slipshod popular writing. A Writer's "purity" is his truth to his own mood' (Bridge, 21–2). Yet, if *pure* raised controversy as a description of Tess in the novel's subtitle, Hardy would certainly recognize that its application to literary production is equally problematic.

More importantly, Hardy's attack on journalism may indicate his uneasiness with his audience. Mandatory education, the mushrooming of cities, the rapidity of print and conveyance, and commercialized newspapers had changed readership as drastically as any consumership. His urban readers, who had identified themselves to Hardy principally through complaints about *Tess* and *Jude* nearly two decades earlier, must have seemed as remote and anonymous as Tess's milk-drinkers. Wanting these journal-readers to distinguish between mere journalism and literature, he concludes his birthday speech by quoting George Sand on the Goddess Poetry: 'Despite her overturned temples and the false gods adored among their ruins, she is immortal. . . .' (Poetry comes from the past, whereas 'hurried descriptive reporting in the newspaper' occupies the present.) Although Hardy's poetry, unlike that of High Modernists such as Eliot and Pound, never excludes a popular audience, he will insist on this distinction between his poetry and journalism.

Only if Hardy were a primitive poet, a vanishing class into which even Hardy's senior, the dialect poet William Barnes, does not fit, could John Lucas's characterization of Hardy – 'that Hardy is the natural poet of a community whose natural modes of utterance are song and dance' (28) – be accurate. Were Hardy unfallen from this nature, then perhaps his ideal audience, like Tess's ideal consumer, and his modernist subject, the 'something primary that he wishes to regain,' could be the same: the Stinsford choir, its hymning congregation, local storytellers, all speakers of colorful dialect, the entire Dorset oral culture. This communal culture persisted into, as it disappeared within, Hardy's early years, so that a natural longing for childhood is reinforced by a longing for a lost culture. Merryn Williams writes of Dorset, 'The county was one of the most backward in England, in the sense of being one of the poorest and least industrialised, and this partly accounts for the survival of many of the old customs and superstitions which Hardy records' (111). We know how often in his poems, with relentless retrospection, Hardy or a surrogate revenant haunts this community and projects, as Seamus Heaney said of Hardy, this 'unperturbed, reliable / ghost life he carried...' (*Station Island*, 34).

Yet, as Lucas puzzles, 'The difficulty is that Hardy never offers any explanation for *why* the past is so different from the present' (48). One cannot answer merely that this culture passed away with Hardy's youth, for which it remains an analogue. Nor have we accounted fully by stating that Hardy had necessarily to turn away from this oral culture into the writer's isolation, although his poems make much of the distinction between inscribing and intoning. Most significantly, the audience to whom Hardy would return through these poetic hauntings had disappeared, and he now faced the anonymous mass of urban readers who had been joined by migrants from Dorsetshire. The insertion of Dorset into a metropolitan market must be more wrenching for the 'natural poet of community' than for other kinds of writers (or for landowners, if not for day-laborers). Hardy's ambivalence about translating his vanishing culture into cosmopolitan literature is palpable in his writing.

When Hardy turns from his hauntings of earlier Wessex, his poems often elegize lost loves or regret accidental partings, as in this stanza:

> I learnt I had missed, by rash unheed,
>   My track; that, so the Will decided,
>   In life, death, we should be divided,
> And at the sense I ached indeed.

(*HCP*, 314)

This unclaimed opportunity was offered the poem's speaker in the form of a letter from an unknown woman, apparently a reader and admirer, whose loving words the speaker first shreds and then attempts to reconstruct, without recovering, however, her name or address. The intensity of Hardy's diction throughout 'The Torn Letter,' which seems excessive and sentimental, may reveal his need to personalize his mostly anonymous urban readership.

Hardy's anxiety concerning his intermediacy between a largely vanished rural culture, fully alive in his memory, and a living but mostly
abstract and disembodied readership finds expression in the 31 engravings
of Hardy's drawings interspersed among the loose gathering of verse,
written over the previous three decades, that formed the *Wessex Poems*
(1898). Compared to other illustrated books of verse, popular at this
time through William Morris's Kelmscott revivalist works, these drawings
are inept, so dark and dense that they sometimes seem objective and
reified rather than illustrative. On the verso facing the title page, the
reader encounters a frontispiece of a churchyard, darkened by countless
cross-grained pen-strokes, with a few lines from 'Friends Beyond,'
a poem placed toward the end of the volume. The opening of Gray's
'Elegy Written in a Country Churchyard'[3] – 'The curfew tolls the knell of
parting day' – is thickened and made palpable in Hardy's borrowing – 'At
mothy curfew-tide / They've a way of whispering to me.' The next drawing we encounter illustrates 'The Temporary the All,' a poem that opens
'Change and chancefulness in my flowering youthtime / Set me sun by
sun near to one unchosen.' The drawing of a church tower on which
a sundial's gnomon casts its shadow toward 5 p.m. – but in stages rather
than consistently dark – literalizes the poem's musings on 'Change' setting
'sun by sun.' Some of the commentaries suggested by other illustrations
are crude, as when 'Her Dilemma,' a poem in which a woman has to
declare to a dying man a love she does not feel, is followed by a drawing
of two humanoids within a vaulted church standing among tombs and
over a subfloor replete with skulls. On the other hand, 'Her Initials' is
enriched by the illustration. The brief poem tells how, when once he
had associated his beloved with a poet's 'effulgent thought,' he had
written her initials in the poet's book beside that thought. Yet,

> – When now I turn the leaf the same
> Immortal light illumes the lay,
> But from the letters of her name
> The radiance has died away!

> (*Wessex Poems*, 21)

Here, Hardy revises the ancient trope, employed by Spenser in *Amoretti*
75 or Shakespeare's Sonnet 55, in which the poet offers the beloved an
immortal encasement within the poem. The irony, of course, of all
these poems is that without name or description in such poems, the
lover's identity fades to the faintest wight's shine in poems that still

bear the poet's name. Hardy not only admits the lover's anonymity, but in the illustration – opened pages of a book of poetry – he places his own colophon, a stylized 'TH,' not within the border surrounding the book, but on the book's page where the beloved's initials might have stood. Hardy thereby exposes the poet's real ambition to 'eternize' his own desire, but he also sides with 'death and all-oblivious enmity,' even if ironically.

In his preface to *Wessex Poems*, Hardy wrote that 'the rough sketches given in illustration, which have been recently made, . . . are inserted for personal and local reasons rather than for their intrinsic qualities' (viii). Hardy might have elaborated that in their density and particularity, the illustrations remain local, objective, and material, resisting translation into universal experience or general expression. In his provocative *Black Riders* (1993), Jerome McGann has argued that

> self-conscious text production like that of Kelmscott and Bodley Head put a frame around romantic writing . . . and thereby . . . the romantic scene discloses itself as a rhetorical display: not the dialogue of the mind with itself, but the theatrical presentation of such a dialogue. (21)

By encasing poems with illustrations, the *Wessex Poems*, as the Kelmscott and Bodley Head illustrated books of the *fin de siècle* did more deliberately,[4] calls attention to itself as an object and to the poems as a product of the material condition of publication, a condition that at once separates the dead object from its living audience and preserves or, even, fetishizes it.

Hardy's interest in making his poetry into an embodiment shifts from illustrations in the *Wessex Poems* to a density of diction in that and subsequent volumes, especially manifest in regional and/or archaic diction. For example, in his third volume *Time's Laughingstocks*, for the retrospective folk subject of the sequence 'At Casterbridge Fair,' Hardy employs variations on the ballad stanza and dialect and otherwise quaint diction. In the final poem in the sequence, the second stanza reads (in imitation of intoning):

> From Clock-corner steps, as each quarter ding-dongs,
>   Away the folk roam
> By the 'Hart' and Grey's Bridge into byways and 'drongs',
>   Or across the ridged loam;
> The younger ones shrilling the lately heard songs,
>         The old saying, 'Would we were home.'

If the *OED* had informed us that *drongs* meant 'unplanted fields' or 'thoroughfares,' rather than 'a narrow lane or passage,' how many of us would be surprised? Without the reader's research, the word remains a six-letter obstruction to meaning – a thing in the line – paired with *ding-dong*, which may mislead us to assume that *drongs* also is onomato-poeic. As if to forewarn us of its different status as 'southwest dialect,' Hardy beribbons the word, which he may have borrowed from Barnes,[5] with inverted commas. Like the 'lately heard songs' – either old songs new to 'the younger ones' or songs actually new at that remote fair-time which would now have the antiquity of 'Eleanor Rigby' or some other Beatles song – *drongs* is a self-reflexive passage to an other time and place.

We witness Hardy experimenting with dialect in the *Wessex Poems*, especially in 'The Fire at Tanter Sweatley's,' which conveys its narratives in lines such as, 'Till he comes to the orchet, when crooping thereright / In the lewth of a codlin-tree, bivering wi'fright' (204). In later republica-tions of the *Wessex Poems*, Hardy makes concessions to his urban readers by changing the title to 'The Bride-Night Fire,' adding the parenthetical half-title 'A Wessex Tradition,' providing a gloss for thirty of the region-alisms, and revising lines, as when in the lines above, *thereright* becomes the more standard *from sight*.

In Hardy's letters and novels, the epistler and narrator employ standard English. Although he might take paragraphs of his letters to discuss, say, the difference between *form* and *stop* as names for hares' and rabbits' nests, respectively (IV, 214), and yield paragraphs of a novel to a Wessex laborer who employs dialect, Hardy's diction remains closer to his urban reader's than to that of his past or region. In the poems, however, even those not ostensibly involved with folk, his *mot juste* will some-times be drawn from that other time and place of rural Dorset. For example, in 'On an Invitation to the United States,' he rejects the new world in the language of the old: 'My ardours for emprize nigh lost.' Meaning 'chivalrous undertaking,' *emprize* is obsolete and *nigh* quainter than *nearly*. In 'For, wonning in these ancient lands, / Enchased and lettered as a tomb,' where the obsolete *wonning* means 'dwelling or abiding in,' the language functions as an adhesive clay from which the subject cannot be extracted, which is also the enchased message of the poem. McGann's characterization of William Morris's three Kelmscott self-publications can also apply to Hardy's poetry: 'The physical composition . . . calls our attention to poetry as a materially-oriented act of imagination. In them "meaning" is most fully constituted not as a conception but as an embodiment' (49), maintaining the distinction

Yeats made in his final letter: 'Man can embody truth but he cannot know it' (*YL*, 922). In the particular embodiments of Hardy's poetry, the density of form and diction imitate formulations of that lost time and place and, thereby, draw Hardy away from his audience to whom he conveys his desire for the past.

If Hardy at once bridges and maintains a distance from his urban audience, his own iron empiricism and rejection of 'superstition,' which still gives him its tug, separate him from that past he is drawn to and yet cannot rejoin. This strong ambivalence – this in-betweenness and isolation – registers in his extreme self-consciousness about his role as observer and about his literariness. For example, the title 'A Light Snow-Fall after Frost' seems to define its poem's topic – the incredibly detailed gradations in the change from a brown to a white landscape. However, as in many other Hardy poems, the details are so precise that before the poem ends our attention has shifted from the advance of snowfall to the mystery of the observer's situation.

This poem then joins a group of phenomenological poems of which 'Afterwards' may be the most successful. In 'Afterwards,' the acute images of occultation, which Tom Paulin has teased out so carefully in *Thomas Hardy: The Poetry of Perception*, become lessons in how to observe, bequeathed to gossiping neighbors to whom the poet is otherwise unknown. The poet's awareness of his role as observer is matched by his recognition that he must represent an oral culture within written forms whose prior uses, unlike speech or song, leave their traces around him. Of the novels, Perry Meisel has written that 'deep furrows of literary precedent . . . line Hardy's text with a precocious anxiety' (31). After enumerating various forms on which Hardy's novels draw, Meisel comments on 'the collision of literary forms, and of other forms of English usage, to which Hardy the latecomer is subject as a narrator.' Meisel's observations seem even more appropriate to Hardy as poet. Hardy's forms often seem the perfect vehicles for particular expressions. However, in their great variety and their occasional misfitting they also call attention to themselves, and we cannot advance far into Hardy's massive *Complete Poems* without feeling we have entered a museum of stanzaic types.

In the brilliant, brief 'In A Museum' Hardy even represents himself as a form of museum, a memory-machine in which the aural song, so important to Hardy's tradition, is plucked out of context and represented visually, as though we might enter museum space to speculate on the didgeridoo and the theorbo exhibited as mute witnesses of their different musical cultures.

[I]
Here's the mould of a musical bird long passed from light,
Which over the earth before man came was winging;
There's a contralto voice I heard last night,
That lodges in me still with its sweet singing.

[II]
Such a dream is Time that the coo of this ancient bird
Has perished not, but is blent, or will be blending
Mid visionless wilds of space with the voice that I heard,
In the full-fugued song of the universe unending.

(*HCP*, 430)

Typically of Hardy, it is the visual negative, the 'mould' of non-being, that evokes the bird, not aurally at first but, under the empirical restraint of the museum, visually, or at least as a visual trace 'long passed from sight.' When he introduces the second, also disembodied songster – 'a contralto voice I heard last night' – the gathering site for these two songs is no longer merely the museum but the poet's auditory imagination and memory. In the second stanza this imagination encompasses 'the coo of this ancient bird,' a sound appropriate not only to an older type of bird such as the dove or pigeon, perhaps even one now extinct such as the passenger pigeon, but also to the first onomatopoeic attempts by ancient man to name birds. In the poet's mind, the 'Here' of this moment and the 'there' of last night expand to an unspecified past or indefinite future – 'is blent, or will be blending' – as time becomes 'a dream,' a spatialization beyond the capacity of the visual – 'Mid visionless wilds' where 'Mid' places him 'at sea' rather than in the middle of – and into the astronomical eternity of 'the universe unending.' Within eight lines, Hardy recreates a sublime experience, one we may associate with the transcendental family but which may now be orphaned and in the fosterage of science. The music of the spheres is replaced by 'the full-fugued song' – the counterpointing of apparent contraries. Placed between the specific locality of 'At the Wicket-Gate' and the homier music of 'Apostrophe to an Old Psalm Tune,' 'In a Museum' evokes an urban experience where museums and fugues cast the poet beyond his local community into a comparativist cosmopolitanism.[6] Once this connection to the local-as-subject, the neighbor-as-audience, and plain-song-as-form becomes attentuated or broken, poetry takes flight (consistent with the radical sense of *fugue*) into vast modernist realms.

Hardy's sense of belatedness, implicit in the museum tableaux of artifacts extracted from their cultures, and his skeptical attraction to the past, history and personal memory emerge most clearly, from the caustic of Emma's sudden death, in the sequence 'Poems of 1912–13.' For example, 'At Castle Boterel' enacts the sequence's paradoxical hauntings – to envision his departed, the poet returns to their old haunts in Cornwall and Dorset – as we see in the poem's opening:

> As I drive to the junction of lane and highway,
>   And the drizzle bedrenches the waggonette,
> I look behind at the fading byway,
>   And see on its slope, now glistening wet,
>     Distinctly yet
> Myself and a girlish form...

(HCP, 351, lines 1–6)

Otherworldly motifs – the encounter at the crossroads, fading images, the 'glistening wet' girl who is almost an *aisling* (a visionary woman more familiar to Yeatsian and Irish readers than to those of English verse) – suggest that the lost lover may have transcended time. More explicitly, the poem counterpoises his radiant moment of personal love, recovered in visionary memory, with the annulling flow of time: 'It filled but a minute. But was there ever / A time of such quality, since or before / In that hill's story?' Early stanzas substantiate this 'minute' through particular and momentary effects: 'We had just alighted / To ease the sturdy pony's load / When he sighed and slowed' (lines 8–10). The palpable and rhythmic images, which particularize and individualize the scene, also suggest those forces that will efface the lover's moment, as if the pony labors under the burden of so many trudgings up this coastal hill. Even by the next stanza, the poet acknowledges that the substance and consequence of this moment are less significant than its motivation by the urgent lifeforce: 'Something that life will not be balked of' (line 13). Claims for primacy of this moment over the continuous march up this hill 'foot-swift, foot-sore, / By thousands more' are maintained, almost solipsistically, by the 'one mind' of the individual lover, as if Hardy is illustrating a Marxist critique of ideology as each person's socially constructed illusion.

The lover's self-assertion, voiced in stanza four, is immediately counterpoised by the claims of expanded time:

Primaeval rocks form the road's steep border,
  And much have they faced there, first and last,
Of the transitory in Earth's long order;
  But what they record in colour and cast
    Is – that we two passed.

(lines 21–5)

At this final dash of hesitancy, the speaker turns from the empirical certainties that rule the outer world to the blind faith governing his inner life. Thus, the poet maintains his image of the lover in the face of 'Time's unflinching rigour,' but in the final stanza the image shrinks because the speaker sinks, as if under 'the burden of the past.'

The poem's form reinforces the poet's ambivalent claim. The rhyme – ABABB – suggests first difference then recurrence, then in a final truncated, strophic line, a turn toward repetition. However, as in the hill's experience of lovers where individuals are replaced within the species, the recurrence takes another rhyme in the same form: CDCDD, and so on to the final short line which voices the poem's ambiguity – 'Never again' – both distinctiveness and obliteration.

We may understand Hardy's interest in 'primaeval rocks' as indigenous. Maiden Castle, the giant chalked figure of Bere Regis, and troves of Roman ruins spawned weekend Victorian archeologists in south Dorset. Such poems as 'The Roman Road' and 'The Roman Gravemounds' suggest that the feet of 'thousands more' trod out of a distant past for Hardy. Such an extended sense of time would have brought Hardy naturally to Lyell and Darwin, whom he might otherwise have tried to invent. Over history's shuffle Darwin privileged both eonian time and the relatively brief time in which, as the catastrophists had argued, variation in a species might emerge or a range of species be exterminated. Through these long and short spans of time Hardy illustrates determinism and coincidence. As in the milk-train episode of *Tess*, however, 'At Castle Boterel' assays the individual's chances in the instant, here as a shard of memory, hauntingly visionary but weighed against the devastating mass of time.

## Translations from the English and Irish past

The gap between the ancient geological formations of Dorset and its prehistoric ruins, on the one hand, and the oral stories and legends of more recent centuries, on the other, is guarded, enforced, and widened by empiricism much more strenuously than in Yeats's Ireland where *dinnseanchas* (narratives that account for place-names) and legends reach back to that distant past. Yet, both writers serve as types of the translator, carrying down, or up, from an ancient but vanishing society orally transmitted stories, tales, even myths. As examples of each poet's use of inherited mythologies, let us compare briefly Hardy's 'The Shadow on the Stone' and Yeats's 'The Fisherman,' both written and published within two years of each other in *Moments of Vision* and *The Wild Swans at Coole*, respectively. For all of Hardy's belief in observation, as Tom Paulin points out, he 'seldom transforms observation into vision' (61). This 'moment of vision' depends on the poet *not* turning his head to observe the source of the shadow that falls on the ancient Druid stone in his garden. Although many of Hardy's neighbors collected Roman and prehistoric souvenirs from the rich middens of Dorchester, until more advanced archeology reached Dorchester in the mid-nineteenth century, prehistoric artifacts were labelled uninformatively as *druidic*.[7] In Hardy's poem, then, the word itself is shadowy, a vague evocation of a past that is less mysterious than obscure and associated with superstition. The final stanza reads:

> Yet I wanted to look and see
> That nobody stood at the back of me;
> But I thought once more: 'Nay, I'll not unvision
> A shape which, somehow, there may be.'
> So I went on softly from the glade,
> And left her behind me throwing her shade
> As she were indeed an apparition –
> My head unturned lest my dream should fade.

(*HCP*, 530)

Set against his own justification as a poet – 'He was a man who used to notice such things,' as he says in 'Afterwards' – his wise passivity yields to his willful blindness, so that *not un*vision substitutes for poetic *dis*closure or *dis*covery. Furthermore, the possibility of multiple truths that resides in poetic ambiguity yields in the penultimate line to a folk elision 'As she were indeed an apparition' which seems to declare in a sort of kailyard subjunctive her presence as a spirit but which really means 'As if she were . . . ,' an illusory truth. Set against Hardy's absolute belief in empiricism, the word *somehow* – as in 'A shape which, somehow, there may be' – points, of course, to the the only truthful observation the poem can make: humans desire unreasonably to transcend the boundaries of death and the limits of a material world. The belief that Orpheus fails to sustain, in the gods' promise of Eurydice's resurrection, Hardy's speaker can maintain only because he knows Emma does not stand behind him, 'throwing her shade.'

Hardy's skeptical empiricism, which separates the poet from his dead lover in 'The Shadow on the Stone,' also separates him from prehistorical and mythological England. According to the English folklorist Neil Philip, 'Of all the major folk literatures, that of England is probably the scantiest' (xiii). As causes for this paucity of folklore, Philip adds to the dominance of scientific thinking the observation that 'the English oral tradition was early destabilized by mass semi-literacy and the wide circulation of cheap reading-matter, offering the concept of a fixed text in place of the oral storyteller's creative reconstruction' (xiv). E. M. Forster has asked:

> Why has not England a great mythology? Our folklore has never advanced beyond daintiness and the greater melodies about our country-side have all issued through the pipes of Greece. Deep and true as the native imagination can be, it seems to have failed here ...
> (Stuart, 75; Forster, 231).

Although Hardy had recourse to tales of local characters, he could not tap into a national mythology.[8] The gap between the measurable present and the mysterious past, which opened with the growth of the scientific method in the seventeenth century, was certainly reinforced by the Reformation that consigned superstition and the old religion to silence and invisibility.

On the other hand, Yeats, in a poem primarily about poetic creation and political antagonism, can suggest a specific story out of Ireland's mythology and prehistory. The title figure of 'The Fisherman' is just as much a figment of the poet's imagination as the shade's source in Hardy's poem. Yeats's poem extends a series of poems such as 'To A Friend,' 'The Dawn,' and the ending of 'The Three Beggars' about the cold disposition of the artist – antithetical to Yeats's natural passionate warmth – toward his subject, and represents Yeats's mask, a character of phase 2 or 3 most unlike Yeats's passionate will at phase 17. Instead of 'not unvisioning' him, Yeats willfully 'call[s] up to the eyes' this fisherman, much as an earlier fisherman in 'The Song of Wandering Aengus' employs magic and ritual to catch or invoke a fish and metamorphose it into a 'glimmering girl.' Yeats can evoke the Irish god of poetry and his poetic pursuit, based on desire and ritual, not only because of his earlier poem but also because of the number of Irish scholars who led from Irish orality into print the mythical Irish pantheon. Beyond being what MacNeice calls, speaking of Yeats's allusions, 'the half-said thing' (41), the allusion to Aengus is unspoken yet nevertheless lodged in the poem for at least some of the audience's orphic retrieval. As said in the Preface, this unspoken context available to an inner audience Hugh Shields, in his book on *Narrative Singing in Ireland*, calls *udár*, a term we shall return to again in Chapter 5.

Yeats's deep structure of story and myth, supplied by Irish storytellers and poets or conveyed by Yeats's daimon, distinguishes him from any English poet of last century. At times, especially in the 1890s and 1930s, Yeats also tapped into Catholic stories of saints and miracles, and this further distinguishes him from Hardy who may bear the pain of his phantom limb of faith but who, nevertheless, in his intermediacy between past and present, oral and literate cultures, vanished auditors and dis-embodied readers, reduces himself to what he calls in another poem 'his body-borne eyes,' a nearly disembodied empiricist. This different attitude toward the body might be traced to the Reformation and to cul-tural differences concerning the Eucharist. As we will discuss in Chapter 5, admission to the privileges of Protestantism required a forswearing of belief in transubstantiation, that the body of Christ adheres to his spirit.

In regard to this difference only, we might look very briefly at contrast-ing poems such as Hardy's 'He Revisits His First School' which differs in its disposition toward the body with the otherwise much more complex poem of Yeats, 'Among School Children.' Hardy began his public edu-cation at age eight. He attended a model school charitably founded at Bockhampton by a wealthy landowner's wife. Childless, she exercised a maternal crush on young Thomas whom, Hardy writes (presumably speaking of a growth of years rather than minutes), she would 'take into her lap and kiss until he was quite a big child' (*ELH*, 23). In the poem the speaker is embarrassed to return in his older body: 'I should not have shown in the flesh, / I ought to have gone as a ghost'; the poem begins, and it continues near the end:

> But to show in the afternoon sun,
> With an aspect of hollow-eyed care,
> When none wished to see me come there,
> Was a garish thing, better undone.

(HCP, 511–12)

Beyond regret for his degradation from Oedipal darling to septuagenarian, Hardy voices his often-stated wish to be a disembodied voyeur, 'putting on the manners of ghosts, wandering in their haunts, and taking their views of surrounding things . . . , a spectre not solid enough to influence my environment,' he says in his autobiography (*HLY*, 275). In part this is a logical extension of Hardy's concept of the poet's function as acute observer and scrupulous reporter: a reduction to eyes, not to be looked upon in their 'hollow-eyed care' but to look out of. Yeats on the other hand, although equally aware of his decline from bearer of pretty plumage to scarer of crows, cannot finally separate the identifying entelechies, 'O Presences,' from their manifestations in the flesh, or know the dancer from the dance. For Yeats, adherence of the body to soul was, at least, one side of a dialectic to which he necessarily returned.

## Yeats's relation to audience

Yeats's convictions about history and the past affect as severely, if differently, his own relation to his audience. He, like Hardy, aligns himself with modernism because, to return to our definition, he 'acts out the loss of something primary that he wishes to regain' and does so through formal strategies that materialize the gaps of modernity. Yeats's interest in origins derives in part from his early, and lifelong, interest in ethnology and philology, topics I'll later take up in relation to Matthew Arnold in Chapter 2. As with Hardy, Yeats's 'loss of something primary' is also entwined with his childhood in Sligo where, he recalls in 1903, he had encountered

> a community bound together by imaginative possessions, by stories and poems which have grown out of its own life, and by a past of great passions which can still waken the heart to imaginative action.
> (*YE&I*, 213)

Although in the year before this essay, he could advise an American midwesterner curious about Irish literature that 'the greater amount of Irish poetry is . . . in the Irish language, & . . . some of the time you mean to spend in study will be well spent in learning that language' (*YCL*, III, 181), in this essay he goes on to say that one could write for this community 'if one had the genius, and had been born to Irish. . . .'

The simple question concerning what Yeats, without Irish, might have derived from the centuries-long poetic tradition in Irish, can mislead us into profound or pointless questions of identity. In the last decade, the topic of translation has become a current and controversial theoretical area. At the same time, poets such as Thomas Kinsella, John Montague, and Seamus Heaney have grappled with these questions practically in the course of translating important Irish texts. Younger poets such as Eiléan Ní Chuilleanáin, Paul Muldoon, and Ciaran Carson, working with translations from the Irish of Nuala Ní Dhomhnaill and others, have incorporated Irish into their own poetry. Consequently, rather than fading away, Irish has entered more intimately and problematically into Irish poetry in English, and the four decades of this book may be seen as a progressive approach toward this intimacy.

Critics disagree about the extent to which Yeats's poetry may register the influence of poetry in Irish: it may distinguish him from other Victorians and Edwardians without being essential to his verse. For example, in a thoughtful essay from 1978, Sean Lucy illustrates that the meters of popular song or *amhrán*, themselves adapted from more formal verse in Irish, drew Victorian Anglo-Irish verse toward a more accentual stanza, employing 'trisyllabic stanzas but with real flexibility' and extending the English pentameter line, often to 14 syllables. Most convincingly, he scans Yeats's 'Cold Heaven' to reveal these Irish traits as well as Yeats's tendency to 'spread the stress' over several syllables – 'ice burned . . . ,' 'love crossed . . . ,' 'Out naked . . . ,' which we read as a unit of thought and not merely two consecutive stressed syllables. Bernard O'Donoghue argues that what he calls 'the great translators of the nineteenth century' – the poets Mangan and Ferguson, J. J. Callanan, Douglas Hyde, and others – toughened the 'effete diction' of Victorian Anglo-Irish poetry. Both he and Sean Lucy speak of the influence of Irish sound effects. Lucy discusses Austin Clarke's campaign to introduce equivalents to Irish sound effects – assonance replacing end rhyme, stopped rhyme, harmonic rhyme, and other devices that influenced Yeats in the 1930s, and thereby require discussion in the next chapter and in subsequent chapters that discuss the growing influence of Irish. Without the Irish language, Yeats initially was drawn to stories, which had followed the countryman's shift to English in the nineteenth century and which he gathered and published in *Fairy and Folk Tales of the Irish Peasantry* (1888), rather than to legends and myths which depended on the original language or on literary translations. Eventually, his interest in the political resources of folklore – to 'waken the heart to imaginative action' – drew him through the translations of Standish James O'Grady's and especially Lady Gregory to the great Irish myth *The Táin* and to its impetuous and violent hero Cuchulain. Accused in the *Freeman's Journal* of wanting to substitute Cuchulain for Christ, Yeats acknowledged that he was personally stirred by this 'conception of the heroic life come down from the dawn of the world' (*YCL*, III, 187, 593).

To the extent that Yeats's dramatic Cuchulain cycle helped reestablish what Yeats called the 'heroic foundations of the race' (592) and contributed to the Irish literary reawakening 'of the heart to imaginative action,' it also failed to provide models for self-governing and ordinance. As Seamus Deane says in his *Short History of Irish Literature*:

> We can discern, in the figure of Cuchulain, the tragic emblem of Ireland's political strife and her dream of cultural unity. . . . Yeats identifies the central problem of his nation's literature. To offer its spiritual history to the world it must transcend the limitations of its origins.                                                      (157)

Where Ireland after the Rising needed an Odysseus or Aeneas, Yeats recovers instead founding figures divided into two types: the Irish figure – magical, impulsive, antinomian, and sexually potent – serves only as a filocide and barren warrior whereas the role of administrative leader is awarded to the John-Bull-like Conchubar: humorless, coldly logical, treacherous, and an aged cuckold. Neither figure can offer Ireland affiliation. Following the colonial separation and alienation of ordnance from ordinance, those different functions of the emerging nation, Yeats, whose poetry always figures cycles as polarities, cannot bring rebel and ruler to the same side of the Irish sea. Finally Yeats's representation of Cuchulain may be read as a critique both of the Irish Revolution and, remembering Padraic Pearse's conflation, of the selective myth of Christ – physically unregenerative but spiritually regenerative through bloodshed and self-sacrifice – on which the Irish theocracy was constructed.

## The changing relation of audience to Yeats and Hardy

Hardy authenticated the journalistic accounts of his award by closing his speech with the peroration I have already cited: 'Poetry itself cannot die. . . . Despite her overturned temples and the false gods adored among their ruins, she is immortal. . . .' On this birthday in 1912, Hardy could hardly have foreseen that this quotation from George Sand might come to be understood less as a reference to Sand's Romanticist sources, such as 'Hyperion,' than as a foreshadowing of Eliot's 'The Wasteland,' a poem whose Modernist vogue would obscure for decades Hardy's subtle simplicity. Nor could he have known that cultural forces and events, some tragic and very imminent, would eventually advance his standing among British scholars and critics relative to Yeats.

After all, 'in 1912, . . . nobody paid any attention to Hardy's verse' (Butler, 51), according to Ezra Pound, who, two years later, would declare of Yeats that 'no one has shown any disposition to supersede him as the best poet in England [sic]' (Jeffares, 1977, 187). Hardy's novels would be reissued from 1912 onward, and thereby further overshadow his poetic efforts, but Yeats had already enjoyed publication of an eight-volume *Collected Works in Verse & Prose* in 1908, which, according to Lytton Strachey, gave Yeats 'pretensions to classical honours.' Strachey begrudgingly conceded that 'it is difficult to think of any other writer of this generation of whom it can be said with equal certainty that he has given proof of inspiration' (Jeffares, 164, 168). Yeats's critical reputation in Britain grew steadily through his reception of the Nobel Prize in 1923 and well into the decades after the Second World War.

Hardy, on the other hand, had received praise for his poetic drama *The Dynasts* but almost no encouraging responses to the three volumes of poetry he had published prior to the awarding of the Royal Society medal at Max Gate. The *Saturday Review* had characterized his first volume as 'curious and slipshod,' 'full of slovenly . . . and uncouth verses . . .' (Gerber, 89). The *Atheneum* declared the second volume 'persistently clumsy' (Gerber, 100), and the *Oxford and Cambridge Review* declared all three volumes a sump for the superfluous acid from the novels, 'drained off in crude and uncertain lyrics' (Gerber, 147). So low was Hardy's stock in certain circles that in 1913 Chesterton could describe him as 'a sort of village atheist brooding and blaspheming over the village idiot' (62).

However, very soon after Yeats's visit to Max Gate, events swept the path for the steady advance of Hardy's poetic reputation. When Hardy expelled Emma from his ceremony, she probably retired to her attic study where she usually remained in retreat from her husband. Generally ignored by Hardy, within six months she would die there in protracted pain from an impacted gallstone. Remorseful and retrospective, Hardy soon responded with a sequence of love poems that many consider his major poetic work. Within two summers, the First World War would begin to render Hardy's grim ironies prophetic and analgesic. The flaw, if not fault, of Paul Fussell's *Great War and Modern Memory* is his failure to recognize sufficiently Hardy's poetic precedence. Arguing that the war's destruction and disillusionment introduce a new ironic tone permanently into British literature, he might more accurately have acknowledged that the war prepared an audience to hear this tone, already present in Hardy's verse.

Yet, more than a tonal shift occurs in the Great War. The decimation of young British males, the homicidal savagery of machines, technology, and chemistry (anticipated in the works of Wordsworth, Browning, Dickens, and other writers of the Industrial Revolution), the torpid stagnancy of trench warfare, the geometric expansion of death, and the betrayal of foot soldiers by the HQ, the war bureaucracy, and the propaganda machine: all this created a break in the English psyche, a loss of faith in the united national purpose, and an emphasis on humanity's material limitations. If this disposition seems already implicit in Hardy's poetry, it finds partial expression in the poetry of the First World War and, as the century progresses, fuller expression in the poetry of major poets such as Ted Hughes and Geoffrey Hill, as if they were venting the repressed nightmares of the first half-century.

If we turn to the most often quoted of the serious poems of the Great War – Wilfred Owen's 'Dulce et Decorum est' – we find a concise expression of a sort of wartime experience not previously offered in English poetry before 1914. Jon Stallworthy points out that in a draft the poem was dedicated 'To Jessie Pope,' who represents a class of poet who regularly in newspaper poems inveigled young men to enlist and 'earn the Empire's thanks.'[9] In a letter to his mother, Owen wrote concerning his title from Horace's *Odes* (III: 2) that 'the famous Latin tag means of course It is sweet and meet to die for one's country. Sweet! and *decorous*!' (Stallworthy, 228) Owen's evident indignation may be directed against a class culture that was both raised on classical, imperial literature and made cohesive by the epoxy of platitudes. From the beginning the soldiers are declassed as 'old beggars' and 'hags' (117). Similarly, the poem tugs against traditional form, as two sonnets lean dependently on each other (the last two lines in one sonnet rhyme only with the first two in the next) and iambic pentameter is disrupted by truncation or extension: 'Bitten as the cud / Of vile, incurable sores on innocent tongues.' The ninth line, which in the sonnet might be the volta or a melting line, can only respond in double spondees to war's emergency: 'Gas! GAS! Quick, boys! – an ecstasy of fumbling.'

In omitting Owen and other First World War poets from his *Oxford Book of Modern Verse* (1936), Yeats quoted Arnold's dictum that 'passive suffering is not a theme for poetry,' but he failed to credit the extent to which much of this poetry is visionary, or at least beyond sight. As point-men on the salients of battle, these poets report on the distress of the body and the profound trauma they had undergone which went beyond reportable seeing. As Owen does here, these poets often recount how eyesight becomes useless:[10]

> In all my dreams before my helpless sight
> He plunges at me, guttering, choking, drowning.
> If in some smothering dreams, you too could pace
> Behind the wagon that we flung him in,
> And watch the white eyes writhing in his face,

The poet recalls the gassed soldier 'guttering,' like Macbeth's brief candle, but also, by suggestion of the homophone, mired in entrails as he drowns within his own body.

If we can enter the poet's nightmare vision, with Jessie Pope and other non-combatants, to that extent we yield to his final admonishment:

> My friend, you would not tell with such high zest
> To children ardent for some desperate glory,
> The old Lie: *Dulce et decorum est*
> *Pro patria mori.*

*Telling*, then, will be replaced by this 'smothering dream.' This nightmare of mechanical warfare, which found partial expression in the First World War poetry, was repressed for a time afterward except in David Jones's *In Parentheses* and in the poetry of Ivor Gurney, who from his mental ward voiced Britain's unconscious nightmare. This repressed nightmare then emerged restoratively in the poetry of Plath, Hughes, and perhaps Hill in the 1960s and onward. In the meantime, fairly or not, Hardy was taken as an exemplar for post-imperial poets, who made modest, non-transcendent claims for poetry, to the exclusion or diminution of romantic poets such as Dylan Thomas or Yeats himself, who sometimes paraded the poet as a shaman in furs.

A third event boosting Hardy's reputation relative to Yeats's among English critics, but one more difficult to document, is Irish independence, achieved only incrementally, as measured by the Rising of 1916, the treaty of 1923, the constitution of 1936, and the entrance into the EEC in 1972, and paralleled by the dissolution of the British Empire and the weakening of English hegemony within an increasingly disunited kingdom. As numerous scholars have argued,[11] the cultural polarity that helped rationalize the British Empire – from national stereotypes to concepts of culture to linguistic, religious, and social differences – also formed the basis for Irish independence and the separation of Yeats from the English canon.

The relation of Yeats's and Hardy's successors to culture take their gradual if irreversible inclinations from 1916's traumatic events. As Yeats came to see in *A Vision*, so nearly all subsequent Irish poets have recognized that they must distance themselves from a Cuchulainoid culture and that they must reinvent their culture to win it from censoring theocracy and physical force. For example, in Northern Ireland during the Troubles, the poets assumed an indirect discourse and a perspective from a province of the imagination while *An Cultúr*, became the Provos' catchphrase in The Falls Road and the H-block.[12] In England, on the other hand, as we've said, the deaths of so many countrymen in 1916, and so many promising poets, made the abandonment of a plain-speaking, empirical poetry seem like an apostasy from the national culture. Poetry, then, took on a commitment to an elegiac, even commemorative culture that no longer seemed so occupied with the role of maintaining class and colonial hierarchies.

Of course for much of the twentieth century, a hierarchical and monocultural standard had come to be employed as the universal metric to judge and exclude different poets. The next chapter, with reference to Berkeley, Burke, Arnold, Yeats, Wilde, and Joyce, will retrace the development of *culture* and analyze how this ideological concept makes a hierarchy of such cultural differences. Of the dramatis personae at the Max Gate ceremony, the third participant, the obliging poet, man of letters, and committee-man Henry Newbolt, plays a crucial role in the advancement of 'culture.' As we shall see toward the middle of this chapter, his leadership of a prestigious literary committee and his authorship of its 1921 report will help enthrone this hierarchical and exclusionary interpretation of *culture*, in which poetry takes on a value disproportionate to its popularity, within the academic and literary institutions of England.

# 2
# The Cultural Value of Poetry

## Henry Newbolt's report

It may have been coincidental that Henry Newbolt would play a decisive if secondary role in devaluing Yeats's reputation among British scholars and critics. However, his appearance with Yeats at Max Gate for that June ceremony was neither accidental nor arbitrary. A vicar's son from Staffordshire, Newbolt had attended public school on scholarship before going on to study classics at Corpus Christi College in 1881. Called to the Bar after Oxford, he spent a decade working for the Law Digest in London. Throughout his university years he had written verse, but his marriage soon after graduation introduced him to a wider literary set that included Mary Coleridge and Robert Bridges. Through Bridges' sponsorship, he managed to publish, with Yeats's first English publisher Elkin Matthews, *Admirals All* (1897), a chapbook of twelve poems. Mostly ballads about English naval victories or colonial heroics, this chapbook included 'A Ballad of John Nicholson' in which the English hero humiliates a 'proud and sly' leader of the Indian 'Mutiny' of 1857 before the ranks of his own Indian captains who can only conclude: 'When the strong command / Obedience is best' (*Selected Poems*, 42).

Patric Dickinson, who edited a 1981 selection of Newbolt's poetry, acknowledges what these two lines suggest: that the enormous success of *Admirals All* arose from its comparison with Kipling's *Barrack-Room Ballads* published five years earlier. Whereas this editor recalls the praise of 'one Cambridge don' that Newbolt wrote 'Kipling without the brutality' (17), more recently the author of a biographical dictionary judges Newbolt's poetry 'too much like diluted Kipling to be any longer fashionable' (Blamires).

In 1901 Yeats himself had praised Newbolt's second volume *The Island Race* (1898) in a letter to Newbolt who, as editor of the *Monthly Review*, was soon to publish Yeats's essay 'Magic.' Yeats ascribed to Newbolt

> patriotism of the fine sort – patriotism that lays burdens upon a man, & not the patriotism that takes burdens off. The British Press just now, as I think, only understands the other sort, the sort that makes a man say 'I need not trouble to get wisdom for I am English, & my vices have made me great'.                                             (YCL, III, 63)

In turn, the publisher of 'Magic,' who told Yeats the essay was 'brilliantly successful' (*YCL*, III, 136), said later of Yeats's conversation that it forced on the hearer 'the impossible necessity of reconciling the world of science with a strongly contrasted world of magic' (Newbolt, *The Later Life*, 6, cited in *YCL*, III, 62).

Newbolt's first volume also included 'Vitaï Lampada' in which the school rallying-cry of 'Play up! play up! and play the game!' braces the remnant of an English regiment about to die in some desert campaign. Newbolt's editor, however, defends this sentimental jingoism of New-bolt's verses with the quaint phrasing that 'all of them had a quality that had been lost to English poetry' (Dickinson, 17), tempting us to add 'Not lost so much as blown away at the Somme.' Newbolt's naive belief that war was a gentleman's game, a belief which foundered with the *Lusitania*, makes this armchair admiral a butt of Paul Fussell's *The Great War and Modern Memory*. From the elevation of Fussell's lofty hind-sight, Newbolt seems particularly fatuous for defending General Haig, Newbolt's schoolboy friend and the unimaginative and intransigent father of the Great War's stalemate.

Yet, Newbolt was a loyal friend to many of his generation's leaders who rewarded him with positions of trust, as did John Murray who invited him to be the first editor of the new journal *The Monthly Review*, a position he held from 1900 to 1904. Soon after its founding in 1906, the English Association – part lobby group, part literary congregation – elected him president. Furthermore, his own efforts to resurrect the Royal Society of Literature, which made him the appropriate delegate to award its gold medal to Hardy in 1912, also secured him an extramural venue for a series of lectures which he delivered as the Society's 'Pro-fessor of Poetry.' These lectures, in turn, formed the basis of his 1917 collection *A New Study of English Poetry*, which returned to fundamental questions – 'What Is Poetry?' – and to social issues – 'Poetry and Educa-tion' and 'The Poet and His Audience.' In this study, among his list of the best living poets – Binyon, Bridges, Doughty, Hardy, Hewlett, Sturge Moore, and Yeats – Newbolt finds no great poets, but he believes, nevertheless, that his age had produced poems of 'orthodox form and size, and of much more than orthodox beauty' and 'for spiritual depth and intensity, as for rhythmical beauty, its poetry is unsurpassed' (23). Although he recognizes the dramatic qualities of Milton, Newbolt asserts – in a judgment that opposes those of Wilde and Yeats as well as of Pound and Eliot – that the best poems 'are the most sincere, those which are most evidently historic records of a soul' (78). Whereas this Arnoldian characterization might restrict poetry to *The Prelude* or *In Memoriam*, in 'Futurism and Form in Poetry' he makes this characterization more inclusive by enlarging the purview of 'the soul':

> Good poetry...is the masterly expression of rare, difficult, and complex states of consciousness, of intuitions in which the highest thought is fused with simple perceptions, until both together become a new emotion.
> (283)

In an important qualification, however, he asserts that the most poignant poetry appears when the poet's imaginative world and 'the life we must ourselves live' are 'nearest.' Armed with such 'purely scientific' principles, Newbolt then considers poetic 'Futurism,' which he defines as 'the revolt against the oppression of the present by the past,' a definition as suitable for Modernist poetry such as Eliot's as for the Italian movement of Marinetti which this essay examines. After granting Marinetti's Futurist Movement a remarkably fair hearing, he compares the innovations of Whitman to those of Marinetti, to the American's advantage, and then thanks Marinetti for exhorting 'us to greater freedom and independence in expression, ... always to the good' (306).

Reading this essay reminds us that Newbolt is an English Liberal and that we have sat through the literary equivalent of a committee meeting in which, ostensibly, the fairest hearing is granted to the widest divergency of views before reaching a foreordained conclusion. We may be cheered by his assertion early in this essay that 'our best poets have all been innovators' who have helped construct a poetic tradition of 'creative freedom' (287), but when we turn to his *English Anthology* of 1921, which includes American as well as Scots writers with English, we find Whitman rendered to two pages while we look in vain among recent writers for work by Hopkins, Edward Thomas, Yeats, and Frost, to say nothing of Eliot or Pound. Similarly, while proclaiming that Croce's emphasis on poetic intention and expression governs contemporary criticism, Newbolt would steer us back to an emphasis on the poets' pact with their audience and to the importance of recognizable forms. Like some hero from his ballads baring his breast to the enemy's shot, Newbolt absorbs the assault of the avant garde in order to hold the line for the status quo.

Clarity of prose and what passed as liberal even-handedness, as well as his growing power as head of the English Association, rather than critical astuteness, must have attracted the president of the British Board of Education to appoint Newbolt in 1919 as chair of a committee to study *The Teaching of English in England*, to adopt the title of the report which appeared in 1921. The 14 members of Newbolt's committee (six of whom were women, nine of whom members of the English Association) included eminent scholars such as F. S. Boas, D. Enright, Prof. C. H. Firth, J. H. Fowler, Arthur Quiller-Couch, George Sampson, Caroline Spurgeon, and J. Dover Wilson, with H. J. C. Grierson, W. P. Ker, Sidney Lee, Walter Raleigh, de Selincourt, Saintsbury, and D. Nicol Smith as adjunct 'witnesses.' Based on questionnaires, interviews, committee discussion, and other evidence, Newbolt wrote most, if not all, of the report (Dickinson, 24) which, in Baldick's judgment, was 'almost... a best seller' and 'a guiding influence upon the development of English studies' (94). Although the report was never implemented officially, it contributed to an alignment of *culture* and literature in Britain, to a more coherent English poetic canon, and, consequently, to the relative marginalization of Yeats and other Irish poets by keepers of that canon.

Neither his central role in that report nor his success as a popular patriotic poet can justify the introduction of Henry Newbolt at such length. Rather, the steady advancement of his literary career (which was fueled by law-clerk fidelity serving for literary genius), his critical judgment (which, as reflected in his anthology, was the vector of unexamined patriotism, snobbism, and decency), and an almost religious commitment to *culture*, seem representative of those maintaining the British literary establishment in these years and influencing, if not determining, the success of poets we are considering in this study. Before reflecting on how *The Teaching of English in England* contributes to *culture* and influences our writers' receptions, we need to see how the concept of culture, which became significant in the Victorian period, impinged both on Yeats and on English criticism. Celebrated, pioneering books first by Raymond Williams and later by Chris Baldick allow me to pass more quickly over the definition and history of *culture* in order to make observations about the mixture of English and Irish notions of culture in poetry's unitary marketplace.[1]

## Yeats's and Burke's oaks

In the same year in which T. S. Eliot introduced the phrase, if not the concept, of 'a dissociation of sensibility' (64), the 1921 Newbolt Report declared:

> The enormous changes in the social life and industrial occupations of the vast majority of our people, changes begun in the sixteenth century and greatly accentuated by the so-called Industrial Revolution, have created a gulf between the world of poetry and that world of everyday life from which we receive our 'habitual impressions.' Here, we believe, lies the root cause of the indifference and hostility toward literature. . . .
>
> (258)

Charged with establishing a 'general or national scheme' (5) for the teaching of English, the committee followed Matthew Arnold in asserting that divisions between the imaginative and empirical worlds within ourselves are projected into or exacerbated by divisions between classes in society. For the solution to these divisions, as for its basic ideology, the Report turned to Arnold: 'Matthew Arnold, using the word in its true sense, claimed that "culture unites classes". He might have added that a system of education which disunites classes cannot be held worthy of the name of a national culture' (6). Although Arnold often addressed questions of culture within a pedogogical context,[2] he never equated a nation's culture with its system of education. Conflating literature and Arnold's definition of culture,[3] as well as culture and religion, the Report argues.

> For if literature be, as we believe, an embodiment of the best thoughts of the best minds, . . . a fellowship which 'binds together by passion and knowledge the vast empire of human society, . . . over the whole earth, and over all time,' then the nation of which a considerable portion rejects this means of grace, and despises this great spiritual influence, must assuredly be heading to disaster.
>
> (253)

If we recall that *religion* and not *culture* initially meant 'to bind back' or 'to bind together'[4] and that no biblical text designates literature as a means of grace, then we would recognize how evangelical fervor has melded distinctions between religion and culture not overtly blurred by Arnold.

In *Culture and Society* Raymond Williams traces the nationalization of *culture* from a term for private intellectual and moral activity to a 'whole way of life' lived by a society (xviii). He finds the first decisive shift in meaning in the writing of Edmund Burke who believed 'all human virtue is the creation of society, and is in this sense not "natural" but "artificial" ' (8). What Williams holds to be the key formulation of *culture* appears in Burke's *Reflections on the French Revolution* (1790):

> We are afraid to put men to live and trade each on his own private stock of reason; because we suspect that the stock in each man is small, and that the individuals would do better to avail themselves of the general bank and capital of nations and of ages.
>
> (Williams, 8; Burke, 183)

Williams goes on to say, 'Seventy years later, this was to be the basis of Matthew Arnold's recommendation of Culture.'

At least from age seven, when he stood on a table to recite Burke 'with great gusto' (*ACP*, 417), Arnold revered Burke as 'the great voice of this epoch' (418), but this was an epoch of 'concentration,' the reactionary period in Britain following the French Revolution. In the preface to his collection of Burke's writings on Ireland (1881), a book largely ignored in its time, Arnold skirts the financial metaphors that Burke, in the *Reflections*, employs for *culture*, but he speaks of Burke's writing as a constituent of culture, both a national trust and a neglected key to the cultural vault:

> To lose Swift and Burke out of our mind's circle of acquaintance is a loss indeed . . . In both cases the unacquaintance shuts us out from great sources of English life, thought, and language, and from the capital records of its history and development, and leaves us in consequence very imperfect and fragmentary Englishmen.   (*ACP*, 286)

Arnold's confusion at this point in his argument concerning Burke's national identity (to say nothing concerning Swift's) – 'Our neglected classic is by birth an Irishman' (287) – originated in Burke's own ambivalence. Born to a Catholic mother and a father who had forsaken Catholicism in order to practise law in a Protestant Ireland, Burke received his formative early education in a Catholic hedge-school before proceeding under the cloak of Protestantism into a Quaker secondary school and Anglo-Irish Trinity College in Dublin. In pursuing a political career in an exclusively Anglican Parliament, Burke 'never feels free over Ireland,' according to the inferential but persuasive argument of Conor Cruise O'Brien in *The Great Melody: A Thematic Biography* . . . of Edmund Burke (xxvi). O'Brien points out that 'Burke's public statements concerning Ireland were few, guarded, cryptic, sometimes evasive. . . . For adequate reasons he did his best to cover his tracks over Ireland' (xxvi–xxvii) (or to recall the Reformation's charge against Jesuits, to equivocate). Arnold's appropriation of Burke as an Englishman could be understood as a generous conciliatory gesture during this period of Anglo-Irish tensions over the Land Wars, but we may as fairly recognize this claiming of Irish writing for an English, rather than international, heritage as a form of cultural imperialism.

If Burke's metaphor for *culture* – 'the general bank and capital of nations and of ages' – continues, as Williams says, as 'the basis of Matthew Arnold's recommendation of Culture,' in Arnold and Burke it remains sublimated or subordinated to, perhaps underlying (but in Burke literally 'in the shade of') botanical metaphors and the idea of cultivation, as a nurturing of nature. For example, in *Reflections* Burke writes of actual banks:

> Even commerce, and trade, and manufacture, the gods of our oeconomical politicians, are themselves perhaps but creatures; are themselves but effects, which, as first causes, we choose to worship. They certainly grew under the same shade in which learning flourished. They too may decay with their natural protecting principles.          (174)

Here, Burke is anxious to ground the Bank of England and the concept of a credit economy, which were instituted soon after the Revolution of 1688, in the same sort of fructifying mysteries as, he believed, nurtured the British constitution before the 1688 settlement.

The organic arboreal metaphor suggested in this passage and shadowed forth elsewhere in *Reflections* becomes explicit in only one passage, which concerns English fellow-travelers of the French revolutionaries, those 'certain societies in London' referred to in the book's subtitle. This metaphorical representation of Britain and its Jacobite sympathizers as a field resounding with noisy grasshoppers bears directly and indirectly on the concept of *culture* and especially on Yeats's relation to Burke and Arnold:

> Because half a dozen grasshoppers under a fern make the field ring with their importunate chink, whilst thousands of great cattle, reposed beneath the shadow of the British oak, chew the cud and are silent,

pray do not imagine, that those who make the noise are the only inhabitants of the field.[5]                                                                    (181)

Although unidentified, in its Yggdrasilian proportions the oak tree can specifically represent only the British Constitution, but it remains general enough to retain associations with ancient habits of British thought, such as the prejudice described two pages later: 'In this enlightened age I am bold enough to confess . . . we are generally men of untaught feelings. . . . Prejudice renders a man's virtue his habit; and not a series of unconnected acts' (183).

The dark rootedness suggested here reinforces other, less direct, references to the oak, which represent its verticality through roots, branches, and growth. However, this passage is otherwise anomalous in representing this version of *culture* horizontally. In this spatial orientation, Burke becomes uncharacteristically like Arnold, who usually represents culture horizontally both in terms of literature that 'has a simultaneous existence and composes a simultaneous order,' in Eliot's phrasing (38), and in terms of educational reforms undertaken at the same time. According to Chris Baldick, as critic of culture Arnold follows his poetic self in reversing axes: '"Not deep the poet sees but wide." Poetry must follow not the vertical axis of probing expressive intensity, but the horizontal axis, by inclusiveness of content, seeing the world steadily and seeing it whole' (27). According to this figuration of *culture*, Arnold would be a horticulturist[6] whereas Burke is an arboriculturist or even, more naturally, a Georgian forester who maintains a laissez-faire stance toward tree growth. This emphasis of Burke's, trusting in the nation's unconscious and its ancient habits, influences Yeats's sense of culture later on in the poet's life.

Yeats certainly was not clambering onto the table at age seven to recite Burke. Even at age thirty, in proposing a 'national literature,' he could not include Burke, Swift, or Berkeley among those who 'have written under Irish influence and of Irish subjects' (*YUP*, I, 360), and nearing forty, Yeats continued to believe these three 'hardly seem to me to have come out of Ireland at all . . .' (*YUP*, 2, 328). By the close of the First World War, Yeats was 'seriously reading Burke,' according to Torchiana's indispensable study (169). As early as 1910, Yeats, in reaction to the effect of the Wyndham Land Act on Lady Gregory and her neighbors, may have been echoing in poems such as 'Upon A House Shaken by the Land Agitation' Burke's praise of a God-ordained 'recognition of a signiory,' a tribute 'performed, in buildings, in music, in decoration, in speech, in the dignity of persons, according to the customs of mankind, taught by their nature' (*Reflections*, 196–7). 'A Prayer for My Daughter' (1919), written in the throes of Burkean influence, probably borrows from passages in the *Second Letter on a Regicide Peace* in which Burke praises aristocratic manners and customs.

In public references to Burke from the 1920s on, Yeats usually places him in an Anglo-Irish triad with Berkeley and Swift and identifies him with his 'British oak,' emblematic of an organic 'nation' deeply rooted in a racial unconscious and manifest naturally 'in custom and in ceremony,' all governed hierarchically in Ireland by 'the people of Burke and of Grattan.' Just as Yeats distorts Berkeley into a lifelong Idealist, he sometimes confuses Burke with the Ascendancy class which Burke actually despised and denounced.[7] Yeats offsets this mischaracterization of Burke by identifying him as Irish and, by association, even as a nationalist – wishful thinking on Yeats's part which Conor Cruise O'Brien has argued actually had its basis in fact. For example, in Yeats's 'The Seven Sages' one sage's family lore places Burke in the house of Grattan, whose Jacobite premises would have felt too uncomfortably seditious for Burke's presence. In that poem, Burke, Swift, Berkeley, and Goldsmith all oppose 'Whiggery,' which Yeats associates with English Positivism and Utilitarianism. In a 1925 speech to the Irish Literary Society, Yeats extols Burke as a national treasure: 'We have in Berkeley and in Burke a philosophy on which it is possible to base the whole life of a nation.' Just as Berkeley's denunciation of English empiricism – 'We Irish do not hold with this!' – unites Irish thought against English, so Burke's oak tree can suggest a natural ecumenism for Ireland, as it can for Catholic Italy: 'In Italy it [religious teaching] takes four forms, that it may not be abstract, and that it may be a part of history and of life itself, a part, as it were, of the foliage of Burke's tree.' In this same speech, Yeats offers his most extended elaboration of Burke's emblem: Burke, 'who restored to political thought its sense of history,' proved 'that the State was a tree, no mechanism to be pulled in pieces and put up again, but an oak tree that had grown through centuries' (*YUP*, 2, 459).

If this oak from *Reflections* . . . allows Yeats to counter post-Enlightenment democracy with an emblem for the unconscious foundation of an organic state, Burke's revision of this tree in 'A Letter to Rev. Dr Hussey' would have been closer to Yeats's own concepts of the antithetical nature of reality. In this letter, written in early December of 1796, Burke warns Bishop Hussey – president of the new Catholic seminary at Maynooth which Burke had helped found – that he should not confuse French intellectual Jacobinism with the deeply rooted Irish nationalism:

The Jacobinism which arises from Penury and irritation, from scorned loyalty, and rejected Allegiance, has much deeper roots. They take their nourishment from the bottom of human Nature and the unalterable constitution of things, and not from humour and caprice or the opinions of the Day about privileges and Liberties. These roots will be shot into the Depths of Hell, and will at last raise up their proud Tops to Heaven itself.                                      (*Letters*, 418)

Disdaining the Philosophes' ruling offspring who would subdivide France geometrically while tabulating human rights, Burke imbues his characterization of the United Irishman with aspects of the sublime, as he himself defined this concept in *A Philosophical Enquiry into ... the Sublime ...* (1756): vastness, perpendicularity, fearsomeness, darkness, sudden changes in light or sound. In contrast to the *levity* of French Jacobites, the Irish rebels represent 'radical evil,' which is baffling to reason. Literally 'radical,' they are deep-rooted, feeding on the 'bottom of human Nature' and entering the 'Depths of Hell,' a vastness that, being perpendicular, therefore exercises 'more force in forming the sublime' (66). Ideas of rootedness and depth imply darkness (70), and the flourishing in 'Heaven itself' implies a sudden shift from darkness to light (73). Finally, contrasting terms and emotive words fulfill Burke's presciption for sublime diction which conveys more of the speaker's emotion than of the object's characteristics (155): the roots, which 'take their nourishment' from humanity, seem serpentine and inhuman; 'the unalterable constitution of things' retains a solidity beyond its actual meaning; 'these roots will be shot into the Depths ...' projects the violence and indefinite agency of evening crime-forecasts; 'at last raise up their proud Tops to Heaven itself,' with its two spondees, has the majesty of those occasional Alexandrines which sprout out of Milton's blank verse.

Although any great oak could serve as a metaphor for the organic, mysterious, pre-Enlightenment state, Burke's arboreal metaphor for the Irish nation in his *Letter to Hussey* – capable of explosive growth – seems much more vital and attractive than his British oak from the *Reflections*, a bovine shelter whose reassuring stasis Burke attributes to 'the cold sluggishness of our national character' (181). In *The Great Melody*, Conor Cruise O'Brien argues that Burke's opposition to irresponsible despotism grew out of his self-identification with Ireland and Catholicism:

Burke was conservative in the 1790s, in relation to Britain, in the sense that he was determined to defend the British Constitution against its

Jacobin and pro-Jacobin enemies. But he was not conservative in relation to Ireland, where the benefits of the British Constitution were
denied to the majority of the population, including his relatives. He
obviously did not want Jacobinism to spread to Ireland. But he was
well aware that the *fear* of the spread of Jacobinism represented the
best hope of securing full Catholic enfranchisement.               (499)

As we will see in the writing of Arnold, Eliot, and Leavis, fear of political
or cultural anarchy plays its important role in the construction of *culture*.

In light of O'Brien's substantial evidence, Burke's first-person posses-
sive, 'our national character,' seems duplicitous on some level, and the
cosmic but psychological oak he shares in confidence with the Catholic
Bishop Hussey appears as an honest, if temporary, expression of how
the Irish state might grow. If, in its vastness and fast sprouting, this oak
projects Burke's fear both of political and theological insurrection,[8] it
also projects his desire for justice for Ireland. It becomes, ultimately,
an emblem of Burke's Anglo-Irish ambivalence, not the same teetering
on a Protestant hyphenated fulcrum Yeats experienced but a temporal
division between his current political persona and his sincere public
conservatism, on the one hand, and a more secret identification with
childhood self and his oppressed people. Thus, the epistolary oak
becomes a clearer *reflection*, in an eighteenth-century sense, of Burke's
soul than the 'British oak' in the *Reflections*.[9]

When Yeats heralds the 'haughtier-headed Burke that proved the
State a tree' (*CP*, 238: 'Blood and the Moon'), he probably refers primarily
to the more placid oak, the bovine shelter of the *Reflections*. Just because
the oak Burke shared with Hussey is more appropriate to Yeats's intention
in this poem to reappropriate Burke as the Irish national philosopher,
this suitability cannot, by itself, give priority to that emblem. However,
we might recognize the deeper affinity of this dualistic oak – branching
from Hell to Heaven, growing heavenward out of hatred – with Yeats's
lifelong Blakean belief that 'without contraries is no progress' and with
such 1930s poems as 'Ribh Considers Christian Love Insufficient' in which,
under Nietzschean influence, hatred and love are necessary contraries:
'Hatred of God may bring the soul to God' (*YCP*, 286).

Yeats would have had access to the letter to Hussey in Matthew
Arnold's edition of Burke's *Letters, Speeches and Tracts on Irish Affairs*
(1881). Although Yeats often vented his nationalist sentiments openly, in
not distinguishing between Burke's oaks Yeats may have been partici-
pating in Burke's own subversive duplicity – a form of post-Reformation
equivocation – which O'Brien characterizes:

In studying Burke, I have often found that, whenever there is an unexpected silence, a failure to refer to something obviously relevant, or a cryptically guarded formulation, the probable explanation is usually to be found at 'the Irish level': the suspect and subterranean area of emotional access to the forbidden world of Roman Catholicism.                                                                                    (450)

Yet, Yeats can guard his own silences or commit his own stealthy misprisions. As one commentator has written, 'When Yeats uses Burke's images, he alters them by the way he selects from them.... The tree becomes other than and more than the merely British oak.'[10] More specifically than the frequent references to trees in Yeats's prose and poetry, one reference in a review of Irish folk tales may echo Burke. Yeats recalls an Irish peasant's vision of 'a great tree' which 'cast a light of imagination on his own dull cattle-minding and earth-turning destiny, and gave him heart...' (*YUP*, 1, 190).[11] What can be demonstrated, however, is that Burke's conversion of the horizontal placid British oak to the vertically dynamic dualistic oak designed for Hussey anticipates not only Yeats's own equivocations but specifically his conversions of Arnold's benign ethnic types of the Englishman and the Irishman to more complex antithetical representatives of their society, projections of Yeats's own ambivalent love and hatred toward his nation and her colonizer.

## Arnold and Yeats

Arnold's essays on Ireland, collected in books in 1865 and 1882, maintain a consistent liberal stance toward England's oldest colony. Writing in the journal *Nineteenth Century* (1881), he said: 'Even to talk of the people inhabiting an island quite near to us, and which we have governed ever since the twelfth century, as a distinct nation from ourselves, ought to seem strange and absurd to us' (*ACPW*, IX, 241). As unwilling as Burke openly to consider alternatives to a union between England and Ireland, in this essay Arnold focuses on England's failure 'to attach Ireland' (243) and advocates 'fair treatment for Catholics...' (269). Striking a Burkean theme, Arnold argues that 'if courtesy is required to cement society,' then the English Philistine who governs Ireland can only dissolve or corrode union. Accepting the Dickensian prototype, Arnold asserts that 'the genuine, unmitigated Murdstone, ... the common middle-class Englishman ... is seen in full force, of course, in the Protestant north; but throughout Ireland he is a prominent figure of the English garrison' (277). With almost no reference to history, Arnold would heal the estrangement of Ireland with the same antidote he opposes to 'anarchy' in Britain: 'transform our middle class and its social civilisation' (284).

No reader of Arnold in 1881 would need to wonder by what agency the Philistine Ascendancy in Ireland, along with the middle class in England, must be transformed. From the publication of *Culture and Anarchy* in 1865, British readers could associate the buzz and drone of Arnold with the sweetness and light of transformative culture. *Culture* is the 'pursuit of perfection' and 'of like spirit with poetry, follows one law with poetry' (*ACPW*, V, 99). Led by the spirit of poetry, culture functions to ameliorate the harshness of the middle class's 'social civilisation,' an objective Newbolt continued to emphasize in 1921. Arnold's cultural pursuit can appear to be more forward-looking than Burke's 'culture' as emblemized by a savings bank or, implicitly, a tree, both drawing on past resources. However, in its association with poetry, which is infused with the Greek spirit, and criticism, which delves for the best that has been thought and said, Arnold's 'culture' assumes its Burkean rootedness in the past. As we will find in the application of Newbolt's 1921 report, in Arnold's argument poetry would be applied as a political instrument to dilate the excessive 'concentration' that restricted both middle-class England and the Irish colony.

Arnold holds that history moves dialectically between such periods of 'concentration' – dominated by law, morality, and the sort of 'strictness of conscience' that characterized the British middle class – and periods of 'expansion' – infused with art, estheticism, and a 'spontaneity of consciousness' that the aristocracy, more than other classes, could afford. Arnold wrote that 'each of these two forces,' which he calls Hebraism and Hellenism, respectively, 'has its appointed hours of culmination and seasons of rule' (472), but both forces also persist in every age and society. I risk this brief summary of *Culture and Anarchy*, which is, after all, a familiar part of our own culture, to draw distinctions between Arnold's related concepts of Hellenism, a temperament which dominates alternate epochs, and Celticism, a temperament which never dominates but which coexists genetically and culturally with the Anglo-Saxon temperament in the British Isles, Arnold giving them a temporal and spatial emphasis respectively.

'On the Study of Celtic Literature,' Arnold's treatise on Celticism and his most extensive writing on Ireland, was first offered in 1865–6 as four lectures at Oxford, in fulfillment of his responsibilities as Chair of Poetry, and then published in the *Cornhill Magazine*. Ostensibly occasioned by a Celtic festival in Wales, the lectures responded, at least in part but more deeply, to the initial Fenian disturbances in Ireland. Based on his readings in ethnology and philology, which he respects as authoritative sciences, Arnold posits certain Celtic racial traits which should not only be recognized as a constituent of but also 'added to' the mostly Saxon temperament of the Englishman. Politically dominant and commercially prosperous, the Englishman manifests a Saxon or German 'genius [which] has steadiness as its main basis . . . fidelity to nature for its excellence' 'with commonness and humdrum for its defect' (351). To relieve his 'dull earnestness,' the English Philistine 'must add something to his strong sense and sturdy morality' (394), but not all Celtic traits are worthy of imitation. The Irish and Welsh remain among, in Arnold's delicate phrasing, 'nations disinherited of political success' (390) because of their immateriality and impracticality, their chronic 'reaction against the despotism of fact' (347). In combing out the strands of Celtic 'genius,' Arnold finds 'sentiment as its main basis, with love of beauty, charm, and spirituality for its excellence, ineffectualness and self-will for its defects' (351). Close to nature with 'something feminine in them,' Celts are therefore attracted by 'natural magic' and 'feminine idiosyncrasy' (347).[12] Although imaginative, delicately sensual, and impressionable, Celts lack the patience and architectonic faculty to complete great art, although they can create lyrics or their equivalent in the visual arts (344). Finally, Celts – 'undisciplinable, anarchical, and turbulent by nature' – exhibit 'not a promising political temperament' which is 'just the opposite of the Anglo-Saxon temperament' (347).

Although Arnold recognizes the weaknesses of the Celt, his attraction to Celticism, if more ambivalent than that to Hellenism, nevertheless seems based on its capacity to release not only the English middle class but himself as well from the excessive 'concentration' of Hebraism. Arnold's assertion in the preface to 'On the Study of Celtic Literature' – 'No service England can render the Celts by giving you a share in her many good qualities, can surpass that which the Celts can at this moment render England, by communicating to us some of theirs' – can be understood as less disinterested and more autobiographical than it at first appears.

In approaching Celticism through ethnology and philology, Arnold recognizes his own amateur status as a scientist and acknowledges his dependence on Lord Strangford, 'hardly less distinguished for knowing ethnology and languages so scientifically than for knowing so much of them' (387).[13] Emerging from its beginnings in the amateur observations of soldiers, missionaries, and other advance-men for European imperialism, the new sciences of ethnology and philology, Arnold argues, now 'can be securely handled only by those who have made these sciences the object of special study' (387). If this stricture would exclude himself, a 'mere literary critic,' it would also exclude his father Thomas Arnold who, as a trained classicist and, from 1841, Regius Professor of Modern History at Oxford, presumed to combine ethnology and philology in his history lectures and, according to George Stocking's *Victorian Anthropology*, to influence 'a generation of Saxon historians' (62). Disregarding newer work by the German philologists Zeuss and Bopp, who located Celtic languages near the trunk of the Indo-European linguistic tree, Thomas Arnold 'insisted much oftener on the separation between us and them [Celts] than on the separation between us and any other race in the world,' thus supporting Lord Lyndhurst's claim that the Irish were 'aliens in speech, in religion, in blood' (300).

At this point in his essay, for the final dismissal of his own father, who was the beloved patriarch of the Philistines,[14] Arnold defers ('let me have the pleasure of quoting...') to the aristocratic Lord Strangford who asserts that Thomas Arnold was merely the victim of the faulty philology of a Hebraic epoch which must give way to the expansiveness of a Hellenic, or Celtic, epoch.[15] According to the inevitable dialectics of his own historiography, Arnold thereby assures the succession of his ideas over his father's concerning both the family of man and his own affiliation. To his father's creation of 'an impassable gulf' between himself and Celts, particularly the Irish, Arnold reacted, a quarter-century after his father's death, with emotionally charged language: his father's theory 'created a profound sense of estrangement; it doubled the estrangement which political and religious differences already made between us and the Irish: it seemed to make this estrangement immense, incurable, fatal' (300). In espousing this newer theory of the Indo-European family of languages, Matthew Arnold finds that 'pregnant and striking ideas of the ethnologists' also lead to 'the true natural grouping of the human race.' More decisively, these views

> establish a...native diversity between our European bent and the Semitic bent, and...eliminate, even in our religion, certain elements as purely and excessively Semitic, and therefore, in right, not combinable with our European nature, not assimilable by it.      (301)

They thereby also create their own 'impassable gulf' between the son's sense of the human family and his father's.

Arnold would veil the oedipal argument with his father by appealing to the newest theory in anthropological thought, this 'science of origins' which teaches 'us which way our natural affinities and repulsions lie' (301). According to this theory, science, conventionally 'a divider and a separatist,' 'recognises in the bottom of her soul a law of ultimate fusion, of conciliation.' Arnold continues, 'She draws, for instance, towards the same idea which fills her elder and diviner sister, poetry, – the idea of the substantial unity of man' (330). Arnold's notions of Celtic cognates displacing Semitic ones and of the eventual discovery of some unified origin, a belief shared by Social Darwinists from Spencer's writings in the 1850s on into the late Victorian era, sounds remarkably like Freud's curious assertions, toward the end of his career in *Moses and Monotheism* (193), that the true lineage of the despised and tormented Jews sprang from the pharaohs. In opposing Thomas Arnold's account of an Anglo-Saxon descent from 'Hebraism,' Arnold has suggested, through the intensity of his language and his essay's strategies against his father, a version of Freud's 'Family Romance,' in which we invent more desirable, liberating precursors to replace our natural forebears. By choosing his temperamental and spiritual family, Arnold escapes from the generic and cultural determinants of being Thomas Arnold's son and a stolid and earnest Saxon. In a similar manner, the youthful Yeats succeeded in separating himself from his father's advocacy of John Stuart Mill and English positivism by claiming links to the Dukes of Ormonde, later by hosting a Daimon out of the thin night air of George Yeats's dreams,[16] but most importantly by inventing a literary religion. The 'family romances' of both Yeats and Arnold release them, on their own parole, from the borstals or H-Blocks of history.

## Joyce's response to Arnold's benign colonialism

More decisively than Yeats, who never seriously studied the differences between languages, Joyce recognized that Arnold's cultural and linguistic standards were tools as useful for exclusion, as for amalgamation, of classes and peoples. Although Arnold opens 'On the Study of Celtic Literature' with some prefatory mocking of journalistic appeals for the expunging of Celtic languages, he nevertheless advocates the peaceful demise of what he believes are the moribund languages of Wales and Ireland:

> The fusion of all the inhabitants of these islands into one homogeneous, English-speaking whole, the breaking down of barriers between

us, the swallowing up of separate provincial nationalities, is a con-
summation to which the natural course of things irresistibly tends.

(296–7)

Arnold proposes establishing a Chair of Celtic, what amounts to a chair
of literary pathology, to study the dead Celtic languages and literature,
but not until the patient has been dispatched: 'Traders and tourists do
excellent service by pushing the English wedge farther and farther into
the heart of the principality; Ministers of Education, by hammering it
harder and harder into the elementary schools' (297). Readers' momentary
relief when they recognize the metaphor as one of woodcutting rather
than of cultural geriatricide dispels when we recall all that arboreal
images represent in the Burkean-Arnoldean tradition. Drawing a parallel
between the passing of the Celtic languages in France and in Wales and
Ireland, Arnold says,

> *Blanc, rouge, rocher, champ, église, seigneur,* – these words, by which
> the Gallo-Roman now names white and red, and rock and field, and
> church, and lord, are no part of the speech of his true ancestors, they
> are words he has learnt; but since he learned them they have had
> a world-wide success, and we all teach them to our children, and
> armies speaking them have domineered in every city of that Germany
> by which the British Celt was broken . . .                    (293)

Some readers will associate Arnold's linguistic series, which he offers in
two more variations, with that offered by Joyce's hero Stephen Dedalus
when he encounters the Dean of Studies in a key scene in *A Portrait of
the Artist As A Young Man*. Whether or not Joyce directly echoes Arnold
in this scene, in the opening of *Ulysses* Buck Mulligan conflates the sweetness and light of Hellenism with the honeyed and waxing pleasures of
hedonism (6).[17] In a passing insight, Stephen identifies Arnold as the
empirical, and therefore visually oriented, horticulturalist of English
education as he imagines one of Buck's accounts of Oxford: 'Shouts
from the open window startling evening in the quadrangle. A deaf
gardener, aproned, masked with Matthew Arnold's face, pushes his
mower on the sombre lawn watching narrowly the dancing motes of
grasshalms' (7). In the hallucinations of the 'Circe' chapter, Buck's version of Hebraism and Hellenism transmute into 'The Siamese twins,
Philip Drunk and Philip Sober, two Oxford dons with lawnmowers. . . .
Both are masked with Matthew Arnold's face' (422). The twins are less
of a comment on the dialectic of Stephen's personal history than on

the stereotypes underlying Arnold's polarized figures of Hellenism and Hebraism; here they become respectively Stephen Drunk, the recycling Celt expanding with blarney and drink, and Stephen Sober, the anal-retentive Saxon concentrating on the 'Buttend of a pencil' and an account book of the self. With their mowers, both merely cultivate lawn order.

In *A Portrait*, however, when Stephen enters the University tardily and converses with the Dean of Studies, we receive a full critique of language's role in bringing English culture to the Irish colony. Because this scene exposes so many of the reactions and strategies shared by many Irish writers and because it has been important to Seamus Heaney and others, we can justify revisiting a much frequented passage in *A Portrait*. Stephen's 'courteous and vigilant foe,' the Dean of Studies, like the founder of Stephen's and Joyce's university, John Henry Newman, is an English convert to the Jesuit order and therefore representative of the two imperial forces that govern Stephen's life. Less than a year later in his fictional life, in *Ulysses*, Stephen will contradict another Eng-lishman's statement that he is his own master: 'I am a servant of two masters, Stephen said, an English and an Italian' (17).

Although his exchange with the Dean of Studies ostensibly concerns esthetics, about which Stephen is rumored to be writing, Stephen attends more to, and later reflects on, the differences in their language. Beginning with – as an image of beauty – an actual fire the Dean lights outside the lecture theatre, the conversation alternates between similes of fire and water. As an illustration of the difficulty of philosophical enquiry, the Dean's first simile of diving into the depths off the Cliffs of Moher must terrify the hydrophobe and non-swimmer Stephen (202). When Stephen quickly shifts to light and fire, the Dean responds with-out irony, 'I see. I quite see your point.' From the vast image of the Atlantic off the Clare coast, they turn to images for containment of water and fire, the bucket and the lamp, but soon Stephen becomes aware of the 'jingle of the words, bucket and lamp and lamp and bucket. The priest's voice too had a hard jingling tone' (203). Now set outside of the conversation by the difference in accents, observing it as well as conversing, Stephen remarks on how meaning shifts with the context of either the literary tradition or the marketplace. Defining terms according to the former, Stephen is misunderstood by the Dean to be speaking in the latter. A member of 'the nation of shopkeepers,' the Dean is imagined by Stephen as having been summoned to the Catholic Church 'like that disciple who has sat at the receipt of custom ....' In embarrassment at his missing Stephen's point concerning the word *detain*, the Dean resumes this figurative discussion, speaking of 'the funnel through which you pour the oil into your lamp.' The word the Dean selects merely as a figure for intermediacy between liquid and fire, Stephen sees from without as a false mediator: 'Is that called a funnel? Is it not a tundish?' Stephen refers to a dish with a spout with which, according to the *OED*, one can draw liquid from a tun or, as in *Measure for Measure*, fill a bottle. The Dean, who confesses he has never heard of the word, wonders if the term is local to Ireland, and Stephen responds, 'It is called a tundish in Lower Drumcondra . . . where they speak the best English' (204). Although the Elizabethan *tundish*, 'now local' according to the *OED*, may have found its repository in Ireland, Stephen's further locating it in 'Lower Drumcondra,' his present home-district in Dublin, simply suggests he will replace citizens of England, represented by this '*senis baculus* . . . a staff in an old man's hand' (201) as the standard-bearer for 'the best English.' Stephen later will ask, of the Dean, 'What did he come here for to teach us his own language or to learn it from us?' (274).

Because this scene centers on difference between English as spoken by an Englishman and an Irishman, it gives a linguistic foundation to Stephen's alienation. Later, Stephen will declare, 'I will not serve that in which I no longer believe whether it call itself my home, my fatherland, or my church: and I will express myself in some mode of life or art as freely as I can . . .' (268–9). Although the Dean is 'a late comer' to Catholicism, he is 'a countryman of Ben Jonson,' and, therefore, Stephen recognizes, 'The language in which we are speaking is his before it is mine.[18] How different are the words *home, Christ, ale, master*, on his lips and on mine!' Apparently random locutions, these echoes of Arnold's word-series approach linguistically crises of divided loyalties induced by English culture. For Stephen, these crises arise from those particular commitments of home, church, and ale-fueled friendships, which distract him from the priesthood of art, as he also struggles with the mastery of Rome and England that demand his allegiance. Stephen dwells on the difference between the Dean's and his use of such words which cause him 'unrest of spirit' (205). Perhaps echoing Ruskin's account in *Stones of Venice* of 'the restlessness of the dreaming mind, that . . . frets and fades in . . . shadows' and creates 'fretwork' (214),[19] Stephen says, 'My soul frets in the shadow of his language.' In that dark gap created when Stephen steps back from the language, his creative fretwork – semantic stonework and word-lacing – will begin.

We might step back, as well, from this scene to recognize how it exemplifies an exchange between colonizer and colonial subject. For the more literal-minded Dean, similes are figures of speech in a rhetorical exercise meant to draw out Stephen's esthetic ideas and, therefore, to educate him. Similes of water and fire that have an efficacious transparency for the Englishman gain opacity for Stephen through a mythic resonance that is part of Stephen's, and by implication the Irish, mind. Mythic references of water and fire, which Joyce places somewhat coyly at the edge of Stephen's consciousness throughout most of the novel, emerge finally as references to the overreacher Icarus's drowning and his father Daedalus's creative forge out of which Stephen will heat and shape through fictive forgeries his own conscience which, in turn, will mold that of his own people.

In his word-play with Stephen, the Dean knows neither the score nor even the game, which has become a parody of the one he initiated. Through the disparity between the Dean's authority and his linguistic skills in this student–teacher relationship, Joyce represents what Homi Bhabha calls a 'hybrid' discourse in a colonial literature:

> When re-articulated by the native, the colonialist desire for a reformed, recognizable, nearly-similar other, is enacted as parody … where mis-readings and incongruities expose the uncertainties and ambivalences of … the discourse of colonial authority.... (Parry, 42–3)

Joyce's literary 'fretwork,' his self-consciousness about language, and his use of play and parody to address an uncertain, multiple audience result from his marginalized colonial situation. Although Joyce's parodic play represents a more rebellious solution to their colonial situation than Yeats's and one more frequently adapted by succeeding generations of poets,[20] Yeats's own self-consciousness about language leads him to adapt and ultimately trope Arnold's racial stereotypes for the Celt and Saxon.

## Wilde's strategies and Yeats's responses to Arnold's stereotypes

Characteristically of his colonial, more specifically his Anglo-Irish, inter-mediacy, Yeats absorbs Arnold's argument about Celts and Saxons ambivalently. Like Oscar Wilde, who agreed with many of Arnold's ideas while resenting his pedagogic perch, from which condescension was inevitable, Yeats adapted many of Arnold's arguments which are rarely ideas so much as notions: Catherine wheels of valued terms, circular definitions, self-quotations, and figurative or metaphorical suggestions.[21] As did his colonial mentor Wilde, however, Yeats often disguised or altered these notions through elaboration or, as Declan Kiberd says in his essential study *Inventing Ireland*, 'the art of elegant inversion' (35).

Not merely a table-talk tutor for the youthful Yeats, Wilde is a crucial intermediary between Arnold's cultural imperialism and the response not only of Yeats but also of Joyce, Flann O'Brien, and other Irish writers. In the last dozen years, Wilde has been the subject of accelerated interest, in the academic areas both of postcolonial studies and of 'queer studies.' Here, I will only summarize some of Wilde's influences on Irish writing. First, as Yeats acknowledges in his autobiography, Wilde introduced him to the idea of the mask (Wilde wrote, 'Man is least himself when he talks in his own person. Give him a mask and he will tell you the truth' (389)). Secondly, to replace Arnold's racist binaries, Wilde substitutes a social distinction, implicitly, between the Irish and English ('For the culture of a country . . . the presence in . . . [the Church] of a body of men whose duty is to believe in the supernatural, to perform daily miracles, and to keep alive that mythopoeic faculty . . . is so essential for the imagination. But in the English Church a man succeeds . . . through his capacity for disbelief . . .'; 'The growth of common sense in the English Church is . . . a degrading concession to a low form of realism' (317).) Thirdly, he pointed to the revolutionary mechanism that William Irwin Thompson calls, in his book by that title, 'The Imagination of An Insurrection.' Wilde argues that language 'is the parent, and not the child, of thought' and that life can express itself only through imaginative forms supplied by art (320, 359); in his more famous phrasing: 'Life imitates art far more than Art imitates life' (307). Fourthly, and a corollary to the above, art is 'a disturbing and disintegrating force' that seeks to disrupt 'monotony of type, slavery of custom, tyranny of habit, and the reduction of man to the level of a machine' (272). Fifthly, he favored the ear over the eye and suggested that a visual monopoly in art limited community and freedom (351). Sixthly, he demonstrated what he learned from Walter Pater, that arguments are best conducted indirectly against an unspecified adversary, so that Wilde can regret 'Nature's lack of design' (290) without mentioning Ruskin and he can close 'The Soul of Man . . .' by asserting that 'the new Individualism is the new Hellenism' without mentioning Arnold by name. Finally, in the autumn of 1890, Wilde augured a fusion of the Aesthetic Movement, already reaching seniority, with the Irish Literary Renaissance, barely conceived, and thereby reminds us of the argument that could be made for his own paternity, in both cases:

> As the creative instinct is strong in the Celt, and it is the Celt who leads in art, there is no reason why in future years this strange Renaissance should not become almost as mighty in its way as was

that new birth of Art that woke many centuries ago in the cities of
Italy.                                                                (396)

From early in the 1890s Yeats recognized Wilde's attacks on Philistinism as guerrilla forays against imperialism. In a review, Yeats wrote,
'"Intentions" hides within its immense paradox some of the most
subtle literary criticism we are likely to see for many a long day,' and
then Yeats suggested that Irish subversiveness may account for the Irish
resistance to fact that Arnold sees as retardation: 'I see in his life and
works an extravagant Celtic crusade against Anglo-Saxon stupidity.
"I labour under a perpetual fear of not being misunderstood", he wrote,
a short time since, and from behind this barrier of misunderstanding
he peppers John Bull with his pea-shooter of wit . . .' (*YUP*, 1, 203–4).

Some of Wilde's posturing can only be labelled as *camp*, an imitation
of a dominant class, in this case English colonizers, that projects an
ambivalence by being both parody and reproduction of an oppressor's
behavior. Yeats's ambivalence may not appear as camp, but he does
manage to contradict Arnold without openly opposing him. For example,
Yeats accepted Arnold's antithetical racial characterizations of Saxons
and Celts but converted the Irishman's 'sentimentality,' his 'chafing
against fact' and 'perpetual straining after mere emotion' which 'has
accomplished nothing' (345), into an existential heroism, an emphasis
on human freedom and the noble and brave act, unmeasured by utilitarian accomplishment. As a reflection of his own Anglo-Irish alienation
from the Catholic majority, Yeats often made his hero a lonely figure,
feeding off his own heart, but from his own colonial difference with
England he imbued his hero with antinomian impulses.

For example, in an introductory essay to Hone and Rossi's study of
Berkeley, we can observe the degree of Yeats's elaboration in his characterization of the eighteenth-century bishop – 'solitary, talkative, ecstatic,
destructive' (xvi) – who accepted his role as an anti-Enlightenment sage
because 'it hid from himself and others his own anarchy and scepticism'
(xvii). Ignoring the amount of time-serving and toadying Berkeley mixed
with his intermittent assertions of principle, some reserved for his journal,
Yeats romanticizes Berkeley through a sort of free association:

> I think of my father, of one friend or another, even of a drunken
> countryman who tumbled into my carriage out of the corridor one
> summer night, men born into our Irish solitude, of their curiosity,
> their rich discourse, their explosive passion, their sense of mystery as
> they grow old, their readiness to dress up at the suggestion of others

though never quite certain what dress they wear, their occasional childish worldliness.                                                    (xviii)

Among interesting variations on Arnold's stereotype of the Irish, we might observe in the penultimate trait a literalization of Yeats's concept of the mask as well as of Wilde's *camp*.

Although toward the end of his essay he associates Berkeley with neo-Platonism, for the most part he recognizes the Bishop's skepticism about a unitary, Newtonian, commonly shared physical world as a practical hard-headedness, an unwillingness to yield to unproven abstractions:

> Born in such community Berkeley with his belief in perception, that abstract ideas are mere words...[with Swift, Burke, and Goldsmith] found in England the opposite that made their thought lucid or stung it into expression.                                             (xx)

Turning Arnold on his head, Yeats recognizes the 'fact,' to which the English Philistine is wed, as a willed abstraction, a fiction necessary for the 'corporate life':

> It is customary to praise English empirical genius, English sense of reality, and yet throughout the eighteenth century when her Indian Empire was founded England lived for certain great constructions that were true only in relation to the will.                    (xix)

By the mid-1930s, sounding like a quantum physicist strained through the mesh of J. W. Dunne's writing,[22] Yeats has reduced Newtonian and Lockean thought to 'the mechanical theory':[23]

> I am convinced that in two or three generations it will become generally known that the mechanical theory has no reality, that the natural and supernatural are knit together, that to escape a dangerous fanaticism we must study a new science.          (*YE&I*, 518)

Yeats continues to quote Arnold, directly or indirectly, over the course of his career. For example, when Yeats explained 'The Literary Movement in Ireland' to readers of *The North American Review* (December 1899), he wrote:

> The popular poetry of England celebrates her victories, but the popular poetry of Ireland remembers only defeats and defeated persons....

Ireland has no pride in her Lawrences and Wellingtons...these belong to the Empire and not to Ireland, whose 'heart beats high' for men who died in exile or in prison.                    (*YUP*, 2, 196)

Yeats may well have had in mind Arnold's snide reference to 'nations disinherited of political success' (390) from 'On the Study of Celtic Literature' or even its epigraph from Ossian – 'They went forth to the war, but they always fell' – which Yeats borrowed for the first title of his poem 'The Rose of Battle' in its 1892 publication. Even Arnold's diction sticks within Yeats's prose, as we see with the word *gay*. When Arnold writes of the Celt's 'gay defiant reaction against fact,' he has already devoted several lines in his text and eight lines in his notes to claiming the word as Celtic in origin, even though his own expert Lord Strangford disagrees. So, *gay* becomes the word Yeats retrieves when he wants to defend the Irish folk-belief in fairies against the skepticism of readers of the English journal *Leisure Hours* who themselves may believe 'that the soul is a little whiff of gas' and other tenets of a scientific faith: 'The fairy populace...gives a fanciful life to the dead hillsides, and surrounds the peasant, as he ploughs and digs, with tender shadows of poetry. No wonder that he is gay...' (*YUP*, 1, 182). As we know, this 'Celtic' word *gay* becomes central in his later life to Yeats's concept of 'tragic gaiety' and, in Yeats's late master-poem 'Lapis Lazuli' to the glittering eyes of the Chinamen, who are masks for Yeats and for every involved observer of art.

In early career, Yeats molds his heroes with subtle reference to Arnold's characterization of the Celt. In presenting the Celt as antidote or mere palliative rather than alternative to Saxon Philistinism, Arnold gelds his Irishman of the sexual excesses that Victorians associated with Catholic Ireland. In 'The Study of Celtic Literature,' he writes reassuringly, 'It is not so much the vulgar satisfactions of sense that attract him as emotion and excitement; he is truly...sentimental' (344). The Celt, then, enters another binary relationship, assuming the natural, impulsive sensual responses insufficiently governed by reason that the Victorians attributed to women: 'The sensibility of the Celtic nature, its nervous exaltation, have something feminine in them, and the Celt is thus peculiarly disposed to feel the spell of the feminine idiosyncrasy' (347). When Arnold entreats, 'Do not let us wish that the Celt had had less sensibility, but that he had been more master of it' (346–7), he skirts the issue of libidinal Eire and her gross national production of children. Particularly alarming to the Malthusians, Irish fecundity confirmed, for Social Darwinians, the primitive nature of this people. Tethered to a middle-class perspective, English Victorian anthropology often associated the Irish and other classes and national types with 'savages.' According to George Stocking:

> The list of social categories thus equated ... in addition to criminals, women, and children, ... included peasants, rustics, laborers, beggars, paupers, madmen, and Irishmen – all of whom were at times likened to savages or to 'primitive' man. ... Governed more by impulse, deficient in foresight, they were in varying degrees unable to subordinate instinctual need to human rational control.                              (229)

In representing the Irish hero as the dangerous sexual renegade, Yeats challenged not only the English middle class's fear of Irish sexual license, implicit in Arnold, but also the restrictiveness of the Irish middle class. In attempting to be more puritanical than the English Victorians, the Irish bourgeoisie denied themselves that sense of contrariness that gave strength to the Irish Georgians – Swift, Berkeley, Burke – who, in their opposition to England, were 'stung ... into expression' (Hone and Rossi, xx). For example, in the 1930s, rather than arguing for the courage and fidelity of Parnell in his relation to Katherine O'Shea, Yeats projects this Anglo-Irish patriot into a popular drinking song where '... stories that live longest / Are sung above the glass, / And Parnell loved his country / And Parnell loved his lass' (309). In poetic dramas, Yeats's hero Cuchulain brings an unassailable, because mythic and pre-Christian, sexual license into sharp contrast with the tidy, moral constraint of his Irish audience. For example, in 1907, that same urban bourgeois audience, which included militant Sinn Feiners, objected to what they saw as the Abbey Theatre's failure to respect the totemic value of the Irish peasant in John Synge's *Playboy of the Western World*. In reaction, Yeats insinuated that they rioted out of impotent envy toward the sexual potency that infused Synge's play, 'that violent, laughing thing' (*YCP*, 593).

In most cases a poem's title serves as a public index that points to or stands in for the poem. The title 'On Those That Hated *The Playboy of the Western World*, 1907,' returns the poem from the myth of Don Juan to a political level that is only indirectly referred to in the fifth line's simile:

> Once, when midnight smote the air,
> Eunuchs ran through Hell and met
> On every crowded street to stare
> Upon great Juan riding by:
> Even like these to rail and sweat
> Staring upon his sinewy thigh.

The stressed opening, set off by commas, reminds us this is a narrative ('Once...upon a time...') of an event already completed – reinforced by an assonantal chiming with the onomatopoeic past tense of *smite* – as it also enacts the first stroke of midnight's toll which plummets Juan from his own riotous living into Hell. Self-confessedly past and fictional, the poem can claim only very indirectly to mirror the current political world, as the excluding simile – 'Even like these...': remote similarity but not identity – confirms. Nevertheless, the similarities become effectively discomforting for Synge's opponents when the reader recalls that the eunuch, like the man of business affairs, sacrifices some humanity to fill – by not filling, for the eunuch – a position of trust. As we are carried forward by the rout of vowels – *u, uchs, ough, on owd, uan* – the enjambment of lines 2 and 3 creates suspense and enforces the crowd's surge. By 'getting a leg over' the end of lines 2 and 3, the eunuchs can stop by line 4 to observe Juan's motion. This gazed upon action, 'riding by,' rhymes with *thigh*, a synecdoche for latent or arrested erotic action and, therefore, an object of sexual fixation.

Finally, the poem reminds us, self-consciously, of its exchange value in the political world. The poem is only *on* the *Playboy* opponents, who are only *like* the eunuchs. Its full effectiveness as insult depends on a close reading for which Yeats, like the Devil or the Commander of Seville in the Don Juan myth, is the transporting intermediary: the poem then discloses hidden layers of insult that correspond to hidden layers of undisclosed repression and sexual motivation in the Abbey rioters and their English equivalents. If in the social world this image of the rioters replaces their own self-concepts, the poem becomes a counter to 'the mirror of malicious eyes' Yeats speaks of elsewhere (*YCP*, 236). In this case, the mirroring exchange between the remote six-line other-world and the more public title and, eventually, between the poem and the actual rioters would be complete and devastating. By accepting and extending the binaries implicit in Arnold and explicit in Arnold's anthropological models, Yeats carries the political struggle with Saxon mentality into the bedroom and the psyche of his enemies. If politically this victory is Pyrrhic, as I suggested in Chapter 1, it is because Yeats found no model for the successor to the hero of the revolutionary stage.

## Shy trafficking: Yeats's and Arnold's poetic economies

As Yeats's borrowings from and reversals of Arnold's writing on culture should indicate by now, we need to read poetically and to attend to metaphors. For example, in 'The Function of Criticism' Arnold's metaphors represent Burke as having made some sort of conversion from the plunging depth and verticality of the sublime to the floating horizontality of a flooded plain: 'It is his accident that his ideas were at the service of an epoch of concentration, not of an epoch of expansion; . . . he so lived by ideas, and had such a source of them welling up within him, that he could float even an epoch of concentration . . .' (244). Caught between the death of Burke's epoch and the suspended birth of an epoch of expansion, Arnold often represents salutary culture, and particularly poetry, as spreading horizontally, not a well or spring but, as in 'The Study of Poetry,' a river:[24] 'The stream of English poetry . . . is the course of one great contributory stream to the world-river of poetry . . .' (307).

In contrast, as metaphors for poetry and imagination Yeats prefers the sort of vertical images Burke employed in the well and tree. Irish landscape with its many sealed passage graves and accidently broached bog-middens must have generated in Yeats a fascination with vertical probings of origins. These interests were strengthened, however, by his early, and lifelong, interest in ethnology to which Matthew Arnold may have introduced him. Yeats's preference for ethnological myth and typology over the historical tracking of human migrations is reflected in his comment on original literatures in one of his earliest published essays:

> In the garden of the world's imagination there are seven great fountains. The seven great cycles of legends – the Indian; the Homeric; . . . and the Irish . . . Every one of these cycles is the voice of some race celebrating itself, embalming for ever what it hated and loved. Back to their old legends go, year after year, the poets of the earth, seeking the truth about nature and man.                                          (*YUP*, 1, 81)

Through the metaphor of the fountain – in the sense of 'source' or 'fountainhead' – which he encountered in Coleridge and Shelley, Yeats can represent his belief that what is drawn from local soil or one's deepest self may also be universal – 'the truth about nature and man.' Following Samuel Ferguson, he excavated beneath the structures of British and Roman empires to find, in the Ulster and Fenian Cycles, 'a fountain' which could still supply 'living waters for the healing of our nation' (*YUP*, 1, 82). If Modernism responds to a hyper-extended time sense and a distrust of history – 'the burden of the past' – by seeking originating points in the unconscious, prehistory, and ritual, then Yeats's Modernism is qualified by his intention, which he declared in an 1892 essay (*YUP*, 1, 255), to de-anglicize Ireland through literature. In 1897 Yeats wrote that 'every new fountain of legends is a new intoxication for the imagination of the world' (*YE&I*, 187). His metaphor of the fountain, fed by an international aquatic table, opposes the Arnoldian metaphor of the mainstream of literature. Beginning with the intention of de-anglicizing Irish literature, Yeats ends both by aligning this literature, through imagination's sources in a collective unconscious, with the neo-romantic, international Modernist movement and by attempting to isolate English poetry in its 'despotism of fact' and the 'dangerous fanaticism' of the 'mechanical theory' (*YE&I*, 518).

Placed so advantageously in the opening of Arnold's influential 'The Study of Poetry' (1879), this figure of English poetry as a stream, and later a mainstream, becomes a commonplace of criticism over the next century, as we will soon see. As Arnold's cultural enterprise becomes institutionalized within school and university curricula and in the metropolitan offices of major canon-forming periodicals and publishing houses, this poetic waterway becomes literalized in the Thames running from Oxford to London as if bearing poetic transports in an insular cultural traffic.

Although neither Arnold nor Yeats wished to reduce poetry to a cultural commodity, they both valorized poetry in relation to their own cultures, often resorting to those binary terms employed by Arnold. For an example from 1886, no more embarrassing than pronouncements by most of us at age 21, Yeats wrote:

> Sir Samuel Ferguson, I contend, is the greatest Irish poet, because in his poems and the legends, they embody more completely than in any other man's writing the Irish character.... This faithfulness to things tragic and bitter, to thoughts that wear one's life out and scatter one's joy, the Celt has above all others.      (*YUP*, 1, 187)

A few months later, at Ferguson's death, Yeats would write that this Ulsterman was 'the greatest poet Ireland has produced, because the most central and most Celtic' and because he wrote by 'the purifying flame of national sentiment' (103).[25] For Arnold, the function of poetry and of culture, generally, was to mollify rather than strengthen Saxon/ Hebraic qualities, which nevertheless still valorizes poetry in cultural rather than in aesthetic terms.

In assigning the value of poetry generally, Arnold usually speaks only of the beneficial ways in which it affects the reader. Individual poems he evaluates in terms of the degree of 'high seriousness' and 'absolute sincerity' relative to other poems. About principles of literary axiology, however, Arnold is usually vague, and had his job as school inspector not led him to involve poetry in pedagogical and curricular questions, he might have followed his own advice to the Scholar Gypsy either to retain silence about his secret lore or to open silent gaps between himself and his society.

Completed before he was thirty, 'The Scholar-Gipsy' probably remains Arnold's clearest attempt to justify poetic reticence and temporize on the poet's behalf. Not ostensibly a poet, the Scholar has abandoned conventional studies to learn the gipsy's 'arts to rule as they desired / The workings of men's brains' (lines 45–6). Should the Scholar reenter contemporary life with its 'sick hurry, its divided aims' (line 204), like Keats's nightingale his 'glad perennial youth would fade, / Fade, and grow old at last, and die like ours' (lines 229–30). Consequently, by a series of gaps, we are separated first from the Scholar's knowledge and then, by time and space, from the scholar himself. Glanvil's book *Vanity of Dogmatizing* (1661), two centuries old, gives an account of the Scholar who existed before Glanvil. Similarly, the Scholar is displaced spatially: the speaker, 'Moored to the cool bank' stares out toward the Scholar's haunt in the Cumner Hills and perceives, in his mind's eye, the Scholar in turn floating on the Thames and retaining yet a further focus: 'leaning backward in a pensive dream /...'/... thine eyes resting on the moonlit stream' (80). At several removes already, the Scholar's focus is an image of change afloat on an image of flux. Finally, in exchange with 'shy traffickers,' the Scholar delivers his goods. Translated by simile into a Tyrian trader, someone whom he can approximate only in his manner of flight, he brings us just to the point of disclosure:

> And snatch'd his rudder, and shook out more sail;
>   And day and night held on indignantly
> O'er the blue Midland waters with the gale,
>   Betwixt the Syrtes and soft Sicily,
>     To where the Atlantic raves
> Outside the western straits; and unbent sails
>   There, where down cloudy cliffs through sheets of foam,
>   Shy traffickers, the dark Iberians come;
> And on the beach undid his corded bales.

(242–50)[26]

Although the trader's surface flight should not be confused with a horizontal sublime, he does pass through the Straits of Gibraltar 'To

where the Atlantic raves / Outside . . . 'the contained market of the Mediterranean. Through this series of substitutions – the Scholar-Gipsy for the
poet, the Tyrian trader for the Scholar-Gipsy, the Rimbaudian zeno-trader
for the closed-marketeer – Arnold distances poetry from 'this strange
disease of modern life, / With its sick hurry . . .' (lines 203–4). Nevertheless, Arnold wants it both ways: as he does in his pedagogic writing, he
still thrusts poetry into an exchange. Awaiting 'heaven-sent moments
for this skill' (50), once he has received these epiphanies, the Scholar
will impart to the world these secrets.[27] Gnostic secrets rather than
mysteries, this knowledge, once acquired, can be taught and transmitted
in a commodities exchange. Until an epoch of expansion has made this
knowledge available, however, it must remain as secret or inaccessible
as the contents of the corded bales.

By not defining poetry or reducing it completely to a utilitarian value,
Arnold avoids equating poetic and other exchanges, but often the language of financial and other economies enters his discussions of poetry.
For example, he concludes 'The Study of Poetry' (1880) by raising the
threat that mass-market reading may eclipse standards and efface good
literature and, especially, the classic. His response sounds remarkably like
Herbert Spencer's answer to threats of the population explosion that
Thomas Malthus exposed. Trusting the human survival instinct, Spencer
insisted that 'a systematic opposition between individuation and reproduction in the organic world . . . inversely correlated . . .' would resolve
the Malthusian dilemma. According to George Stocking,

> If the Irish potato famine was evidence that the pressure of fertility
> still operated in modern life, Spencer nevertheless looked forward
> to a day when the discipline of labor to gain a living would have
> produced a race in which each pair would have only two children
> to reproduce themselves, and the pressure of population would dis-
> appear entirely.                                                      (221)

In a parallel argument, Arnold reassured his readers: 'Even if good literature entirely lost currency with the world, it would still be abundantly
worth while to continue to enjoy it by oneself. But it never will lose
currency with the world. . . .' He concludes with some of Spencer's
logical softness: 'Currency and supremacy are insured to it . . . by the
instinct of self-preservation in humanity' (327).

Unlike Wallace Stevens, who said that poetry was a kind of money,
Arnold never equated poetry with currency. However, when he employs
the terms in proximity, as in the statements above, works of literature

that are vying for the readers' attention assume a relation to the classic which is analogous to the relation of currency and of commodities to a universal standard of gold or silver. If we consider his discussions of literary 'touchstones' and of the classic, we can recognize that Arnold deliberately developed this analogy. When he writes that he assays recent literature by 'using the poetry of the great classics as a sort of touchstone, to correct this estimate,' he sets passages side by side to see if any gold rubs off.[28] Until time and criticism dispel the personal and historical estimates, the literary work, awaiting the 'real estimate,' circulates as a potential classic. In a certain sense, however, the classic itself no longer circulates. Arnold writes of Shakespearean and Miltonic poetry, 'We all of us recognise it as great poetry, our greatest, and Shakespeare and Milton as our poetical classics. The real estimate, here, has universal currency' (319). Like a gold standard, the classic is elevated above local currency and a market in which values fluctuate. T. S. Eliot, who identified 'maturity' (occurring at a good moment, seasonable, ripe) as the essential quality of a classic, adapts Arnold's dialectic to an organic model and removes the classic from the imitation and competition of subsequent generations. According to Eliot, the great poet or author of the classic 'tends to exhaust the ground he cultivates, so that it must ... be left in fallow for some generations' (*ESP*, 125).

  In all such systems of value and exchange, according to Jean-Joseph Goux, 'a hierarchy is instituted between an excluded idealized element and the other elements, which measure their value in it' (3). If we extend Goux's homological argument to include literary canons and culture, then the centrality of poetry to culture and the fetishizing of the classic within literary hierarchies necessarily raise these questions of measurement and standards that Yeats decried. Once the utility of poetry had become an acceptable topic, through discussions of its role in school curricula, it follows that literary standards must be established. Macmillan, for example, the publishers of Arnold, Hardy, and Yeats, published Francis Palgrave's *Golden Treasury of English Songs and Lyrics* (1861), with the objective, suggested by its title, of setting aside 'a true national anthology' and thereby introducing a standard into a British Isles poetry market that boasted 'some twenty-thousand respectable versifiers' (Morgan, 63). In his preface, Palgrave promised that 'so far as the standard of Excellence kept in view has been attained ... a similarity of tone and manner ... will be found throughout: – something neither modern nor ancient, but true in all ages, and like the works of Creation, perfect as on the first day' (531). Order will be imposed on both the curriculum and the market by this ageless poetry, which, in the words of Alexander

Macmillan, 'will never cease to command the ear and – pray note the merchant spirit, strong even in high moods in the British shopkeeper – the purse of thousands everywhere' (Morgan, 62). As an extension of these objectives, Macmillan later initiated a *Golden Treasury Series* of selections from standard authors for which Hardy was represented in 1916 in a thin volume suitable for carrying into the trenches.[29]

In arguing for the establishment of literary standards, Arnold admits voices of dissent on the issue of 'the classic.' For example, as a *concessio* 'The Study of Poetry' quotes Charles d'Héricault's persuasive criticism:

> The cloud of glory playing round a classic is a mist as dangerous to the future of a literature as it is intolerable for the purposes of history. . . . It hinders us from seeing more than one single point. . . . It puts a statue where there was once a man, and hiding from us all trace of the labour, the attempts, the weaknesses, the failures, it claims not study but veneration. . . . Above all, for the historian this creation of classic personages is inadmissible; for it withdraws the poet from his time, from his proper life, it breaks historical relationships, it blinds criticism by conventional admiration, and renders the investigation of literary origins unacceptable. It gives us a human personage no longer, but a God. . . .                    (*ACPW*, IX, 164)

Against this assertion that the classic falsifies history and the processes of creation Arnold offers no real response. He merely asserts that these possible negative effects are less important than an unencumbered appreciation of the work, 'to feel and enjoy . . . to appreciate the wide difference between it and all work which has not the same high character' (309). In the next century, Eliot would acknowledge that the immediate recognition of the superiority of the classic – for him a matter of that work's 'maturity' – required the reader's prior disposition toward that work: 'To make the meaning of maturity really apprehensible . . . to the immature, is perhaps impossible' (*ESP*, 117). The classic then exhibited a trait understood only by the class or group that possesses it. If Eliot is correct, we may then doubt the efficacy of teaching the classics to the literarily underprivileged, but we would be overlooking their uses for mob control. As if advocating a kind of tear gas, in 1860 the educator H. G. Robinson promoted literary education because 'it actually forces an awareness of class inferiority upon its unrefined readers, making them ashamed of their "insignificance" before the intellectual leaders of the race, and numbing their own creative capacity' (Baldick, 67).

If the classics can help nurture the populace of a growing democracy, as Arnold believed, or reduce them to a savage's torpor, as Robinson advocated, that reading public, comprised mostly of Arnold's Philistines, can also use the classic, Oscar Wilde maintained, for reactionary purposes: 'The fact is the public makes use of the classics of a country as a means of checking the progress of Art. They degrade the classics into authorities. They use them as bludgeons for preventing the free expression of Beauty in new forms' (273).

Wilde, like Eliot, Arnold, and his exaggerators such as H. G. Robinson, recognizes that the classic and the canon function to restrict freedom and clothe political values in esthetic dress. Rather than denying the validity of Arnold's idea of the classic or a canon of superior works, Yeats – politically conservative within Ireland – promotes his own English canon composed of English radicals or Irish patriots such as Swift, Blake, Shelley, Morris, and Rossetti, most of whom had been challenged by Arnold and would soon be excluded by Eliot or Richards or Leavis.

Yeats does depart from Arnold's emphasis on the consumption of poetry's sweetness and light and its consequent cohesive effect on a population threatening to become unglued. In 'The Function of Criticism ...,' when Arnold speaks of *currency*, he refers to an active circuit of exchange among thinkers, poets, and audience:

> I say *current* at the time, not merely accessible at the time; for creative literary genius does not principally show itself in discovering new ideas, that is rather the business of the philosopher. The grand work of literary genius is a work of synthesis and exposition, not of analysis and discovery.

He goes on to define the poet's function as 'dealing divinely with these ideas, presenting them in the most effective and attractive combinations...' (*ACPW*, III, 260–1). Inescapably commercial, Arnold's gerunds *dealing* and *presenting* contrast with Yeats's ironic *trade* which – in 'Irish poets learn your trade' or 'Yet now it seems an idle trade enough (*YCP*, 327, 81) – veers away from the possible synonym *exchange* toward an emphasis on craft, or making, and on expressiveness.

In Yeats's poetic economy, 'a community bound together by imaginative possessions' (*YE&I*, 213) supplants the 'business of the philosopher' of Arnold's economy as the origin of the poet's topics and ideas. Elsewhere, Yeats contradicts Arnold in arguing that Irish heroic poetry 'is not, as a great English writer has said, "a criticism of life," but rather a fire in the spirit...' and, again, that Irish folk tales 'are not a criticism of life but rather an extension...' (*YUP*, 1, 84, 187). Yeats believed Arnold's linking of philosophy and poetry drained poetry of its imaginative strength, as he suggests in a review of William Sharp's alter ego Fiona Macleod: 'Ten years ago Miss Macleod would have asked herself, "Is this a valuable and sober criticism upon life?" and we should probably have lost one of the most inspired... one of the most intense poems of our time...' (422). As if still in an oral culture, the poet receives inspiration from the people, transforms it imaginatively, and returns it immediately to the people:

> Does not the greatest poetry always require a people to listen to it? England or any other country which takes its tunes from the great cities and gets its taste from schools and not from old custom may have a mob, but it cannot have a people.... To have even perfectly the thoughts that ... can be got from books, the precision that can be learned at school, to belong to any aristocracy, is to be a little pool that will soon dry up. A people alone are a great river....    (213–14)

Once again Yeats seems to have inverted Arnold's metaphors to the Irish advantage.

Just as Yeats's inversions suggest that he deliberately reflects and counters Arnold, so, one could argue, the effort to free Ireland from the cultural hegemony of English language, literary canons, 'received pronunciation,' urban art and music, and even sports, which could name itself in its infancy the Celtic Revival and the Irish Literary Renaissance, found its deliberate and self-conscious focus because Arnold had advocated a similar deliberate focus for English *culture*. One could even argue that Yeats's emphasis on poetic craft arises from the necessity to purge the Irish canon of its most artificial or rhetorical writers, such as Moore and Davis, in order to project a standard for its new literary canon that could eventually compete with England's standard. With centuries of Irish literature available to him only in translation and with a very youthful Irish literature in English, Yeats compensated for Ireland's disadvantage relative to English literature by rhetorical ploys, and even propaganda. For example, he returns to Burke's tree metaphor to argue the inevitability of Ireland's literature overcoming England, as a young tree must eventually grow from 'unity to multiplicity, from simplicity to complexity...' and outlive an aged one (*YUP*, 1, 268). 'We are gardeners,' Yeats says, 'trying to grow various kinds of trees and flowers that are peculiar to our soil and climate' (269), thereby making an Arnoldian case for a distinctive, home-grown literature.

Superb critics and readers at times, both Arnold and Yeats engage in the employment of bodies of literature for what they see as the political advantages of their own countries. As, at times, the colonized but rebellious subject or, at other times, the intermediary between Anglo- and Irish cultures, Yeats seems to play the game of culture according to Arnold's rules, trying, like some great West Indian cricketer, to subvert and master the English game imposed on him. What is understated, much less understudied, is the fact that Yeats's literary works, like other Irish literature even more antagonistic to England, had to depend on the goodwill and the corporate mechanism of English publishing houses.

## Irish bards, Scots publishers, and English editors

The 'New Irish Library,' of which Yeats was the first editor – and which he believed was crucial to the next, ideological stage of the struggle for Irish independence – owed its existence to the young publishing house of T. Fisher Unwin and to Yeats's advocate and friend there Richard Garnett. By the time Yeats's adversary, the aged and stodgy Irish patriot Charles Gavan Duffy, with the backing of old-line nationalists, assumed control of the 'Library,' which had been his original project, Garnett had become too remote from the, mostly underground, mechanisms of Irish politics to restore Yeats's editorship. Garnett's weakness as an ally of Yeats illustrates a general pattern of English publishers failing worthy Irish writers. In late Victorian London, British ignorance of Irish politics, as in Garnett's case, or an unconscious ideological bias, rather than any deliberate blacklisting, account for the exclusion of Irish writers who later established their merit. However, in the case of Macmillan's rejection of Yeats in 1900, as Warwick Gould has convincingly established, a strong racial bias in one of the readers and the desire for political revenge in the other account for this injustice by one of London's major literary publishers.

Macmillan Press was founded in 1843 by two Scots brothers, who were themselves outsiders by nationality, class, and education. Beyond publishing Hardy and Arnold, the Macmillans proved after the rejection of Yeats to be remarkably open to Irish writers such as Sean Lysaght, Stephen Gwynn, AE, and James Stephens who were Macmillan authors by 1912. After the First World War, Macmillan enlisted Padraic Colum (1922), Sean O'Casey, Lennox Robinson (1925), Eimar O'Duffy (1926), George Shiels and F. R. Higgins (1927), Katharine Tynan (*Collected Poems*, 1930), Frank O'Connor (1931), John Eglinton (1935), Paul Vincent

Carroll (1938), Joseph Hone (*W. B. Yeats*, 1942), and, perhaps surprisingly, Patrick Kavanagh in two volumes (1936, 1947). Yeats did not join Macmillan's list until 1916 because hostile reports by two readers, Mowbray Morris and John Morley, blocked his acceptance. Morris characterized Yeats's work as 'unreal, unhuman and insincere' and categorized him with Maeterlinck, Ibsen, and the Pre-Raphaelites as 'eccentric.' Evaluating a volume that included 'The Song of Wandering Aengus,' 'The Song of the Old Mother,' 'The Cap and Bells,' and 'The Secret Rose,' John Morley, who with kinder words had once rejected Hardy, wrote that Yeats's poems were 'neither more nor less than a pure negation of the human understanding.' He concluded, 'It is to me sheer nonsense. I do not say it is obscure, or uncouth or barbaric or affected – tho' it is all these evil things; I say it is to me absolute nullity . . .' (220–1). Charles Morgan, author of Macmillan's commissioned history and innocent of the readers' darker motives, said that these reports bespeak 'a mind closed against imaginative writing not of its own school' (222).

Recently, Gould pointed out evidence of Morris's anger over Yeats's letters in March of 1900 to the Irish papers protesting a proposed visit of Queen Victoria to Dublin and summoning nationalists to 'a monster protest meeting' (47). The linking of Yeats's name with Maud Gonne's during the run-up to this visit would not have escaped the notice of the second reader John Morley. As former chief secretary for Ireland, liberal politician, and editor of three journals who sometimes supported controversial writers such as Swinburne, Pater, and Thomas Huxley, he might be thought to be more open to Yeats's writing. Yet, as Gould discloses, three years earlier Maud Gonne had organized Irish voters in Newcastle to defeat this advocate of Home Rule because he would not support amnesty for all Irish political prisoners. In his two books on Edmund Burke he is not above stereotyping the Irish, and words in his report such as *barbaric* assign Yeats to outsider status. The mention of 'treason' in Morris's report on Yeats's poems and the seething tone of Morley's report both clearly spring from political, if not also ethnic, hatred.

If such hatred increases the vitriol of these reports, their rejection of Yeats by Morris and Morley also reveals a thorough confusion of literary values with class and sectarian presumptions. Charles Morgan concludes that 'both write with the dangerous vehemence of men who feel that their citadel is being undermined' (222). The kind of domestic realism they valued and the positivist presumptions they shared would be threatened by Irish writing such as that of Yeats, Joyce, Flann O'Brien, and Beckett which broadens or flits from the perch of reason.

## The course of culture from 1921

This confusion becomes institutionalized within the best-selling 1921 report which openly advocated an ideological role for poetry within 'English' culture. One paragraph of Newbolt's report even seemed to summon the so-called Pylon School – Madge, Auden, and MacNeice – of the 1930s to their urban settings and contemporary subjects:

> The enormous changes in the social life and industrial occupations...
> accentuated by the so-called Industrial Revolution, have created
> a gulf between the world of poetry and that world of everyday life
> from which we receive our 'habitual impressions'....Here too lies
> our hope; since the time cannot be far distant when the poet...will
> invade this vast new territory, and so once again bring sanctification
> and joy into the sphere of common life.                    (258)

Chris Baldick, who quotes the passage above, pronounces the 1921 Newbolt report a 'guiding influence upon the development of English studies, particularly in the schools, but also in the universities through the work of I. A. Richards' (94).

Small wonder, then, that with almost Masonic tendentiousness, such major English critics of poetry between the wars as Richards, F. R. Leavis, and Middleton Murray depreciated Yeats's Romanticist and modernist tendencies with more or less direct reference to his Irishness. For example, in 1928 I. A. Richards wrote:

> A weakness of the modern Irish school (even) at its best, in Mr. Yeats...
> may be that its sensibility is a development out of the main track.
> It is this which seems to make it minor poetry in a sense in which
> Mr. Hardy's best work or Mr. Eliot's *The Waste Land* is major poetry.
>                                                           (197)

Speaking of poetic languor in *The Wild Swans* volume, Murray wrote that 'it may be that Mr. Yeats has succumbed to the malady of a nation' (Jeffares, 1977, 218). Auden had the good manners not to ascribe Yeats's interests in the occult to his Irish origins: they are 'Southern Californian,' he wrote, but he added with wit and English class condescension that they certainly are not 'the kind of nonsense that can be believed by a gentleman' (*Eminent Domain*, 111).

One can argue that the 1921 Newbolt Report institutionalized an opposition to the sort of poetry Yeats wrote by inventing Leavisite cadres before F. R. Leavis himself appeared. The Report asserted that:

> The Professor of Literature in a University should be...a missionary... not merely to the students...but still more toward the teeming population outside the University wall.... The fulfilment of these obligations means propaganda work, organisation and the building up of a staff of assistant missionaries.   (259)

In the next decade F. R. Leavis began his career as editor of *Scrutiny* and long-time lecturer at Cambridge and her fringes. Sharing with Yeats and Eliot a sense of the Industrial Revolution's deleterious effects on society, he promoted culture's clerisy where Arnold had championed its laity. As a stabilizing alternative to Yeats's 'dream-world,' Leavis's evocation of a 'minority capable...of appreciating Dante, Shakespeare, Donne, Baudelaire, Hardy,' upon whom 'the implicit standards that order the finer living of an age' (*LFC*, 15) depended, seems questionable.

> The minority capable not only of appreciating Dante, Shakespeare, Donne, Baudelaire, Hardy...but of recognising their latest successors constitute the consciousness of the race.... Upon this minority depends our power of profiting by the finest human experience of the past; they keep alive...tradition.... Upon them depend the implicit standards that order the finer living of an age, the sense that... the centre is here rather than there.   (*LFC*, 15)

Through the process of discrimination that occurs in reading George Eliot, D. H. Lawrence, or T. S. Eliot, this minority will come to locate and fix 'the centre.' Curiously, Leavis seems to extend these requirements for sympathetic recognition to his own writing at the end of this passage in *For Continuity*: 'By "culture"...I do not suppose myself to have produced a tight definition, but the account, I think, will be recognised as adequate by anyone who is likely to read this pamphlet.' By whatever shibboleth, a core of students and scholars at Cambridge responded to this challenge and gathered around *Scrutiny* to oppose mass culture in British schools with a Leavisite program of discrimination and recognition. As Catherine Belsey explains, the main effect of this program was the 'making of hierarchies':

> The leaders of the community are to be properly equipped to recognise a hierarchy of subjectivity, mysteriously given to individuals, and

judged on the basis of a knowledge not open to rational argument. By this means, a ruling élite provides itself with a sensibility which is the source and guarantee of its right to control and administer experience.                                           (Widdowson, 129)

To understand where and how Yeats settles in this 'hierarchy of subjectivity' we can turn to Leavis's major discussions of him in *New Bearings in English Poetry* (1932) and *Lectures in America* (1966, 1969). In *New Bearings* he does specify some cumuli of critical criteria: the essential quality of a poet is 'the need to communicate something of his own' (11); poetry matters when a poet is 'more alive than other people, more alive in his own age' (13); the poet is 'unusually sensitive, unusually aware, more sincere and more himself than the ordinary man can be'; and 'his capacity for experiencing and his power of communicating are indistinguishable' (13). Such criteria may seem too blunt to inscribe a critique, but in fact they are fashioned to favor T. S. Eliot over the Victorian poets generally and Yeats specifically.

At a time when many British critics acclaimed Yeats the major living poet in English and Edmund Wilson judged him 'perhaps the only poet of the first magnitude' (Jeffares, 1977, 38), Leavis avoided explicit derogation of Yeats. He preferred to destabilize Yeats by emphasizing one of the poles between which Yeats 'vacillates.' He argues that from his Victorian debut, Yeats has been 'preoccupied with the creation of a dream-world' (10). Yeats's weakness – this appetite for 'Transcendental Beauty' – is counterpoised, Leavis concedes, by a potential strength, an ironic recognition that this 'reality' must be illusory, and that even if it could be reached it would leave human longing unslaked' (37). On the other hand, 'Yeats differs from the Victorian romantics in the intensity with which he seeks his "higher reality."' 'The difference,' Leavis adds, 'we have attributed to his being Irish' (40). Just as great poets spring from great cultures in a timely epoch, so may genius founder in a cultural bogland: 'For Mr. Yeats Irishness... means that his dream-world is something more than private, personal and literary; that it has, as it were, an external validation' (34). Finally, Leavis asserts that Yeats's use of symbol drawn from magic and hermeticism 'is commonly felt to be an unsatisfactory element in his later verse, and to come from an unfortunate habit of mind' (49). Behind the clouds of 'is commonly felt,' 'an unsatisfactory element,' and 'unfortunate habit of mind,' we glimpse not only the association of the Irish and magic, recycled from Arnold, but also certain unestablished assumptions: (1) that the experience, for which a poet must have 'capacity,' is of the boot-to-stone variety Samuel

Johnson offered in refutation of Berkeley, rather than also imaginative experiences shaped by the conditions of one's life; (2) that language must match – in order to convey almost transparently – experience rather than entering into or shaping that experience; (3) that the poet – 'more sincere and more himself than the ordinary man' – possesses a self which he can walk like a dog to sniff a reality he remains apart from and unabsorbed by; (4) that what is 'commonly felt' of the world by our senses and empirical beliefs based on reports of the senses are more realistic and a better guide through this life than other systems of belief.

We may understand more clearly and fully how these assumptions weigh not only against Yeats but also against most Irish poets if we consider Leavis's *Lectures in America* where he undertakes a discussion of Yeats's Byzantium poems. He begins, again, with qualified praise for Yeats's 'genius' and the 'variety, range and flexibility' of his poetic (61). He then regrets that Yeats allowed 'his extra-poetic habits' to undermine the 'kind of convincingness and inevitability that comes of ... a complete sincerity ...' (65). He continues:

> To explain what I mean by 'extra-poetic' habits I need only point to *A Vision*, that representative of a life-long quasi-creative addiction which was not sharply or surely distinguished by Yeats from his real creative concern. (65)

The same degree of spiritual preoccupation labeled an 'addiction' in Yeats becomes simply a 'doctrinal frame' when it appears as Anglo-Catholicism in Eliot's *Four Quartets* or when it appears as a deeply held priestly vocation in Hopkins' poetry, a poetic topic beneath Leavis's mention in *New Bearings*.

Leavis then turns to poems he admires – the two Byzantium poems and 'Among School Children' – to praise and limit Yeats. In his reading of 'Sailing to Byzantium,' his recognition of Yeats's ambivalence between the generational world and a world of artistic permanence – this 'ambiguity turning into irony' – probably advanced our understanding of the poem in 1966, the year of this lecture. He admires the irony of Yeats's reduction of 'monuments of unaging intellect' to a mere 'clockwork' bird. He continues:

> The duplicity of the last line gives the completing touch to the irony: *Of what is past, or passing, or to come*. This retains, inevitably, something of the solemn vatic suggestion that emanates from the foregoing

poem. But what in its immediate context of the closing half-stanza it
evokes is court gossip.                                                          (69)

A further irony and possible further reference for the third line, one
noted by other readers, is the sixth line, 'Whatever is begotten, born,
and dies,' a sequence it reverses. This should lead us to other reversals in
the poem: 'fish, flesh, or fowl' (5) reorders 'the young,' 'birds in the trees,'
and 'salmon-falls' as they appear above; in a historical Byzantium, the
opening lines of stanza III would read: 'O sages in a gold mosaic wall /
As if you're standing in God's holy fire'; then six lines later, 'artifice of
eternity' makes more sense when translated into 'eternity of artifice.'
Such reversals characterize the mirror of art into which Yeats passes
with the demonstrative pronoun that opens the poem. He imagines
being in another, timeless place, and the poem characterizes that otherworld of imagining we carry with us, which must always reference this
world, as the last line indicates.

Although Leavis admires Yeats's conversion of ambivalence to irony
in 'Sailing to Byzantium,' he treats Yeats's divided self, his concern for
masks and roles, not as legitimate representations of the dissolving
Humanist self, and certainly not as colonial role-playing, but as weaknesses, as failures to find his 'centre of unity' (75). Leavis writes, 'Yeats's
habit of cultivating attitudes and postures ... makes one – if an Englishman, at any rate – remark that Yeats is a fellow-countryman of Wilde,
Shaw and Joyce' (75). Perhaps Leavis hadn't the resources in 1966 to
understand how colonialism may have forced on these writers a self-
consciousness about Irishness, an uncertainty about audience, questions
about the various languages and discourses thy spoke, and an awareness
of how social forces construct our various selves. Nevertheless, he holds
them to a standard of sincerity and unity of self that derives from his
line of English social criticism.

Leavis's nostalgic Englishness, his messianic view of the cultural role
of literature, his positivist criteria for literature, and his views on Yeats
all descend on and pervade the next generation of critics and scholars
which Leavis himself characterized in terms of standards for value. In
*For Continuity*, Leavis compared the judgments of 'a very small minority'
on whom the 'discerning appreciation of art and literature depends'
to gold; he then compares the endorsements of these judgments by
a somewhat larger minority to the currency underwitten by this gold,
metaphors which seem particularly nostalgic because offered in the year
his nation abandoned the gold standard. The success of Leavis's movement, through writings of his advocates such as Denys Thompson, in

shaping secondary education in Britain down nearly to the present is attested to by many critics, such as the Sheffield lecturer Frank White-head:

> More than from any other printed source, . . . from *Revaluation* and from *The Great Tradition* . . . English teachers, and ultimately their pupils, learned how to develop and apply their own reading-capacity to poems, prose and novels. . . .                    (Whitehead, 147–8)

The journal *The Use of English*, which succeeded *English in the Schools*, carried the message of *Scrutiny* and Leavis into secondary-school teaching. Leavis's influence spread beyond the schools into other literary institutions, as Stuart Laing records: 'During the fifties and sixties *Scrutiny's* legacy was apparent in every field of literary criticism and education. . . . The presence of Leavis was felt both through his published criticism . . . and through his appetite for controversy.' Laing goes on to mention the Leavisite coloring of the seven-volume *Pelican Guide to English Literature* (Sinfield, 1973, 146–7).

While Yeats's reputation was still weathering Leavisite attacks, in the 1970s, the poetry of Hardy was enjoying the support of a remarkable critic and of a growing number of admirers, for many of whom Hardy was the major British poet of this century. In 1972 poet and critic Donald Davie asserted this claim most boldly in his *Thomas Hardy and British Poetry*: 'In British poetry of the last fifty years . . . the most far-reaching influence, for good and ill, has been not Yeats, still less Eliot or Pound, not Lawrence, but *Hardy*' (3). Ultimately, Davie rests his case on the following distinction between Hardy and Yeats:

> Hardy appears to have mistrusted, and certainly leads other poets to mistrust, the claims of poetry to transcend the linear unrolling of recorded time. This . . . sets him irreconcilably at odds with for instance Yeats, who exerts himself repeatedly to transcend historical time by seeing it as cyclical. . . .                    (4)

John Lucas argues persuasively that if we set Davie's book within the context of his later writing, an implicit counter-thesis emerges that explains the parenthetical comment above that Hardy's influence works 'for good and ill.' Lucas asserts that Davie's subtext, which 'is very much one to be *inferred*, and is by no means lying out in the open,' implies that 'if something is badly wrong with English poetry – and Davie is sure there is – the root cause can be traced back to the particular kind of modesty which Hardy's poetry embodies' (138). This 'modesty' – the belief that poetry is not transcendent – appeals to New Historicists who would see poetry, like all human enterprise, as grounded in material causes. Ironically, then, if Lucas's inference is accurate, Davie's book, itself, becomes a major factor in the elevation of Hardy, as Blake Morrison acknowledged in a 1989 interview in the *Irish Literary Supplement*. He said, 'Davie's *Thomas Hardy*...is one of those rare pioneering arguments....' He continues:

> There's far more interest among English poets in Hardy these days than in Yeats.... [Yeats] is perceived as marginalized or 'not British.'... as alien, too, because of his theosophy, because of fairies, *A Vision*....                                        (Johnston, 'Q&A,' 19)

Although Morrison's terms incorporate basically the same empiricism/ magic polarities by which Arnold characterized Celtic and English literary traditions, we may, nevertheless, weigh the difference of these traditions and the appropriateness of some such distinctions. The difficulty arises with words such as *alien, marginalized*, and *not British* from the mouth of a self-styled leader of the London literary establishment: literary editor of the *Observer* at the time of this interview, and later of the *Independent*, poet and author, and co-editor of a major anthology.

If Morrison's statement that 'there's far more interest...in Hardy these days than in Yeats' is still accurate of living English poets at the turn of the century, as it seems to have been of critics, we might suppose that British booksellers would conform to this preference. We know they did around the time of Hardy's death: in 1928–9, Macmillan published 1000 copies of *The Tower* and 1500 of Yeats's *Selected Poems* while printing over 50 000 copies of ten various volumes of Hardy's poetry. From the time of Davie's promotion of him in 1972, Hardy receives more space than Yeats in major anthologies from England in the last quarter-century. For examples, Helen Gardner in *The New Oxford Book of English Verse* (1972) and Philip Larkin, with his ghost-editor Ian Hamilton, in *The Oxford Book of Twentieth-Century English Verse* (1973) prefer in nearly three to two proportions poems by the poet 'nobody read in 1912' to poems by the Irish Nobel Laureate. Consequently, when we turn to the British readership, we can only be surprised that after a half-century of critical battering by Leavisites, Yeats's poetry sells well beyond Hardy's. Macmillan offers these results:[30] between 1951 and 1991, Hardy's *Collected* and its successor his *Complete Poems* have sold 43 000 copies; between 1950 and 1988, Yeats's *Collected Poems* has sold over 176 000. The British reading public's apparent independence of critics and academics is supported by evidence from other publishers, such as that of the Penguin Classics Series, where two-thirds of its 900 titles are translations from Greek and Roman, almost none of which is used in academic courses. We might, at least, hypothesize that a very large group of literate British book-buyers pursues its own culture independently of the literary critic.

Apparently, in drawing this contrast between Yeats and Hardy, Morrison expresses the view almost exclusively of critics:

> Yeats is seen as posturing and worked up from artificial rhetoric and stilts. Hardy is not on stilts, and Yeats is. That's how it is perceived in a tradition that is still dominated by Larkinesque ordinariness and which is therefore highly repelled by Yeats.      (Johnston, Q&A, 19)

Yeats, himself, recognized his own stiltedness, in 'High Talk' and 'The Circus Animals' Desertion,' two poems published in the last month of his life. While 'Circus Animals' mocks only 'Those stilted boys,' the youthful lovers in his early verse, 'High Talk' – in equating Yeats's persona or mask with Malachi Stilt-Jack, the stilted man in the circus procession – can serve as a proleptic response to this tradition of assimilation that would exclude Yeats.

From its startling first line with its 15-syllable lines and self-mocking tone, this disguised sonnet seems anything but stilted, at least until the last couplet. The second quatrain gives us the colorful melange of wild nature and the unnatural – ponies, bears, and, necessarily, a performer on stilts

> Because women in the upper stories demand a face at the pane
> That patching old heels they may shriek, I take to chisel and plane.

> (*CP*, 343–4)

Yeats's spelling *stories* for *storeys* suggests a deliberate pun or even a series of puns: the circle of bluestockings who were the core of Yeats's admirers ('patching old heels') require in their private reading ('in the upper stories') the personal and tragic lineaments of the poet ('a face at the pane'). This final couplet either enacts Yeats's stiltedness or perhaps parodies it ('when they mock us, that we mock again,' he had said in an earlier poem), and this uncertainty of Yeats's intention may be a weakness in the poem. In the final quatrain, the 'Processions' that open the poem become process itself, the succession of life from great-grandad on down, that gains momentum and urgency from the tumble of dactyls followed by spondees: 'All metaphor, Malachi, stilts and all. A barnacle goose / Far up in the stretches of night; night splits and the dawn breaks loose.' Recalling the line from *Ulysses* – 'God becomes man becomes fish becomes barnacle goose becomes feather bed mountain' (for Joyce, the cycle of life)[31] which is based on the medieval belief that barnacle geese spring from the sea – Yeats's high-flying surrogate can be read as 'all metaphor' itself, in the term's radical sense of 'bearing change.' This metamorphosing mask – Daddy-long-legs, Malachi Stilt-Jack, barnacle goose – in the final couplet changes again, radically, into the sea-god: 'I, through the terrible novelty of light, stalk on, stalk on; / Those great sea-horses bare their teeth and laugh at the dawn.' These startling *neigh*-sayers must belong to Manannan MacLir, the Protean sea-god of Irish myth, or to Poseidon.

In place of the order Yeats sought in life and maintained in his poetry, this poem admits the flood that breaks the monumental art that Davie desires. As Thomas Whitaker explains in his convincing treatment of this poem's final line, the horses of Poseidon ramp where the wisdom of Athena might reign or rein in (234–5). During the last eight months of his life, Yeats wrote poems of 'an old man's frenzy' appealing for 'a mind' that could 'pierce the clouds' or descend to 'the foul rag and bone shop of the heart.' In 'High Talk,' his assuming a mask not only elevates the poet's perspective above nature and the ordinary to the plane of artifice, where his stiltedness is exposed, but also, paradoxically, opens the poet to the metamorphosing processes of life, a destabilization as dangerous as the turbulent sea, Yeats's standard image for anarchy and disorder.

Rather than a final position, Yeats's terminal disposition towards disruption is his last corrective pull against order grown rigid, not so much in Irish theocracy or British postcolonialism, as in poetry that, lacking a public voice or a heroic dimension, has settled for domestic certainties or ironic disappointments of conventional expectations. Several of Yeats's 1930s poems insist that poetic language must disturb and renew, as well as create, order – a conviction shared of course by many poets and a number of influential critics from Neitzsche to Morse Peckham to Julia Kristeva. Yeats's notion, manifest in 'High Talk,' of poetry having to disrupt the symbolic order to create a passage for 'the real' and for true poetry, came naturally to other Irish writers, such as Wilde, Joyce, Flann O'Brien, and Beckett, all of whom did their 'fretwork' in the shadow of the colonizer's English. Recently, this impulse to unsettle descends to the work of English poets such as Roy Fisher, Peter Reading, and Carol Ann Duffy and even of canonical English poets, such as Ted Hughes and Geoffrey Hill, enough to have challenged the poetry of 'civic sense,' 'political reponsibility,' and 'Larkinesque ordinariness,' espoused by Arnold, Newbolt, and Leavis, and of all 'those who hanker for the rigid in a world of flux,' as Davie characterized himself (*Thomas Hardy*, 176). As Chris Baldick has written of Arnold, Eliot, Richards, and Leavis: 'Order or harmony becomes the key term uniting these critics against ... centrifugal forces propelling the world to chaos' (212–13).

Yeats's denunciation of 'the mechanical theory' and his appeal 'to study a new science' grew as much from a cultural 'rebellion against the despotism of fact,' when these 'facts' maintained colonial rule, as from his own peculiar genius. In other Irish writers, scientific skepticism may express a Catholic reliance on mystery, braced by a resistance to what is seen as the materialism of Anglican culture. On the other side of the Irish sea, Hardy's presumed demystifying of nature and Davie's desire for monumentality also grow out of a cultural climate. If, in the choice Arnold offered between culture and anarchy, Yeats saw the need occasionally to prefer anarchy or to explore the 'nothingness' of chaos, he responded to a need felt by intellectuals from various cultures and disciplines who were not politically bound to the Newtonian faith. Like other Irish writers, Yeats hardly had to be infused with quantum or chaos theory to entertain the possibility of other and micro-worlds, which are governed by other temporal systems. Of these otherworlds, Paul Muldoon has written:

> One of the ways in which we are most ourselves is that we imagine ourselves to be going somewhere else ... something out there to which we belong, that our home is somewhere else ... there's another dimension, something around us and beyond us, which is our inheritance.                                                   (Haffenden, 141)

At least from the eighth century Irish writers have charted these voyages into the imagination. Although this is one way the Irish literary tradition offers Yeats and other writers that 'external validation' of which Leavis complained, Leavis and his followers have ignored the validity of this world as thoroughly as a hidebound Newtonian might ignore the quantum physics' multiple and 'little worlds' with their variant laws.

If in a somewhat different sense Yeats also believes with Berkeley that *esse est percipi*, at least as we participate in multiple worlds, our emotions and points of view condition, if not shape, them. If these seemingly anarchic worlds ultimately are ungovernable by science, then ultimately, chaos becomes more like a Hebraic nothingness than like the Greek magma from which universes are born. In that case Yeats also knew (I will argue in Chapter 3) that 'nothing makes poetry happen,' as Auden would say of Yeats, in so many words.

# 3
# The 1930s: Yeats, Auden, and Others

## The emergence of Auden

The juncture of politics and poetry in the 1930s has attracted much critical attention to this era, especially in England. Irish writers suffered from new censorship laws at the beginning of the decade and the isolation of neutrality toward the end, and consequently some of its most promising poets – including Austin Clarke, Denis Devlin, Brian Coffey, Thomas MacGreevy, and Samuel Beckett – lived abroad for all or most of the decade. Whereas the 1930s involved its writers in such dramatic oppositions as Fascism and Communism, the proletariat and the bourgeoisie, engagement and estheticism, and points along the spectrum of sexual politics, it also focused these conflicts in reportable events, such as Depression-era unemployment and the Spanish Civil War. The writers themselves characterized their era as the postwar period and then forebodingly as the period between wars, and this self-conscious literary decade may have been the first to terminate itself by declaring its own demise and by contributing to its own postmortem, through the disavowal of its major principles, the closing of its most illustrious journals, and the departure from Britain of some of its major figures.

English poets' perception of their public role – to transmit early warnings of fascist aggression – led them to repress mourning and postmortem reflection on the First World War, except in the somewhat marginalized poetry of Ivor Gurney and David Jones. The poets' sense of being temporally and spatially between – two wars, mourning and moving on, reactionary and radical politics, public rhetoric and private disclosure, local and transinsular audiences, the graveside and immortality – creates an ambivalence about their allegiances that contributes to different levels of poetic discourse within single poems. Such ambivalence and multiple levels of discourse, which characterize colonial and postcolonial Irish writing throughout the century, seem important to English poetry especially in this decade.

In vaulting over the 1920s and braking at the 1940s, we neglect the major achievements of Pound and Eliot who, after all, are American, rather than British or Irish, poets. Nevertheless, they can enter this narrative of the 1930s – respectively – as a major influence on contemporary or future writers as diverse as Yeats, Bunting, Kinsella, Davie, and Raworth, and as the pioneer avant garde poets and major editor-directors in the century. Necessarily but less justifiably, such focus relegates the real achievements of Lawrence and Graves to the status of poetic influences, and mostly later in the story. Nevertheless, the decade may earn its attention in this book by the fact that most of the important poets of the surrounding decades either emerge or expire in the 1930s.

Acclaimed at different levels of distinction, Auden, Spender, Basil Bunting, David Jones, and Dylan Thomas all attract British readers' attention during this decade. With the publication in T. S. Eliot's *Criterion* of the closet-drama *Paid On Both Sides* and then from Eliot's editorship at Faber & Faber of *Poems*, both in 1930, Auden seems so suddenly to appear – 'like an earthquake or volcanic eruption' Walter Allen said (51), in recording the impact on himself of *Poems* – that the process and labor in Pound's injunction to 'Make it new!' seemed already rendered into an achieved condition: the *new*. Both enabling and responding to Auden's career, unusually talented editorial midwives proclaimed this state of newness. Michael Roberts published two anthologies of new poetry: *New Signatures* (1932) and *New Country* (1933); Geoffrey Grigson founded the journal *New Verse* in 1933 and edited it until its demise in 1939; in 1936 Roberts' collaborator on *New Signatures*, John Lehmann, began the semi-annual journal *New Writing* which lasted until the end of 1939.

It may seem curious that the emerging British writers, nearly all leftist in politics, saw the deaths in this decade of those older, politically reactionary writers – D. H. Lawrence, T. E. Lawrence, Yeats – not as the clearing of deadwood from another epoch's growth but as the passing of pioneers and pathfinders. As Stephen Spender said in recalling the 1930s:

> To my generation, Joyce, Eliot, Yeats, in his later poetry, and Lawrence stood for the modern in literature. They seemed revolutionary in their writing, which was what we cared about, and we gave little thought to their politics.
> (5)

Perhaps because the Irish literary tradition in English was far less cap-acious than the English, the emerging Irish poets witnessed the death of Yeats and, just beyond this decade, of Joyce with more mixed and intense feelings. A decade after Yeats's death and employing a metaphor familiar from Burke, Austin Clarke spoke for most of those younger Irish poets:

> As far as the younger generation of poets are concerned, here in Ireland, Yeats was rather like an enormous oak-tree which, of course, kept us in the shade, and did exclude a great number of rays of, say, the friendly sun. . . .                                    (Rodgers, 85)

In the first annual Yeats lecture, T. S. Eliot either ignores Yeats's Irish successors or assumes Yeats's deleterious effect on them when he says, 'Certainly, for the younger poets of England and America, I am sure that their admiration for Yeats's poetry has been wholly good' (248). Yet, out of the stultifying cultural conditions of post-Treaty Ireland in the 1930s, significant poets slowly emerged with the knotty enduring quality possessed by, say, Edwin Muir in Britain. The poetry of Austin Clarke, Patrick Kavanagh, Denis Devlin, and Padraic Fallon appeared only sporadically, if at all, in English journals or newspapers in the 1930s – although Clarke and Kavanagh attempted literary careers in London[1] – and remained underpublished or ignored by British publishers. As if the Irish Sea were a time-warp, major Irish journals – *The Bell*, *Envoy*, *Lagan*, *Rann*, and *Poetry Ireland* – appeared and disappeared one decade after England's 1930s in a delayed echo of their British counter-parts.[2] Nevertheless, if we except Auden and perhaps MacNeice, one can make a strong case that these Irish poets emerging so inconspicuously in the 1930s have endured as well as those British poets more celebrated in their time.

One might argue that, after Yeats's death, this exception of Auden makes the scale dip pendulously and unbalances any comparison of English and Irish poetry. The very attention Auden's poetry has drawn from superb readers and scholars such as Monroe Spears, John Fuller, and, especially, Edward Mendelson not only clarifies but even constructs – because Auden's difficulty requires pioneering readers – this poet's high stature. With respect to popular attention from university students and informed readers, however, Auden's involvement with so many crucial issues of his time, and even of ours, and therefore his suitability for Culture Studies brings him readers with little interest in or capacity for merely analytical interpretations of his poetry.

Well before Culture Studies became a preoccupation of English depart-
ments, the early career of W. H. Auden had been historicized so thoroughly that the poet has nearly vaporized into this construction called
the 1930s. A quarter century ago, during the US's bicentennial, Britain
began recovering this crucial decade through the 'Young Writers of the
Thirties' exhibition in the National Portrait Gallery and through the
publication of Samuel Hynes's cogent study of *The Auden Generation*
(1976) and A. T. Tolley's *The Poetry of the Thirties* (1975), which had just
appeared. This awakening of attention to such a bracketed era must
have made *The English Auden . . . 1927–1939*, published in 1977, seem
almost inevitable rather than an overemphasis of one stage of a career
on the basis of biographical and national, rather than poetic, consider-
ations. These books were followed, most notably, by Bernard Bergonzi's
compendious *Reading the Thirties* (1978) and Valentine Cunningham's
exhaustive elaboration *British Writers of the Thirties* (1988). These works
analyze how 'Auden' is promoted beyond the poetic partnership entitled
MacSpauday to the name of the firm, how this poet undertook some of
his age's intellectual preoccupations – Marxism, Freudianism, Christian
existentialism – and how his very style, the Audenesque, tinctured the
poetry of many of his contemporaries. Concerning this style Bernard
Bergonzi points out:

> The central paradox about the Audenesque is that, although by the end
> of the thirties it was disseminated throughout the English-speaking
> world, and can be called a collective style, its origins lay in one man's
> very personal, even idiosyncratic vision of reality.          (50)

In introducing his bulgingly comprehensive study of the 1930s, Cunningham declared, 'All texts and context will . . . lose their separate identities,
collapsing purposefully into each other . . .' (1). Indeed, his index lists
over 450 topics, mostly non-textual, associated with Auden, only five of
which receive more than three pages of discussion. In such an amalgamation, 'Auden' may suffer the fate of 7 Middagh Street, the Brooklyn
boarding house whose artistic menagerie Auden governed benignly in
the early 1940s but which 'bulldozed . . . became part of the Brooklyn–
Queens Expressway' (Farnan, 25), part of a carriageway that offers us
easy transport to where Auden no longer exists.

  In this study of the exchange between British and Irish poetry, we
must take a considerably narrower approach to Auden's poetry: the
byway connecting Auden's verse to that of Ireland's Yeats and MacNeice,
Austin Clarke, and Patrick Kavanagh. By this path we may reach a clearer

understanding not only of this generation of Irish poets but also, in Chapters 4 and 5, of Kinsella, Mahon, Longley, and Muldoon, Irish poets affected by Auden's influence in later decades. Equally important and crucial to any idea of poetic exchange, we can specify some conditions and strategies Auden shares with Irish writers and thereby clarify his intention and even certain poems. Most significantly, unlike Spender, Madge, Muir, or Graves, for example, Auden shared with Yeats's Irish successors certain problems of tone that arise from the poet's uncertainty about his audience.

Before devoting most of this chapter to these two topics – the similar ways in which the eccentricities of these Irish poets and of Auden affect tone and questions about the value of poetry – we should examine the evasive complexity with which Auden challenged his early readers of *Poems* (1931) and dazzled his first reviewers. Because this style has often been characterized, we might begin with Bernard Bergonzi's succinct summary:

> In the 1930 *Poems* we find Auden experimenting with an elliptical, 'telegraphese' manner, by omission of the definite article ... the opposite pole to what became Auden's normal practice ... : copious use of the definite article; unusual adjectives and adjectival phrases, and surprising similes, which have a reductive or trivialising effect; and personified abstractions. (48)

As a consequence of these techniques, we more often know what a poem 'concerns' than what it means, and such partial knowledge is hard-won and, often, the gift of earlier acute readers such as Mendelson. In 'The Watershed,' for example, which begins:

> Who stands, the crux left of the watershed,
> On the wet road between the chafing grass
> Below him sees dismantled washing-floors,
> Snatches of tramline running to the wood,
> An industry already comatose,
> Yet sparsely living. A ramshackle engine

$$(EA, 22)^3$$

we feel that we have entered private territory, a sense confirmed by Auden's review-essay in the *New Yorker* in 1965:

> Between the ages of six and twelve, I spent a great many of my waking
> hours in the construction and elaboration of a private sacred world,
> the basic elements of which were a landscape, northern and lime-
> stone, and an industry, lead mining. . . . It is no doubt psychologically
> significant that my sacred world contained no human beings.
>
> (*AF&A*, 502)

In conformance with such a prescription, the poem seems, at first, devoid
of industry, active nature, and, if what appears as an opening sentry-
challenge succeeds, people. However, the initial commanding question
'Who stands?' quickly revises to a generalization – even an invitation –
that 'whoever stands the crux left of the watershed' – a particular place
and moment of convergence and division – may experience the gravity
of decay in a disused industry. In the poem, this occurs not as active
falling but as arrested action, mostly vertical, displaced into gerunds and
participles and nouns converted from verbs: 'Below him sees dismantled
washing-floors / Snatches of tramline running to the wood.' Although
no humans remain to dismantle, wash, snatch, or run, an engine 'raises
water,' apparently without human agency, and stories of the heroic dead
are chosen and recounted by an unspecified historian.

In the second stanza, the auditor who was invited into this imaginary
space, is warned to 'Go home, now, stranger,' because 'This land, cut off,
will not communicate' to one who prefers living faces in an actual world.
Nevertheless, in spite of the speaker's denial, nature and personification
and human desire edge into the poem:

> Beams from your car may cross a bedroom wall,
> They wake no sleeper; you may hear the wind
> Arriving driven from the ignorant sea
> To hurt itself on pane, on bark of elm
> Where sap unbaffled rises, being Spring;
> But seldom this. Near you, taller than grass,
> Ears poise before decision, scenting danger.

When lights from the conveyance of the auditor, who is after all the
public, probe the secret, ghostly interior and 'wake no sleeper,' we are
as skeptical as we might be that in Hardy's 'Nobody Comes,' certainly
a predecessor to this poem, the car 'with lamps full glare,' which 'whangs
along in a world of its own,' 'has nothing to do with me' (*HCP*, 743).
The denial of pathetic fallacy in 'the ignorant sea' only invites personification of nature which is 'unbaffled,' the old use of *hurt* as 'hurtle

itself onto' innervating *pain*. Consequently, the denial of life in this imaginative plot animates the scene and creates the poem, as if it came to the hand unbidden.

Although 'Watershed' is not willfully cryptic – some fully understood secret hidden from the reader – as some reviewers seemed to believe, it does, nevertheless, suggest some undisclosed topos of origination. It vaguely concerns an idea about art which Auden learned from Shakespeare, and probably Shelley and Yeats, and articulated in *The Sea and the Mirror*. As in Shakespeare's 'Sonnet 106,' which ends 'For we, which now behold these present days, / Have eyes to wonder, but lack tongues to praise,' by denying poetry's capacity to incorporate or impinge upon the here and now, the poem draws life in. Shelley's fear that 'vacancy' crowns Mont Blanc or Yeats's alternative belief that the human's world springs from 'his bitter soul' are severer forms of this creative site from which Auden would banish life only to have it return, even from its hidden history of industrial tragedies. As we shall see, this idea finds more complex expression in Auden's poems of the late 1930s.

In psychological terms, the poem's very reticence invites and occludes discussion of this 'private sacred world' as a maternal landscape which – with damaged shaft, reluctant pump – provides for 'the many dead' their 'final valley,' like Gaea reincorporating her dead children. In this regard, the placement of the reader 'On the wet road, between the chafing grass' seems strategic and characteristic of Auden's objective disposition toward nature. Distracted by the fricatives and sibilants of 'chafing grass,' one can forget that even this action, a wet rubbing, is withheld until the 'stranger' departs from the road that runs 'between' the fields.

The sort of discussion of landscape and 'the thematics of the Mother' (214) that Neil Hertz conducts in regard to Courbet and Flaubert could be elucidating in regard to Auden's landscape. 'Watershed' might then be read in light of Auden's more open discussion, later in his life, of his relation to his mother. For example, in a review of J. R. Ackerley's autobiography, Auden concludes that Ackerley 'did not belong to either of the two commonest classes of homosexuals, neither to the "orals" who play Son-and/or-Mother, nor to the "anals" who play Wife-and/or-Husband (*AF&A*, 453). According to Carpenter, Auden who 'thought the feminine streak in him grew from identifying with his mother,' was enrolled in the 'orals' (12, 48). In his letter to Byron, Auden confesses: 'We imitate our loves: well, neighbours say / I grow more like my mother every day' (*AEA*, 191). And in 'New Year Letter' (1940), he writes that he has stood in his post-industrial Midlands landscape 'Upon the edge of shafts and felt / The deep *Urmutterfurcht* that drives / Us into knowledge all our lives' (*ACP*, 182). Following this experience of the uncanny – a terror related to the mother but perhaps also a multilingual pun – 'the reservoir of darkness' stirs and a voice from this abandoned mine says in German that his mother would not come back, that, as *Das Weibliche*, she remains with him as his duty and his love (*ACP*, 183).

## Homosexuality and Auden's sexual identity

The psychological sophistication of Auden's 'New Year's Letter' springs from his comprehensive and intense reading in Freud, Ellis, Groddeck, and others. Less than a half-century earlier, the field of study was just emerging and the topic of homosexuality, which must have focused Auden's psychological interests, hardly had a name to speak. According to Alan Sinfield, the trials of Oscar Wilde in the mid-1890s not so much exposed the identity of the homosexual as constituted or discovered that identity. After Oscar Wilde's sensational trials in 1895, which led to his conviction for sodomy, 'inversion,' according to Jonathan Dollimore, 'was being used increasingly to define a specific kind of deviant sexuality inseparable from a deviant personality.' Sinfield establishes by scholarly elaboration Dollimore's point that 'the homosexual had become a species of being whereas before sodomy had been an aberration of behaviour' (67). Although sodomy was a capital crime from the reign of Henry VIII until 1861, sodomites were shadowy and undefined, if not hanged, presences. Jeffrey Weeks has found – late into the nineteenth century –

> among the Metropolitan Police and in high medical and legal circles, . . . the absence of any clear notions of a homosexual category or of any social awareness of what a homosexual identity might consist of. . . . [Therefore] the adoption in the last decades of the nineteenth century of words like 'homosexual' or 'invert', both by sexologists and by the homosexuals themselves, marked as crucial a change in consciousness. . . .                                                   (101–2)

Although Havelock Ellis's *Sexual Inversion* (1897) made its case for medical causes for homosexuality, the Labouchère Amendment (1885) to the Criminal Law Amendment Act, under which Wilde was prosecuted, and subsequent amendments and acts from 1898 and 1912 still hovered as legal threats over the private lives of Auden and his friends coming to age after the First World War.

   History could neglect both the anxiety and the sense of pioneering adventure with which adolescents in the 1920s approached the sexual boundaries thrown open after the First World War. Beyond inducing moral disillusionment, the War had depleted the pool of men available for marriage, given women greater independence, and opened new realms of sexual experimentation, both in the cities and in the universities.[4] Auden was just behind the avant garde in crossing these borders, coming to Oxford, as he confessed in his 'Letter to Lord Byron', as 'the tail . . . / To that debauched, eccentric generation' (*EA*, 195) celebrated by Waugh in *Vile Bodies* and *Brideshead Revisited*. Once released from the repressiveness of boarding school, Auden – with 'a matter-of-fact, hearty appetite' (Carpenter, 63) – acquired homosexual experiences at Oxford and on weekends in London, as well as an assured, if not altogether contented, sense of his own sexual identity. Although sexual intimacies deepened his friendship with Isherwood and Spender (Osborne, 52), his literary support-group included, if rarely women, heterosexual men and homosexuals with whom he was not intimate.

In what must now be seen as early stages in the formation of homosexual models and stereotypes, Auden accepted from his psychological and, later, religious readings a view of his sexual proclivity as 'sinful' and 'unhealthy' (e.g. Carpenter, 105). This self-incriminating view and a liberal denial of difference on the part of those reviewers who perceived Auden's sexual allegiances probably account for the critical diffidence, if not indifference, to the homosexual aspect of his poetry.[5] For example, Alan Rodway's statement about Auden's homosexuality – 'Its influence on his work, were it not known of, would be literarily imperceptible; known, it is negligible' (18) – is unusual only in its succinctness.

Few critics acknowledge the effect of Auden's homosexuality on his writing. Bernie Benstock argues that Auden's practice of revising severely and deleting whole poems from his work was a self-censoring that arose from social disapproval of homosexuality. 'It is now apparent that W. H. Auden lived his entire life, if not in abject terror, then at least in constant apprehension,' he concludes (226). Clive James may offer the strongest rebuttal of statements such as Rodways's, above. James's eleven-page *Commentary* response to Auden's passing, entitled 'On His Death,' reappears in *At the Pillars of Hercules* (1979) but, I believe, in no collection of essays on Auden. James argues that although Auden was the master of concrete detail, 'this talent was the very one which could not be used unguarded to speak of love.' Consequently, 'he was forced from the concrete to the abstract.' James then concludes, 'The need to find an acceptable expression for his homosexuality was the first technical obstacle to check the torrential course of Auden's unprecedented facility. A born master of directness was obliged to find a language for indirection' (26).

James first conducts his argument through one of Auden's strongest early poems 'The Wanderer,' about which he says, 'The homosexual's enforced exile is strongly present, although never explicit' (27). James then relates each stanza of the poem to issues in Auden's life rather than looking closely at what he calls Auden's 'elliptical suggestiveness.' We might complete James's reading to show why a poem that begins 'Doom is dark and deeper than any sea-dingle' is not simply about the fall and judgment (*doom*), the displacement of all humans from a bucolic comfort ('dingle') into an estranging element ('sea-dingle'). The second line, 'Upon what man it fall,' does sound selective, also reminding us that *man*, in itself, can be partial. If we look more closely at lines 11–13, we see that James's phrase 'elliptical suggestiveness' may minimize Auden's indirection:

> Or lonely on fell as chat,
> By pot-holed becks
> A bird stone-haunting, an unquiet bird.

During the moment we entertain the notion that *chat* may be the mad monologue of the lonely or that *fell* is cruel or fallen or see the *pot* in *pot-holed* or read *beaks* or *pecks* for *becks* (in other words, substitute the more familiar approximate word for these regional words), we obtain an unexpungeable image of a creature, a bird of Auden's region, driven by hunger in the manner of the wanderer who will encounter 'Bird-flocks nameless to him.' A decade later in 'Mundus et Infans,' Auden's poem says of the child: 'has he not a perfect right / To remind us ... / ... we had never learned to distinguish / Between hunger and love?' (*CP*, 253). This is not *suggestiveness* so much as carefully arranged sublimations (including bird for wanderer) in Freud's sense,[6] an inescapable net of associations, whose holes or empty spaces snare the reader.

James challenges us especially in his reading of these lines of the second stanza:

> There head falls forward, fatigued at evening
> And dreams of home,
> Waving from window, spread of welcome,
> Kissing of wife under single sheet;
> But waking sees
> Bird-flocks nameless to him, through doorway voices
> Of new men making another love.

James concludes, 'Only tiredness could make the doomed traveller dream the banalities of hearth and wife: awake, he is once again involved with real love. And real love is a new love, with all political overtones fully intended' (27). Attractive because revisionary, this reading overlooks the poem's emotional investment in home: 'Waving from window,[7] spread of welcome' evokes so many welcomes – greeting arms, the laden table, love's enfolding and dilation – that we can feel invited to recall that in the Anglo-Saxon work from which this departs, the lines read, 'He dreams that he is greeting and kissing his liege-lord, and laying his hands and head on his knees' (Kershaw, 11).[8]

The dream of homecoming returns in the final stanza with an intensity James neglects in his emphasis on the anxiety and shame expressed in the fourth and fifth lines from the end: 'From thunderbolt protect, / From gradual ruin spreading like a stain;'[9] James then makes this convincing point:

> The spreading ruin is something closer to home than the collapse of Europe. There was fear in Auden's pride about his condition. Fear of the police and fear that the much-trumpeted corruption might be a fact. (28)

In spite of his guilt, which would soon harden into a conviction that his homosexuality was sinful, Auden believed in grace, which he often called *luck*, and therefore in his own candidacy for the unearned homecoming the final lines anticipate: 'Bring joy, bring day of his returning, / Lucky with day approaching, with leaning dawn.' Maintaining the consistency of his argument, James misconcludes that Auden 'doesn't really expect luck to be granted or his kind of day to dawn' (28). However, because of the absence of articles before *day*, the second *day* is upon us before we recognize, suddenly, that we anticipate *daylight*, this day, and we lean – with the household, the wanderer, and the long light of an early-spring English morning – toward this breathless closing.

If James overstresses this one side of Auden's ambivalence,[10] nevertheless his argument that homosexuality forced Auden to become a strategic writer rather than a lyricist of 'unprecedented facility,' his selection among the early poems of convincing illustrations of homosexual concerns, and his emphasis on the theme of the 'homosexual's enforced exile,' make this essay an invaluable complement to more thoroughly argued essays by more established critics of Auden. For example, in a thoughtful, but equally partial, essay on 'The Voice of Exile: Auden in 1940,' Samuel Hynes examines 'The New Year Letter' to account, in part, for what he sees as Auden's 'voluntary exile.' He argues that Auden left Britain in January 1939 'to go in quest of a life that would be a parable of the condition of Modern Man. . . . Questing was on his mind, because that's what he saw himself as doing: journeying to meet the future' (34). Yet, from the very early 'Nor was that final . . . ,' wisely dropped from the *Collected Poems*, homosexuality is often seen as another state into and from which one crosses clandestinely, and consignment to the boundaries of either homosexual or patriotic allegiance exclusively is a banishment. For example, when Auden composed a sonnet sequence entitled *The Quest*, soon after his arrival in New York, many of the poems recount enforced exiles. In 'The Crossroad,' for instance, the empty 'here' recalls places of parting: 'Two friends who met here and embraced are gone, / Each to his own mistake. . . .' The poem continues, 'So at all quays and crossroads: who can tell / These places of decision and farewell / To what dishonour all adventure leads' (*ACP*, 224).

## Yeats, Wilde, and Auden: queer and colonial margins

This 'note of crisis, of banishment, banishment from the heart, banishment from home,' in the words of James Joyce, Auden shares with the Irish writer. As Edward Said has observed:

> The decolonizing native writer – such as Joyce, the Irish writer colonized by the British – re-experiences the quest voyage motif from which he had been banished by means of the same trope carried over from the imperial into the new culture and adopted, reused, relived.
>
> (211)

We can recognize a similar conversion of this trope, reflect on similar ways that Auden and Yeats are marginalized by critics, assess Yeats's influence on Auden and, in turn, see Auden's special attraction both for MacNeice and other Irish contemporaries and for Irish poets of subsequent generations. Yet, we still may be unable to define precisely whether the relation of Auden as homosexual to Irish poets as colonial or postcolonial writers is metaphorical, homological, or cognate. First, the terms *colonial* and *postcolonial*, as reigning fashions, are questionable and sometimes unhelpful. Ireland, especially Northern Ireland, is both colonial and postcolonial, as well as European. In space and time, Irish poets and Auden are eccentric to the same center, sharing a similar history of exclusion from an identical center of power, whereas if non-European colonial writers suffer from similar methods of exclusion, they do so in relation to a different center or from a situation much less approximate to that center.

If we begin by comparing Auden's situations to Wilde's, we come close to recognizing in the English class system a central antagonist to both the homosexual and the Irish colonist. Both emerged as distinctive types in the mid-nineteenth century, just as with the help of anthropology, ethnology, and psychology the British middle class and the bourgeois family were seeking foils against which they could identify and qualify themselves for their new leadership roles. Acccording to Raymond Williams, the imperialist rationalization for one man's right to govern another derives from a belief in the colonizer's superior capability of conquering nature (Parry, 54). By extension then, and in reference to the Freudian model, he who governs his own nature can claim the right to govern the homosexual who, allegedly, cannot.

More to our point, both Auden and Wilde, the homosexual and colonial writer, would have become sensitive to how often power unjustly protects property – through marriage or colonial rule – whereas the English heterosexual may be both blind to the operations of the marriage mart, because of romantic notions, and ignorant of how English hegemony privileges him. Auden confided in his 'Letter to Lord Byron' that he admired Jane Austen's depiction of 'the amorous effects of "brass,"' when she revealed 'with such sobriety / The economic basis of society' (*EA*, 171). In Wilde's incursions into rough lower-class establishments, his 'feasting with panthers' (Ellmann, 389), he was employing sex to transgress class as well as sexual taboos. And Isherwood, who with Auden cultivated relationships with working-class youths in Berlin, entered working-class bars with his friends 'like traders who had entered a jungle' (28). Isherwood decries those who allow sentimentality to blind them to the cash basis for these relationships: 'But this was a colonial situation, nevertheless' (32). For the colonial and homosexual writers, such lack of illusion about power relationships may tune their ears to nuances of condescension and keep them alert to the need to address different audiences differently, often at the same time.

Having sat as an ephebe at Wilde's dinners, where a dining and work table were indistinguishable, Yeats learned much from the older writer about the role of ambiguity in managing his savage colonial ambivalence and in addressing at once two audiences with two sets of expectations. While reviewing Wilde's stories in *United Ireland* in 1891, Yeats confided to his Irish nationalist readers, 'I see in his life and works an extravagant Celtic crusade against Anglo-Saxon stupidity.' He then quotes Wilde on his self-protective mask: 'I labour under a perpetual fear of not being misunderstood' (202–3). If his auditor only laughs off his paradox, Wilde succeeds in masking the seriousness of his duplicitous enterprise. Whereas many English wielded their language unselfconsciously if proprietorially, Wilde, from his homosexual and Irish bases of identity, would have come to understand the exclusionary strategies of power and how language enacts and hides these strategies. Although George Steiner has argued that 'the subject of difficulty in poetry . . . has moved to the very centre of aesthetic experience since the late nineteenth century' (47), he does not recognize, among his four kinds of poetic difficulty, the sort of politically motivated poetic duplicity – a preliminary, political form of *camp* – that Wilde employed.

Because of a probable influence on Auden, Wilde's 'language for indirection,' in Clive James's phrase, particularly his method of arguing indirectly in a dialogue or other fictionalized form against an unspecified adversary, needs illustration. Assuming a Darwinian model, Wilde argues in 'Soul of Man Under Socialism' that 'there is no evolution except towards Individualism. . . . Under Individualism people will be quite natural and absolutely unselfish . . .' (285). His argument projects an echo:

> Individualism does not come to man with any sickly cant about duty . . . or any hideous cant about self-sacrifice. In fact, it does not come to man with any claims upon him at all. It comes naturally and inevitably out of man. It is the point to which all development tends.                                                                 (284)

This converts the neo-Platonic idea of Walter Pater – English esthetician, Oxford tutor of Wilde's, and instigator of this indirect argument against an unspecified opponent which he employed successfully especially against Arnold – into a Blakean idea about man's creative spirit. Here Wilde echoes the conclusion of *Studies in the History of the Renaissance* (1873): 'For art comes to you proposing frankly to give nothing but the highest quality to your moments as they pass, and simply for those moments' sake.' However, Wilde substitutes the Philistine phrase for justifying capitalism – 'natural development' – for the esthete's 'highest quality' as the unexamined term. In a similar manner, Auden sometimes employs echoes to refute those writers he admires most. For example, as Mendelson discloses in his reading of 'Fish in the unruffled lakes,' Auden represents love in terms of Yeatsian images of fish, swan, and lion, only to lift this love beyond universal nature into the contingency of the actual human choice: 'Last night should add / Your voluntary love' (*EA*, 163; Mendelson, 214).

Even later in the decade, Auden reveals similarities to Wilde. As he appears to progress toward clarity, he incorporates into his poems the sort of generalization he often tested on hearers or adherents in conversations or monologues. The biographer Charles Osborne characterizes these verbal explorations: 'Like many of those renowned for their conversational powers, he was disinclined to converse, preferring to harangue. Like Wilde, he was a performer, though his manner was decidedly more Johnsonian than Wildean' (37). In his writing, however, although Auden employed paradoxes, as in the close of 'In Memory of W. B. Yeats,' he preferred aphorisms. In considering late-1930s poems such as 'Musée des Beaux Arts' and the elegy to Yeats, I will argue that when he brought aphorisms into poetry, they often became ironic. Sweeping or exclusive generalizations – 'nothing . . . ,' 'never . . . ,' 'not one . . .' – become contingent, situational, and relative to a limited context, not in the manner of Samuel Johnson, clinging to the flotsam of absolutes, but of the colonial and sexual double-agent Wilde arguing relative to the Protean moment.

The complexity of Auden's contending bases for self-identification – poet, Englishman, homosexual – approached that of Wilde – writer, Irish nationalist who was dependent on British institutions and audiences, and homosexual – who possessed, Eve Sedgwick speculates,

> an exquisitely exacerbated sensitivity to how by turns porous, brittle, elastic, chafing, embracing, exclusive, murderous, in every way contestable and contested were the membranes of 'domestic' national definition signified by the ductile and elusive terms England, Britain, Ireland.                                                                 (151)

She goes on to compare Wilde's complex allegiances to Roger Casement's 'heightening and contrastive braiding together of exoticizing British imperialist/anti-imperialist, with Irish nationalist, with homosexual identifications and identities' (152).

For the English who brought both Irishmen to trial, homosexuality was, if not confused, at least associated, with treason (Sinfield, 194). Although Auden's patriotism was questioned from the Parliament floor soon after his departure for America (Carpenter, 291), more recently and without the excuse of a national crisis Tom Paulin links Auden with two infamous spies – homosexual and contemporary with Auden – and recommends that we try to 'see Auden as adopting the kind of strategy which Burgess or Philby adopted and to explore the idea that he too was a defector both from his class and, in 1939, from his country' (76).

From an Irish point of view, Paulin might raise similar charges of defection against James Joyce, especially if we recognize that as his countrymen were dying in the war against Britain for independence, Joyce was composing the Cyclops and Sirens episodes of *Ulysses* with what can be seen as blistering satires against Irish nationalism. Both Joyce and Auden chose self-banishment because they saw their commitment to art being opposed by the commitment to nation or colony. This opposition confronted Auden through hostile reviews, spearheaded by those of the Leavises and *Scrutiny*.

## Quest or banishment? Critics' role in Auden's emigration

Among the encomiastic reviews that greeted Auden's poetic debut in 1930, an anonymous reviewer for the *Times Literary Supplement* struck this sour note:

> Many passages in it are baffling, if not unintelligible, because they lack that measure of normality which makes communication between one individual and another possible. For mental idiosyncrasies, if they are extravagantly indulged, isolate a writer as completely as if he spoke in an unknown tongue.... The manner of his invitation is often so peculiar to himself and so eccentric in its terminology that, instead of communicating an experience of value to us, it merely sets our minds a problem in allusions to solve. (Haffenden, 90; Gross, 129)

In a 1983 publication, John Haffenden identified this reviewer as F. R. Leavis. Leavis's terminology – 'measure of normality,' 'mental idiosyncrasies ... extravagantly indulged,' 'peculiar,' and 'eccentric' – and the emphasis on communication suggest those issues concerning tone and the English audience that Leavis will raise against Auden in a series of negative reviews. Especially in the light of later reviews by F. R. and Q. D. Leavis, the implications of this Leavisite language will appear indelicate or even bigoted when applied to a homosexual poet who, central to his own circle, remains eccentric within the English tradition.

Soon other critics would relate Auden's style to childhood concerns and a few, mostly the Leavises and their deputies, would charge him with a failure to mature and to live up to his early promise. In a review of Auden's third publication *The Orators* Leavis raises the central issue of secrecy and privacy using the sort of money metaphors that Auden will soon adopt for poetry: 'Again and again it is evident that he has not taken enough trouble to make his private counters effective currency'

(Haffenden, 101). Anticipating such criticism, Auden himself had offered his editor a preface to *The Orators* that began, 'I feel this book is more obscure than it ought to be,' but Eliot, probably knowing the futility of such apologies, rejected this preface.

Meanwhile, the *New Verse* editor Geoffrey Grigson, as truculent as Leavis and as devoted to Auden as Leavis was to Eliot, counterattacked in July 1933:

> Dr. Leavis, it seems, cannot recognize creative generosity until years have passed. . . . *Scrutiny*, if Dr. Leavis wants some plain criticism, is too adolescent, too self-righteous, too ready to accept the naivetés of ledger-criticism informed with a little sour yeast of Eliot and Lawrence. . . .                                                    (2)

As we shall see, this could only deepen Leavis's belief that Auden's reputation was enlarged by a conspiratorial clique.

At the close of 1936 in a more strident *Scrutiny* review of *Look! Stranger*, Leavis attacks Auden's lack of organization which, he deduced, led to 'an embarrassing uncertainty of tone and poise. . . .' He concludes by decrying the 'group-world,' which included presumably Auden's circle of Oxford supporters and *New*-publication editors but not Auden's editor at Faber & Faber, T. S. Eliot. Prior to this conclusion, he strikes a keynote for all subsequent *Scrutiny* attacks on Auden:

> Since so much of his emotional material and his poetic aura, glamorous or sinister, comes fairly directly from childhood and schooldays, the borrowing can hardly have any other effect on us than that of implicit self-diagnosis. For Mr. Auden still makes far too much of his poetry out of private neuroses and memories – still uses these in an essentially immature way.                            (Haffenden, 223)

Derived from Freud, *immature* became a coded reference to homosexual behavior. One's eyes strain to find in Leavis's writings reference to Freud or Ellis, to say nothing of Homer Lane or Georg Groddeck or others by whose writing Auden constructed his psychological concepts. Within a dozen years of the first translations of Freud, Auden had been exposed to his writing through his father, who, from the early 1920s, drew on Freud's writings in his medical practice. By the mid-1930s, however, Freud was sufficiently in the intellectual atmosphere to supply terms and certain concepts that enter into F. R. and Q. D. Leavis's reviews of Auden. Freud asserted that the infant enters life disposed toward polymorphous perversity and innate bisexuality and becomes socialized through repression and/or sublimation. Usually enforced indirectly through social stereotypes and institutional nudging, this process of socialization was sometimes delayed in Britain by all-male boarding schools where youthful homosexuality was fairly common. A practitioner of athletic training himself,[11] Leavis would probably have maintained the conventional prescription of discipline and self-control for one to mature into heterosexuality. In any case, Leavis or other *Scrutiny* reviewers offer this presciption to Auden with increasing insistence in their successive reviews: Auden 'was peculiarly in need of the check . . . [of] criticism' (1933); Auden's 'poetic aura, glamorous or sinister, comes fairly directly from childhood and schooldays'; 'essentially immature'; 'the failure of Mr. Auden's talent to mature' (1936); and he expresses 'unbalanced, immature enthusiasms' (1945).

Henceforth, Leavis, in his own person, wrote rarely of Auden and then only in a tone of lockjawed dismissal. In 1940 in his saddest review, he depreciates in less than a page one of the most enduring volumes of this century, *Another Time*, with the regret that 'Mr. Auden is still adolescent . . . he has nothing more like maturity to offer than before.' Among the elegies to Yeats and Freud, 'Musée des Beaux Arts,' 'Spain 1937,' 'Rimbaud,' and a dozen other anthology pieces, all of which he ignores, he can 'judge in favour of one or two things' which are 'September 1, 1939' and a mediocre poem he misunderstands (IX: 1, 200). His preference for the latter ('What we have to learn, / That we love ourselves alone: / . . . / Every living creature is / Woman, Man, and Child') because it seemed to praise heterosexual marriage suggests that Auden's homosexuality may have distorted Leavis's critical talents much as Leavis implied it had Auden's.

In 1950, when Leavis reissued *New Bearings*, his influential 1932 study of poetry, he took a few perfunctory sentences to explain that he omitted discussion of Auden's poetry from the first edition because 'the promise, as I saw it, could not be asserted without a weight of qualifying and privative emphasis' (227). His spleen awakens, however, when he reflects on Auden's admirers who 'spoke of him as having superseded T. S. Eliot.' In Arnoldian terms, he dismisses them 'as the failure of the function of criticism' and 'as the disintegration of the educated reading public' (229).

Perhaps in reaction to such attacks, from which he himself had suffered severely, Stephen Spender reflected back from the mid-1960s and made the strongest case against *Scrutiny* by any of its contemporaries:

*Scrutiny* took none of the risks involved in charitable judgment. . . .
Their frequent policy with young writers was to destroy a reputation
before it was made. . . . Moreover, the publication of their literary
periodical was also bound up with theories of education. Young men
reviewing were given editorial instruction as to the lines on which
they should attack other young writers. . . . In pointing out how
immensely concerned Eliot was, I want to emphasize that there are ways
of encouraging literature other than being intolerant to beginners. . . .
[Over the next few years] the power of English teachers will extend
beyond the universities to the B. B. C., the British Council, and to literary periodicals. They really have to choose between the methods of
*The Criterion* and those of *Scrutiny*'.                                    (208)

To be fair to Leavis, we might acknowledge that his central concern
in these attacks on Auden and his set is that coteries, weighing class and
social concerns over literary concerns, seemed to him to dominate literary judgment. So successful has Leavis been in establishing the canon in
secondary schools and influencing school-leaving exams that we can
forget how marginalized he remained at Cambridge, where he retained
no regular position, and how many comfortable sinecurists in the literary
establishment must have condescended to him as an earnest, evangelical
yeoman. As D. W. Harding has written in defense of Leavis:

He often had to go against a large, loosely associated body of the
right people, whether literary journalists and their cultivated friends
or academics engaged in English studies. . . . It was when feeble or
objectionable work was widely over-valued that he made his attacks,
desperately fierce with anxiety as he saw the basis of sound judgment
being undermined.                                               (190, 193)

In a letter to *The Listener* in the mid-1950s, Leavis himself complained,
'For the twenty years of its life *Scrutiny* had to contend against the hostility, overt and covert, intense and wholly unscrupulous, of the academic and literary worlds, or of what I think it reasonable to call the
Establishment . . .' (*Letters*, 54).

Having acknowledged this degree of justice in Leavis's defensive posture, we must recall a footnote toward the end of *New Bearings* where he
boasts: 'I may say that this placing of Auden has been enforced in
*Scrutiny* by detailed criticism in more than half a dozen reviews, coming
from half a dozen hands' (227).[12] Among the most savage of these reviews,
no doubt approved or even assigned by Leavis, was one by his partner

and wife Q. D. In a review of MacNeice's *Modern Poetry* and three auto-biographies, she went out of her way to make explicit what must have been for a number of years this couple's pillow-talk about Auden (not that their private life should be open to scrutiny). After quoting MacNeice on Auden's 'not unfriendly contempt for the female sex,' she adds, of the Auden circle, 'It is no use looking for growth or development or any addition to literature in such an adolescent hot-house' (76).[13]

So saying, she raises for all but the innocent or obtuse the perilous subject of Auden's homosexuality and the possibility of a collusive network of homosexual reviewers and editors, which within the gossip of some heterosexuals was called 'the homintern' and which Auden's heterosexual supporter Grigson also threatened to expose, chillingly, by publishing in *New Verse* simply a list of 'the aggresive homosexual excluders' without designation or heading (Grigson, *Recollections*, 154). Toward the close of the Second World War, *Scrutiny* intensified its attack in a review by L. G. Lienhardt of *For the Time Being* which includes 'For the Time Being' and *The Sea and the Mirror*, two serious long poems, the second major by nearly everyone's standard. As if reading from a *Scrutiny* manual, Leinhardt regrets that Auden's 'technical facility has been lav-ished upon . . . boyish fantasies and unbalanced, immature enthusiasms' (345). He continues, striking Leavis's second note: 'His separation from the circle in which that tendency was formed came too late to enable him to discard his public character and see what values of his own he could substitute for those of the group which made his reputation' (349). With the blunt pugnacity, if not the roundhouse spelling, of the Marquess of Queensbury, who wrote to 'Oscar Wilde posing Somdomite' at the Albemarle Hotel, Leinhardt or the editors of *Scrutiny* entitled this long review 'Auden's Inverted Development.'

Leavis's exposure of his personal prejudice through increasingly less veiled innuendoes follows the progression of his criticism of Yeats which we considered in Chapter 2. Regardless of the effect of such criticism on readers of poetry, it would have had to remind Auden and Yeats, among many such reminders, that their identifications as English poet and/or English citizen, respectively, were qualified, and those qualifications would become increasingly severe for Auden as the 1930s progressed. As Weeks demonstrates, 'During the 1930s, particularly, homosexual offences became a particular preoccupation of the Public Morality Council . . . [leading to] a major trend of increasing prosecutions on a national scale' (220). Weeks uncovers another pattern, which must have emerged pain-fully for Auden, 'of an increase in the prosecution of buggery related to whether or not Britain was at war or in a state of social turmoil' (100), presumably because homophobia disrupts homogeneity. Although we know how alertly Auden monitored the approach of war, we are forced to imagine how acutely he felt the concomitant marginalization. It is easier to picture his response to two insistent summonses from Geoffrey Grigson, his strongest poetical advocate, for poets to come to the center of public action. In March of 1938, in reference to Yeats's 'Lapis Lazuli,' just printed in the *London Mercury*, Grigson wrote, '*All things fall and are built again.* How comfortable! We have no right to listen to Yeats, no right at least to stay outside . . .' (*New Verse*, no. 29, 22).

Especially with his growing disenchantment with activist poetry, Auden may well have empathized with Yeats's powerful response to war's demands on poetry, both poets being necessarily *outside* the English heartland because of their colonial and sexual identities. In the 1938 autumn issue, only a few months before Yeats's death and Auden's departure for Manhattan, Grigson proclaims 'the end of poetic isolation' and declares that 'the only justified retreat is the loneliness in the centre and not on the edge. Unless a poet can be there sometimes at least, he has no right to exist and no claim to be tolerated and need expect no good man to listen to him' (nos 31–2, 2). Acknowledging that war had already taken the lives of poets in this decade, we must nevertheless recognize the irony that this 'harsh invasion of the private life by public crises that is so definitive a part of the experience of the "thirties generation"' (Hynes, 100) should arrive from his most supportive editor like a conscription, and therefore expulsion, notice to the poet after whom the age is named.

Edward Mendelson, concurring with Isherwood, dates Auden's decision to emigrate from the performance of his play about mountain-climbing: 'He had known for more than two years, since finishing *The Ascent of F6*, that he would eventually leave England' (346). Because of his mother's deliberately withheld love and his resultant hunger to be heroic in his mother's eyes, the hero of this play cannot withstand demands on his talents and control his own life. In the play's ending, which Auden and Isherwood never could get right, the hero scrambles to the summit to confront, not the demon of the mountain, but the figure of his own mother, in whom we see projections of Auden's over-demanding mother.[14] Isherwood recalls that Auden offered reasons for his departure many years later in a BBC interview – 'England for me was becoming impossible. I couldn't grow up. . . . English life . . . is for me a family life, and I love my family, but I don't want to live with them' (Isherwood, 315–16) – which we might recognize as a 'language for indirection' appropriate either to Auden's situation or that of a colonial writer. He also said, 'I knew then that if I stayed, I would inevitably become a member of the British establishment' (Carpenter, 195). It is with some insight then into the relationship between maternal and colonial dependence that Yeats wrote to the director of Auden's play about revising its conclusion: 'Why not let the white garment fall to show the mother, or demon, as Britannia. That I think would be good theatre – a snow white Britannia' (Haffenden, 21).

## Auden: poetry and questions of value

If entertained long enough, our questions about poetic tone lead to questions about poetic audience and, eventually, arrive at questions about community which Eliot, Leavis, D. H. Lawrence, and Auden himself made into a major issue of this decade. Within these discussions, the bedrock question remains 'what is the good of poetry?' Because the issue that destabilizes nations and disrupts communities is economic and because this is a question of value, questioners often dress their inquiry about poetry in economic terms. Significantly influenced by Marxism and colonialism respectively, British and Irish poets of the 1930s saw questions of poetic value as not merely parallel or homological to questions of the general economy but as merging into and conditioned by these larger economies which, through much of the 1930s, were in crisis. Economic conditions in both Britain and Ireland, as well as their international relations, forced both nations to overemphasize community. Having won only a partial independence from Britain in 1923, the Irish Free State transferred its struggle from military backalleys and boreens to economic and moral arenas. In 1932 under the leadership of de Valera, Ireland reneged on its treaty obligation to pay £3.13 million per annum for money borrowed from Britain in the turn-of-the-century land acts that transferred property to Irish sharecroppers. In retaliation, Britain imposed on Irish farm goods a tariff, which was used to repay this debt, and Ireland, in turn, imposed duties on British coal, cement, and other goods. What Ireland lost in the health of small farms, as exports dropped from over £43 million in 1929 to under £17 million in 1936 (Mowat, 431), they gained in national independence and a sense of self-worth. With a timing born of a captive nation's vigilance, on the day after Edward VIII abdicated his throne in 1936, the Irish Dail effaced the British monarch from its constitution in preparation for its proclamation of complete independence in 1937. Such independence remained political and nominal, however, because the Irish pound stayed pegged to gold and sterling and then, when Britain went off the gold standard, to the pound sterling, and Britain remained the major market for Irish goods and source of Irish imports.

Because 'postcolonial' Ireland remained a colony of Britain – economically, now, if not clearly politically – this nation maintained its policies of de-anglicization by purging itself of decadent British influences. Ireland maintained its war with Britain, therefore, by enforcing by statute what it saw as its moral advantages. With a copse of consenting hands and a pen's ripple, the new government passed a censorship law and decrees against divorce and birth control and became from 1928 a land where marriages were insoluble and pornography and offensive publications – and, later, news of Nazi atrocities – never circulated, as if the Irish government was already pursuing de Valera's dream, proclaimed in a famous St Patrick's Day speech in 1943, of making Ireland a 'land whose countryside would be bright with ... the laughter of comely maidens' (Lee, 241). Publications found offensive by the Censorship Board, such as works by Joyce, O'Casey, O'Connor, Clarke, and many other Irish writers, could not be read by their countrymen nor could these writers comfortably earn their living at home. In other ways, the oppressive nature of the Irish theocracy forced the writers to maintain toward their own government the adversarial relation that some of them had first established toward British rule. The Irish nation continued to define itself as not-British and, especially, not-English, a position which – enforced by wartime neutrality and censorship – drove this nation into extreme isolation. Reacting to save their intellectual lives, writers such as O'Casey, Beckett, Brian Coffey, and Francis Stuart emigrated across the Irish sea. Others, already polyglot and catholic by upbringing, listened to short-wave radio, smuggled books from the Continent, and otherwise looked toward Europe for literary models and so, in many cases, from their provincial locations adopted international modernist stances.

Although a nuisance, Ireland hardly figured among the major problems of Britain which between the wars was being supplanted by the United States as the chief economic force in the world. Divided horizontally by a slow postwar recovery and by the depression that resulted in unemployment and low wages, the British economy was also riven vertically between bankers centralized in the City (originally separated from the general economy to serve the Empire)[15] and industrialists in the Midlands, London, and, increasingly, in southeast England. British poets, consequently, felt pressures to address social issues and the looming international crises which temporarily distracted poets from a national mourning for the losses of the First World War. Pressures from a conservative literary establishment to renounce international modernism, however, helped to maintain a traditional – basically a failed Georgian – poetics.

As if Marx were right, all aspects of British society seemed driven by and to drive the economy. Having deemed previous departures from the gold standard unsuccessful and sometimes seeming to confuse commitment to the gold standard with patriotism, Britain nevertheless saw its gold reserves drained by payment of a war debt to the United States. Even the symbols of British sovereignty were devalued as other nations' loss of confidence in the British pound was exacerbated in mid-September of 1931 by a 'mutiny' in Invergordon, Scotland, of a large fleet of the British navy. One week later, Britain abandoned the gold standard and the stilted exchange rate of the pound, and allowed the pound to settle at a lower rate more conducive to the export of British goods. Whatever the homeopathic effects of the pound's reduction, the severance of the printed paper money in one's pocket from the mythic security of gold must have affected the British folk imagination similarly to, but to a lesser extent than, gold debates in nineteenth-century America.

Of these Marc Shell has written: 'The paper money debate was concerned with symbolization in general, and hence not only with money but also with aesthetics... the relationship between the substantial thing and its sign' (6). Speaking of this same debate, David Harvey elaborates in terms that may bear more directly on the exchange between writer and reader in the 1930s than on participants in the general economy:

> But it was now registered as a downright antagonism between the financial system (the whole structure of credit moneys and 'fictitious capitals') and its monetary base (gold and other tangible commodities that give a clear physical meaning to money).... All of these shifts created a crisis of representation. Neither literature nor art could avoid the question of internationalism, synchrony, insecure temporality, and the tension within the dominant measure of value between the financial system and its monetary or commodity base.
>
> (262–3)

Harvey sees in this shift from commodity-based local currencies to international credit either one cause for or a symptom of the shift to modernism.

In 1911, at a crucial stage when much of English literature might have looked pre-modernist to an outsider, André Gide spoke to Saint-John Perse about his admiration for English, 'the denseness of such a concrete language ... its pleasure in trying to reincarnate the thing itself. ...' In comparison:

> French, a more abstract language ... tries to signify rather than represent the meaning, uses words only as fiduciary symbols like coins as values of monetary exchange. English for me was still at the swapping stage.
> (601)

Twenty years later, British literature was approaching its own 'crisis of representation' as we see in the violently opposed responses to Eliot's poetry. The young Auden, lacking the quiddity and clarity of Hardy or whomever Gide had in mind, seems closer, if not to French abstraction, then to the use of words as fiduciary coinage that Gide describes. Quoting from Perse's recollections, Donald Davie, in his book *Articulate Energy* (1971), advocates this 'fiduciary' relation between readers and modern poets such as Yeats. In a later essay (1980), however, he would deny its appropriateness for the youthful Auden's relation to his enthusiastic supporters.

Nevertheless, I would argue that *fiduciary* – even in its narrow sense of describing a currency exchange based on trust – serves as a very helpful term for understanding the responses of Auden's readers – mostly patient in the midst of uncertainty – to that 'language for indirection' we discussed earlier in this chapter. Deeply ambivalent, he needs to communicate yet fears the consequence of full disclosure. In the opening lines of his early poems Auden appeals for our trust: in secret missives or orders from the HQ, he con*fides* in us; his tone is con*fidential*. Although the poems reserve their secrets or even mysteries, they also offer us memorable lines and phrases that are portable. For just one example, the poem that begins 'The strings' excitement, the applauding drum,' written when Auden was 22, concludes:

> This longing for assurance takes the form
>
> Of a hawk's vertical stooping from the sky;
> These tears, salt for a disobedient dream,
> The lunatic agitation of the sea;
>
> While this despair with hardened eyeballs cries
> 'A Golden Age, a Silver ... rather this,
> Massive and taciturn years, the Age of Ice.'
>
> (*EA*, 32)

By readers then or now, this poem could be understood not as a parody of Hopkins' 'The Windhover' but as a precocious contrasting of Auden's faithless, Positivist age with Hopkins' world in which humdrum work or humble sacrifice could still reflect Christ's love, if only momentarily. Because enough phrases are memorably epigrammatic – 'salt for a disobedient dream' and the final line – we trust that the poem will eventually clarify, both in its meaning and in some metaphysics, the belief, or even assumption, underwriting this poem.

Davie remains very skeptical of the grounds for the youthful Auden's appeal to his audience, 'in the sense of . . . grabbing its fitful and short-winded attention,' and he discounts Auden's minted phrases: 'For in hindsight one can see it as predictable that the decade which began with the phrase-making of W. H. Auden would end with the phrase-making of Dylan Thomas' (*Kenneth Allott*, 7). On the other hand, Auden projected a confidential integrity that won him enthusiastic support, as we see in this statement in 1933 by Harold Nicolson, who would later denounce Auden for his emigration to the US: 'A man like Auden with his fierce repudiation of half-way houses and his gentle integrity makes one feel . . . terribly Edwardian and back-number, and yet, thank God, delighted that people like Wystan Auden should actually exist' (Hynes, 125).

One of the earliest proponents of this fiduciary reading of Auden – this taking on trust his apparent confidences – was C. Day Lewis in his *A Hope for Poetry* (1934). Day Lewis, including himself as a source of hope, asserts that 'where the community is swollen, spiritually disorganized and heterogeneous . . . [the poet] is bound to be obscure, for he is talking to himself and to his friends – to that tiny, temporarily isolated unit with which communication is possible . . .' (37). As a trustee in that inner audience, Day Lewis recalls, as a parable he needs to translate for us, a particularly memorable passage from the hero's diary in Auden's *The Orators*:

> It wasn't till I was sixteen and a half that he [an uncle] invited me to his flat. We had champagne for dinner. When I left I knew who and what he was – my real ancestor.

In what Day Lewis praised as 'one of the great moments of the book,' this passage conveys to him the 'feeling that each of us has some personal link with the past, some natural or quasi-supernatural being from whom we draw power. . . . We claim for these "real ancestors" only this:

that great men, heroes, men who have seemed to live at a higher pressure than the rest, can brim over into posterity' (3–4).

We blush with hindsight at Auden's betrayal of Day Lewis's trust. A number of uncles pop up in *The Orators* such as the two who visit their nephews in the Do family: 'Now Do-a loved to bathe before his breakfast / With Uncle Dick, but Uncle Wiz...' The uncle of this 'great moment of the book,' Uncle Henry, the hero's 'real ancestor,' who has been dishonored in some mysterious death, remains a model to the young hero because, in the uncle's mysterious phrase, 'I have crossed it.' Our latter-day supposition that the transgressed border is social and sexual rather than political is confirmed by a passage in Isherwood's *Christopher and His Kind* in which Christopher visits his rich uncle Henry in 1930 London and, 'by making it clear to Henry that they had the same sexual nature' (36), educes from him a monthly stipend that allows Isherwood to live and write in Berlin.[16] According to Eve Sedgwick, even in Wilde's day, *uncle* 'was a common term for a male protector in a sexual relation involving economic sponsorship...' and 'offering a degree of initiation into gay cultures and identities...' (59).

If Auden, on fairly rare occasions such as this, slips from a 'language for indirection' into a code, he has some justification in face of the laws that would cast him out, or into prison. On the other hand, Davie's brief against Auden's phrasemaking and the resultant credulousness of his audience seems supported by this example. At times, Auden's portable phrases and epigrams may be seen as coins, lovely in their design and minting, that are underwritten neither by the golden treasury of the English poetic tradition nor by a comprehensive new fiduciary system that rewards the reader's trust. In this one regard, Leavis may have been accurate when he wrote of *The Orators* that Auden had 'not taken enough trouble to make his private counters effective currency' (Haffenden, 101).

One can approach Auden's English career as just such an effort to establish a reliable fiduciary poetic relationship with his audience and to write poems that rendered, in a phrase Auden borrowed from Yeats in 1936, 'the thoughts of a wise man in the speech of the common people' (*EA*, 360). Such an approach establishes the dialectical plot of Mendelson's *Early Auden* in which divisions within Auden and between Auden and his audience are never dissolved but rather resolved by '*accepting division itself*' (Mendelson's emphasis): 'If a divided self or a divided society could not be made whole, at least each part might consent to learn from each other, and might yet make a vineyard of the curse' (359). Where Mendelson finds acceptance, I find in Auden's poetry a permanent ambivalence which undergoes permutations. Psychoana-lytically, as Jean Laplanche reminds us, ambivalence occurs in

> specific conflicts in which the positive and negative components of the emotional attitude are simultaneously in evidence and insepar-able, and where they constitute a non-dialectical opposition which the subject, saying 'yes' and 'no' at the same time, is incapable of transcending.                                                  (28)

Before returning to Auden's relationship with Yeats and with MacNeice and other Irish poets, we might reflect on several stages in Auden's approach to his audience and on his poetic efforts to create 'effective currency' and through such reflections recognize the persistence in 1940 of Auden's deep ambivalence, not fully acknowledged in Mendelson's dialectical teleology, between simple wise disclosure and a reticent ambiguity. Auden reaches his most optimistic portrayal of poetic exchange in a poem of the mid-1930s rather than of the decade's close. The poem that lends its opening to the title of the 1935 British volume *Look, Stranger!* may offer Auden's fullest representation of poetic exchange, between poet and reader, the senses and external reality, memory and the present moment, the present and the future, and between poetic economy and the world's traffic, as we begin to see in the first stanza:

> Look, stranger, at this island now
> The leaping light for your delight discovers,
> Stand stable here
> And silent be,
> That through the channels of the ear
> May wander like a river
> The swaying sound of the sea.

(*EA*, 157–8)

Although the poem has attracted a number of excellent close read-ings,[17] I follow Mendelson closely enough to quibble with him. We might understand the poem's opening imperative as addressed less to 'a double for the poet himself,' as Mendelson asserts, than to a double-as-reader who will learn to estrange himself from a scene so that it does not remain merely familiar and therefore undisclosed. What the poet animates by projecting as 'leaping light' becomes introjected in the reader as 'delight.' If the island is Great Britain rather than, say, the Isle of Wight, then the setting must be Dover, conventional site of patriotic sonnets about Britain in crisis, but especially Arnold's 'Dover Beach' in which the shift from sight to sound (Arnold's 'Only . . . / . . . / Listen') and thereby from space to time, memory, and history, Auden's poem imitates: 'And silent be, / That through the channels of the ear / May wander like a river / The swaying sound of the sea.'

Mendelson, catching Auden's play on *sound*, says, 'The mind acts as a microcosm of what it observes. The sound of the large body of water moves in the ear like a small body of water, and both sounds move aimlessly' (339). Yet, in commerce and poetry *channels* not only restrict *sound*, they provide passages for controlled, not aimless, exchange. In the poem exchange is represented so extensively, especially in the swapping and borrowing of rhyme, slant rhyme, internal rhyme, assonance, and consonance – all animated by a pausing and surging rhythm – that exchange almost becomes a principle of creative perception, the exchange between observer and scene. We see this especially in the second stanza where rhyming exchanges tend to demarcate and alliteration to dissolve or oppose limits: 'Here the small field's ending pause / Where the chalk wall falls to the foam, and its tall ledges / Oppose the pluck / And knock of the tide.' The following enjambed line – 'And the shingle scrambles after the suck- / ing surf . . .' – deliberately reshapes Arnold's lines, 'Listen! you hear the grating roar / Of pebbles which the waves draw back and fling' – lines which lead to thoughts of sequence, the past, and 'the eternal note of sadness.' Although Auden's lines move forward in time, to the extent that Arnoldian echoes register, this future as represented in 1936 carries that degree of foreboding.

The poem concludes with a Wordsworthian projection into future memory:

> And the full view
> Indeed may enter
> And move in memory as now these clouds do,
> That pass the harbour mirror
> And all the summer through the water saunter.

Here the visual reflexiveness of sky and water represents the relation of present scene and future memories much as they do in Wordsworth's 'I Wandered Lonely As a Cloud,' but Auden's imprecise consonant rhyme – *har/bour; mir/ror; wat/saunt* – and the insistent falling rhythm in *enter, clouds do, harbour, mirror, summer, water,* and *saunter* add to the slight note of foreboding.

This final stanza begins by transporting us both offshore – 'Far off like floating seeds the ships / Diverge on urgent voluntary errands' – and, through a shipping itinerary and a seminal future, forward in time. Mendelson seems accurate in pointing out that the second line in this stanza 'abjures all sensory metaphors' (339). Reflecting on these divergent ships, Mendelson asserts that 'implicit in the poem are challenges to its author to find his own urgent errand, to leave his poetic isolation behind him...' (339–40). However, Mendelson exaggerates the difference between this image of willed action and what he calls the 'passive sensory impressions of unconscious natural objects,' because he restricts 'sensory' to sight. The exchange of sounds – *erge/urge*; *ver/vol*; *erge/gent*; *ary/erra*; *on/un/and* – and the acceleration of the pyrrhic swell of unstressed syllables (*un•ta*) before cresting in the amphibrach (*ry er•rands*) duplicate the aural exchanges and tempo of the poem's other lines.

To the extent that commerce is rendered rhythmic and auditory – 'That through the channels of the ear / May wander... / The swaying sound of the sea' – the poem suggests the primacy of measured language and the fact that all commerce floats on, in Ciaran Carson's term, the Briny Say. Regardless of how separate poetic and commercial economies may seem in reality, within this poem the natural economy of alternations and the political economy of divergence are part of 'the full view' created in the poetic relationships with the poem. The occasion for the poem underscores, somewhat ironically, the decade's tendency to make poetry an economic handmaiden: it was written for a British Travel Association film to help attract that larger economy to seaside holidays (although most of it was later dropped from the film – see Carpenter, 186, and Mendelson, 339).

Although economics contributed less to Auden's extensive reading in the 1930s than did psychology and religion, he must have been familiar with the ideas of J. M. Keynes (who produced one of his plays), W. H. Beveridge, and other economists popular with the government. Even in discussions of literature he often employs economic language, as in a 1933 review of books by Leavisites – 'We live in an age in which the collapse of all previous standards coincides with the perfection in technique for the centralised distribution of ideas' (*EA*, 317) – and he represents the value of poetry in terms of the poet's exchange with his or her audience. For example, writing for children in 1932, he said that words are a means of exchange, 'a bridge between a speaker and a listener...,' and 'while speech begins with the feeling of separateness in space..., writing begins from the sense of separateness in time, of... I shall be dead to-morrow, and you will be active in my place, and how can I speak to you?' (*EA*, 304, 305–6). In this same *Outline for Boys and Girls* . . . , he says we write to be read and for the pleasure of verbal making, and other motives fall well behind these two.

For the next few years, certainly through the publication of 'Look, Stranger . . .' in 1935, Auden will come closer to the ideal of this bridge of poetic words than he did in early poems or than he will in the popular, much-anthologized poems of 1940. When he tells his reader in 'Look, stranger . . .' to 'Stand stable here,' he is not incorporating the readers so much as yielding his place so that he can stand in the reader's public space. Perhaps the best expression of this exchange, a deepening of Auden's concepts in the *Outline*, would be Georg Simmel's exploration of the motives for an exchange like the poet's, in which a poem that the poet values in itself for its craft and truth can only become complete in exchange. Simmel writes:

> Society is the supra-singular structure which is nonetheless not abstract. . . . Exchange, as the economic realization of the relativity of things . . . lifts the individual thing and its significance for the individual man out of their singularity, not into the sphere of the abstract but into the liveliness of interaction, which is, so to speak, the body of economic value.                                                      (69)

When the commodity the poet brings to society is comprised of deeply personal and even illicit ideas and emotions, the bridge-crossing that leads to a valuable exchange can also exact its toll.

Auden's simple 1932 text on value and poetry-as-a-bridge reads as a primer for the more sophisticated writing in Christopher Caudwell's *Illusion and Reality* published in 1937 just months after the young Marxist poet-activist was killed in the Spanish Civil War.[18] In his 1935 anthology *The Poet's Tongue*, Auden wrote: 'One of the motives behind poetry is curiosity, the wish to know what we feel and think. . . . Curiosity is the only human passion that can be indulged in for twenty-four hours a day without satiety' (329). In responding to the 'average' man's preference for golf or sight-seeing over poetry, Auden offers poetry as an ultimate commodity.[19] Two years later, Caudwell's book asserts: 'Poetry externalises emotion. . . . Emotion is minted – made current coin. Feelings are given social value. . . . Poetic dreamwork is [labor] because one produces social commodities . . .' (218). As in a dream, the poem projects 'man into a world of phantasy which is superior to his present reality.' He continues, 'Only by means of this illusion can be brought into being a reality which would not otherwise exist' (30). Poetry molds reality because, as a means of exchange, 'poetry moulds the instincts to reality...' (219). While poetry indirectly feeds, as it is fed by, reality, it remains aside from reality. The poet, however, is socialized by this process: 'Just as the producer of material goods for society brings them to the common market, so the artist or the scientist brings his special experience to the ideological market in a fashioned form' (191).

In reviewing Caudwell's book in May of 1937, Auden praised it extravagantly as 'the most important book on poetry since the books of Dr. Richards, and, in my opinion, [it] provides a more satisfactory answer to the many problems which poetry raises' (*New Verse*, no. 25, 20). Auden refused to criticize the book because, he says, 'I am not competent to do so, and secondly because I agree with it.' In the next year, Auden introduced his *Oxford Book of Light Verse* with a historical 'decline and fall of poetic communities,' which in its stages approximates closely that offered in detail in chapters 4–6 of Caudwell's book. Both critics track the beginning of the poet's alienation from his audience to the Renaissance, but whereas Caudwell traces the pathology of the poetry to the progressive loss of solidarity with the community, Auden believes a degree of remoteness from an audience is positive for the poet:

> The more homogeneous a society, the closer the artist is to the everyday life of his time, the easier it is for him to communicate what he perceives, but the harder for him to see honestly and truthfully, unbiased by the conventional responses of his time. The more unstable a society, and the more detached from it the artist, the clearer he can see, but the harder it is for him to convey it to others.     (*EA*, 364)

As I have suggested, within the 1930s, Auden's meaning was most accessible in poems from *Look, Stranger!*, the 1936 volume (for example, 'Look, Stranger,' but also 'Now from my window-sill,' 'A shilling life,' 'Casino,' 'Fish in the unruffled lakes,' and songs from *The Ascent of F6*) and in poems published very soon after (*Letter to Byron*, 'Spain 1937,' and the earlier poems of *Another Time* (1940)) all of which can reward the reader's trust. However, some of the most popular poems from the next volume *Another Time*, specifically the elegies and 'Musée des Beaux Arts,' conceal more difficulties than first appear and even form a commentary on modernist difficulty. To clarify this point, it seems most helpful to reflect on the poem most often explicated of all Auden's poems, 'Musée des Beaux Arts.'

The poem's title, which seems to announce merely a space or occasion for musing, actually suggests the poem's subject, not suffering but a particular way of musing on suffering or on any serious subject within the museum setting or within a modernist poem. Robert Langbaum has succinctly characterized the archeological and psychological impulses behind modernism as the intention to 'dig below the ruins of official tradition to uncover in myth and underground tradition, an inescapable because inherently psychological pattern into which to fit the chaotic present' (10). As Hugh Kenner has argued, high modernist poetry such as that of Pound and H. D. was deeply influenced by these poets' countless hours in London museums, and the roots of modernism extend from the Enlightenment when museums emerged.[20] The modernist poem, such as *The Cantos* or 'The Waste Land,' like the museum, displays language, images, or artifacts from various cultures independently of their historical contexts, thus apparently introducing difference but actually insinuating or, even, proclaiming a universal human nature.

By opening with an exclusive, and easily refutable, generalization – 'About suffering they were never wrong, / The Old Masters...' – the poem establishes the kind of restricted truth it will offer. First, the statement that the Old Masters always represent humanity's indifference to suffering is untrue. Any approach to the several Brueghel works in room 44 in the Musées Royaux des Beaux-Arts in Brussels must carry observers past a number of paintings proclaiming the centrality of Christ's suffering or the martyrdom of Stephen or Lawrence or other saints, subjects which attracted Auden in a museum ('I would look at a painting of the Crucifixion before a painting of a still life...' (*EA*, 357)). One wonders even if the term 'Old Masters,' usually reserved for Italian painters of the cinquecento, is appropriate for Brueghel. Nevertheless, like a single painting purchased or purloined from its cultural context and placed among other paintings,[21] the poem composes from various non-indigenous elements its own truth, and it does so by the same sort of indirection and displacement he praises in Brueghel's paintings: '... how well they understood / Its human position; how it takes place / While someone else is eating or opening a window or just walking dully along.' Whereas we might expect an explanation of *how* the suffering takes place, the five occurrences in the poem of the word *how* evade the meaning of 'in what manner' to substitute other senses of the adverb / conjunction, as we see in the enjambment above where a promise to explain converts to a line expanding to 22 syllables explaining '*that* it takes place / While someone else is eating,' etcetera. In the second stanza, we are told that 'the dreadful martyrdom' must, by necessity, occur 'Anyhow in a corner,' meaning both that it must occur *nevertheless* and *in any manner* so long as it is out of the way. Just as activities such as eating or waiting or skating occlude the specific gruesome activities behind words such as *dreadful martyrdom*, so insignificant nouns displace names of victims dying 'Where the dogs go on with their doggy life and the torturer's horse / Scratches its innocent behind on a tree.' In the poem's and the painting's understatement of the massacre of the innocents, which eventually leads to Christ's death on a tree, the insignificant backside is foregrounded, as they say.

Similarly, in the last stanza's account of Brueghel's 'Landscape with the Fall of Icarus,' the Ovidian story of the son of the maze's architect, whose flight terminates when he flies too close to the sun, is relegated to traces in the words *amazing* and *disaster* (against the sun-star). The poem ends with a statement on necessity and suffering:

> . . . the sun shone
> As it had to on the white legs disappearing into the green
> Water; and the expensive delicate ship that must have seen
> Something amazing, a boy falling out of the sky,
> Had somewhere to get to and sailed calmly on.

Yet, this fourth line from the poem's conclusion discloses that this state-ment about suffering is undercut and limited by its manifestation in a work of art, that before the enjambed line reaches the suffocating *water*, it must pause at *green*, thus reminding us of the painted representation and its placement in a decontextualized series of paintings whose only significant relationship is metonymical. The poem then forms a critique of modernist poetry rather than, as Michael Riffaterre would have it,[22] a critique of estheticism or art-for-art's-sake. Although Auden is not yet ready to declare that 'poetry makes nothing happen,' a message that will resonate in complex ways across the elegies and the masterwork *The Sea and the Mirror*, he is ready to suggest how statements made by art, especially modernist art, no matter how well phrased and moving in their expression of a truth, are distanced from the real contexts that would imbue them with more than a conditional truth.

## Auden and Yeats

Having embarked for his new home in the United States in January of 1939, Auden could have been forgiven for believing history altered as he crossed the forty-fifth meridian. After all, the day of his arrival in New York harbor, the 26th, turned out to be the coldest day of the year, the day after Spain had fallen, and two days before W. B. Yeats, the most important member of Auden's literary avunculate, would die in the hills of Provence. The tribute for Yeats he published in the *New Republic* in March and the *London Mercury* in April, like most elegies in English, concerns not so much the dead as – in more valuable tribute – the state of poetry after this death. Probably in response to his private ambivalence about his English audience and his responsibility to them in time of crisis, as much as to the anticipation of a public version of this debate in Parliament and British papers concerning his departure from England, 'In Memory of W. B. Yeats' finally attempts to settle Auden's ambivalence in his most memorable, unequivocal, and concentrated line, 'For poetry makes nothing happen: it survives . . .' As if he had for-mulated a prophylactic against early-1930s activist rhetoric, to which he had contributed, and late-1930s protestations that poets should be patriots, Auden repeated this statement in a spring essay on Yeats in the *Partisan Review*, in 'New Year Letter,' in his notes for a book *The Prolific and the Devourer* (never published in his lifetime), and in several letters to friends.

Nevertheless, a closer look at the elegy can suggest that his assertion that 'poetry makes nothing happen,' like the general 'argument' of 'Musée des Beaux Arts,' is a conditional statement, true only paradoxically in its situation in the poem. Consequently, we should explore 'the valley of its saying,' itself a tourist site for explicators, where we observe first of all the familiar Audenesque displacements: winter is dead; the day is dying; statues are disfigured; mercury has sunk, and 'all the instruments agree / The day of his death was a dark cold day' (*EA*, 241). While these lines may seem much less evasive than the displacements of early poems (indeed they find justification in the elegiac convention of mourning nature, as well as in the actual weather conditions that accompanied notice of Yeats's death), they may in fact derive from Yeats's own imagery for declining temperature, for coldness, and ultimately for that anti-thesis to his own hothouse romanticism: that idea of the constructed or achieved self he called the mask.

After attempting prototypes of the mask in 'To A Friend Whose Work Has Come to Nothing,' 'The Dawn,' and 'The Three Beggars,' Yeats achieves his clearest image of 'simplification through intensity' (*A Vision*, 90) through the figure of the fisherman, an inhabitant of phase 3 which is the opposite of Yeats's phase 17. In 'The Fisherman,' the public Yeats scattered among his detractors finds a unifying image in 'This wise and simple man' for whom Yeats would write a 'Poem maybe as cold / And passionate as the dawn' (149). Thereafter in Yeats's poetry coldness rep-resents death but also the other, antithetical state which draws him out of his natural self and with which he achieves momentary union in the accomplished poem.[23]

To extend this suggestion that Auden honors Yeats by incorporating a key image from the dead poet's writing, we might recall that the elegy's last section appears in the stanzaic form, unusual for Auden, of section V of 'Under Ben Bulben,' which had appeared on 3 February in the *Irish Times* and the *Irish Independent*. The rhythm of 'Earth, receive an honoured guest' follows the trochaic trimeter with the extra stressed syllable of Yeats's last testament: 'Irish poets, learn your trade,' and so on. Furthermore, in the conclusion of the poem, as John Fuller asserts, 'The river is transformed into the sacred life-blood of Yeats's poetry . . . to become in the final stanza a healing fountain (the unfrozen pity of stanza 6, and a melting inversion of the snow-covered proleptic statue of the opening winter scene of Part 1)' (289). We recognize as well that Auden converts the hydrodynamics of poetry from the English river to the Yeatsian fountain discussed in Chapter 2.

If this is plausible, the elegy's climactic phrase, 'poetry makes nothing happen' may also translate one antithetical notion derived from Vico and Berkeley, from which Yeats frequently vacillated, that mankind creates history, and even life and death, from his own imagination:

> Death and life were not
> Till man made up the whole,
> Made lock, stock and barrel
> Out of his bitter soul,
> Aye, sun and moon and star, all
>
> ('The Tower,' *CP*, 198)

Quoting these lines, Louis MacNeice asserts that, in opposition to British empiricism, Yeats ignores Berkeley's comments on 'the mind of God' and appropriates the Irish philosopher as a sort of solipsist (148). MacNeice quotes other verses of Yeats – 'Whatever flares upon the night / Man's own resinous heart has fed' and 'Man has created death' – to clarify Yeats's paraphrase of Vico's assertion in *On the Boiler* that 'we can know nothing . . . that we have not made' (126).[24] We would be consistent with this reading of the elegy as a work partly constructed from Yeats's own rhythms and ideas, which seems to be Auden's intentions in other elegies, such as those for Freud and James, if we interpreted 'poetry makes nothing happen' to mean that poetry creates life ('comes about by chance') out of the imaginary antithesis of the objective world.[25] This leaves open the possibility that once it has 'happened,' poetry can affect our disposition toward history – 'persuade us to rejoice,' 'make a vineyard of the curse,' and teach us to accept necessity and 'to praise' – and thereby establish an imaginative precondition to historical action. Auden's last stanza then may, at least, leave open the answer to Yeats's question in 'The Man and the Echo': 'Did that play of mine send out / Certain men the English shot?'

Even if we recognize that Auden's insupportable generalized exclusions in these two poems – 'never . . . ,' 'nothing . . . ,' – invite contradiction and closer reading, a reasonable person, such as even myself, could be skeptical of this interpretation of Auden's most famous aphorism. In spite of Auden's tendency to exercise this phrase in public after its invention for 'In Memory of W. B. Yeats,' it works best, as it was probably intended to originally, within the poem itself in tension with those statements about what poetry can achieve in bracing and even altering the heart of the reader.[26] The insight that art serves life more efficaciously indirectly and at a certain distance finds its first overt expression in 'In Memory of W. B. Yeats.' Auden never directly credits Yeats with this idea which he might have acquired from 'Sailing to Byzantium,' as I read it, or 'Lapis Lazuli.' In response to Yeats's restrained enthusiasm for Auden's poetry, a certain ambivalence toward Yeats by Auden would be a reasonable response. Auden's 'The Public v. The Late Mr. William Butler Yeats,' published in the *Partisan Review* the spring after Yeats's death, can be read as a clever dramatized argument for Yeats's greatness in which the prosecution concedes certain faults which are overridden by a superior defense. In fact, certain of Auden's charges – an indifference to 'the great struggle of our time to create a juster social order,' an inability to recognize poetic gifts in others, a disbelief in science – must have adhered fixedly in Auden's final judgment. Nevertheless, Auden defends Yeats on the grounds toward which he, Auden, is immigrating: that a certain excitement and sincerity in the poems will recreate similar feelings in others, regardless of their political differences with Yeats; that the strength and clarity of his poems are 'parallel linguistic virtues' to brotherhood and intelligence in democracy; and therefore that poetry never meets or directly enters into history to which it maintains a homological and reflective relationship.

Nine years later, in a *Kenyon Review* essay, Auden expressed his indebtedness to Yeats without this dialogue, dissent, or much apparent ambivalence. In characterizing 'Yeats As An Example,' he asserts that 'one whole side of Yeats, the side summed up in *A Vision*, has left virtually no trace' (188–9). Then in a playful swipe at Isherwood and Gerald Heard, at home in Hollywood, he labels Yeats's occult 'so essentially lower-middle class – or should I say Southern Californian – so ineluctably associated with suburban villas and clearly unattractive faces.' Yet, he justifies Yeats's anti-scientific bias as a necessary defense of imagination and his myths as indigenous beliefs that bound him to his people. Finally, Yeats bequeaths his successors two genuine but somewhat modest innovations that can be imitated. He introduces a range of metrical variations – well illustrated by Auden – that liberate contemporary poetry from 'iambic monotony'; he transforms the occasional poem from being either an official, impersonal performance or a trivial *vers de société* into 'a serious reflective poem of at once personal and public interest' (113). By citing, as an example of this subgenre, 'In Memory of Major Robert Gregory' rather than 'Easter 1916,' '1919,' or 'Meditations in Time of Civil War,' Auden avoids exactly identifying the type of personal historical poem that Hynes says was Yeats's legacy to the 1930s and which Auden had tried – in 'September 1, 1939' for example – and, according to his own judgment, failed to adapt.

In spite of Auden's ambivalence, Yeats seems crucial to the most important change of course in the younger poet's career, his distancing of poetry from history. And then, recalling the earlier argument of this chapter, ambivalence was the common disease that determined Yeats's mask and Auden's ambiguous stance toward his audience. Although Yeats's expression of his ambivalence would differ from Auden's, Auden would have understood Yeats's confession, quoted more fully in Chapter 1, that in spite of English persecution of the Irish he owes his soul to Shakespeare and that 'my hatred tortures me with love, my love with hate' (*YE&I*, 519).

## MacNeice's intermediate eccentricity

This expression of ambivalence nearly finds its match for intensity in the poetry of Yeats's most prominent Anglo-Irish successor, the Belfastman Louis MacNeice. However, having spent most of his schooldays and adult life in England, the mixed expressions of love and hatred are usually directed back across the Irish Sea toward Ireland. His vitriolic denunciations of Ireland occur in the war poem 'Neutrality' – in which 'The neutral island facing the Atlantic' finds its counterpart in 'The neutral island in the heart of man,' but in which both turn inwardly backward, averting attention from the fact that 'off your own shores the mackerel / Are fat – on the flesh of your kin' (*McCP*, 203). In the earlier poem 'Valediction,' Ireland offers generally legacies of 'arson and murder' and, specifically to MacNeice, 'indifference and sentimentality.' If he must accept this inheritance as part of his nature, he can impose a gap – through a daytripper's perspective and ironic observations – between himself and his motherland, 'And become as one of your holiday visitors / And however often I may come / Farewell, my country, and in perpetuum' (*McCP*, 53).

Of Belfast – 'devout and profane and hard' – he confesses, 'This is my mother-city, these my paps,' and concedes, 'Cursèd be he that curses his mother. I cannot be / Anyone else than what this land engendered me' ('Valediction,' 52). In an early poem, the city seems dominated by its Protestant patriarchy:

> The sun goes down with a banging of Orange drums
> While the male kind murders each its woman
> To whose prayer for oblivion answers no Madonna.
>
> ('Belfast,' *McCP*, 17)

Whether the Madonna, represented by a 'garish Virgin,' remains silent in the face of Catholic prayers or in response to the disregard of Protestants, she hardly seems exalted here (or served poetically by this awkward final inversion). In a note to *The Poetry of W. B. Yeats*, MacNeice suggests that Irish nationalism, as represented in the icon of Cathleen Ní Houlihan, may be traceable 'to a mother-fixation, even to an Oedipus complex, England representing the father. Any such study should also weigh the effect of the Virgin Mary upon Ireland' (138). In his own life, however, MacNeice associates his Ireland both with the father, the loved and feared Anglican bishop who withdrew from his son after his wife's death, and that wife, Louis's mother who entered hospital when her son was five and died when he was seven. She figures indirectly in 'Last Before America,' a poem about the West of Ireland, to which MacNeice often refers as a pre-natal territory of dream and the unconscious:

> Both myth and seismic history have been long suppressed
> Which made and unmade Hy Brasil – now an image
> For those who despise charts but find their dream's endorsement
>
> In certain long low islets snouting towards the west
> Like cubs that have lost their mother.
>
> (*McCP*, 227)

In *Irish Poetry After Joyce* I concluded that the cartographic appropriateness of the image of the cubs – otherwise outweighed by the historical and zoological inappropriateness of this image for Western Ireland, where bears were non-existent and children, not mothers, emigrated – becomes reinforced and ratified by the poet's own deep maternal longing.

Although the depths and recesses of MacNeice's ambivalence await full exploration, his credentials as an Irish poet have been carefully qualified and effectively reclaimed by Edna Longley and then Peter McDonald, as well as by Anthony Roche, Tom Paulin, and others. Without looking further at MacNeice's poetic expressions of Irishness, then, we might turn to *The Poetry of W. B. Yeats* to see how MacNeice employs the older poet to distance himself from Yeats's English detractors and to situate himself in relation to English and Irish poetries. First, MacNeice acknowledges sharing traits with Yeats derived from their common Anglo-Irish background: the effects of loneliness, concern for family, an anarchist individualism, a sentimentalized view of Irish history, a 'half-envious contempt for England' and of the English, 'an inferior race,' members of a nation associated with materialism while Ireland is spiritual (47). What appears, in the balance of the book, as critical scrutiny, 'rigorous, . . . offering Yeats no quarter, no deference,' in the words of Richard Ellmann's foreword to a 1967 reissue, amounts actually to a skillful concessive argument. As we saw in Chapter 2, English critics would marginalize Yeats simply by equating his Irishness with 'eccentricity' – 'a development out of the main track . . . minor poetry . . .' (I. A. Richards); 'Mr Yeats has succumbed to the malady of a nation' (Murray); Yeats found in his Irishness 'an external validation' for his 'unfortunate habit of mind' (Leavis).[27] Just at that marginal point, MacNeice takes up Yeats's defense, asserting that unlike 'most of the poets of the Nineties . . . Yeats escaped because he harnessed the aesthetic doctrine to a force outside itself which he found in his own country' (38). He continues, 'It was Ireland that saved him from becoming the slave of these things' ('theosophy on the one hand and Nineties aestheticism on the other') (49–50). The style of early Yeats, derived from Pre-Raphaelite and late-Romanticist English poetry, found its bracing corrective in the atmosphere of Irish landscape, 'cold light and tumbling cloud.' 'In reviving Irish literature he revived himself. . . . It was Ireland that gave body to his poetry. His escape from England coincided with his escape from adolescence. His adolescent poetry is his *English* poetry' (52).

At a time when most English readers continued to judge Yeats in terms of his 1907 selection,[28] MacNeice was intent on presenting *The*

*Tower* (1928) and *The Winding Stair* (1933) 'as the highest achievement of Yeats's genius' (135). Furthermore, MacNeice makes the case that, in spite of his idiosyncrasies, Yeats had a greater affinity than Eliot with poets of the 1930s who

> stood with Yeats for system against chaos, for a positive art against
> a passive impressionism. Where Eliot had seen misery, frustration, and
> ruins, they saw heroic struggle – or, sometimes, heroic defeat – and
> they saw ruins rebuilding.                                    (224)

To maintain the elder Yeats as this sort of heroic model for the 'Auden Generation,' MacNeice needed to offer some defense of Yeats's highly criticized selections in *The Oxford Book of Modern Verse* (1936) in which many of these contemporaries were neglected or slighted. Perhaps in the most extreme of these dismissals of Yeats's anthology, Geoffrey Grigson wrote in *New Verse*: 'Our great respect for Mr. Yeats cannot prevent us from saying that his anthology is eccentric, reactionary, narrow, frequently stupid, often ridiculous ... as a view of the best poems between 1892 and 1935 ... cuckoo' (nos 23, 21). Devoid of the leathery sophistry that a defense of this selection would have required, MacNeice quotes approvingly the best bits from Yeats's Preface and obliquely defends the selections as a consequence of Yeats's 'child-like liking for simple poetry of the folk type,' of which the selections are 'much better than his selections from more intellectual work' (167). Whereas Yeats wrote much complex poetry, 'he found most contemporary sophisticated verse repugnant.' The simple poetry, which Yeats saw 'as coming from the people ', 'was more easily found in Ireland. ...' MacNeice then continues to explain Yeats's complex use of the refrain, thus reminding us that even Yeats's curious tastes arise from traditions that are rooted in the people's imagination and that nourish his own poetry.

Finally, MacNeice corrects the degree of overstatement in Auden's phrase 'poetry makes nothing happen':

> The fallacy lies in thinking that it is the *function* of art to make things
> happen and that the effect of art upon actions is something either
> direct or calculable. It is an historical fact that art *can* make things
> happen. ... Yeats did not write primarily in order to influence men's
> action but he knew that art can alter a man's outlook and so indi-
> rectly affect his actions.                                    (225)

Because MacNeice may be overlooking the indirection that Auden himself may intend by this overstatement, MacNeice's correction helps us locate his own poetry more accurately than it does Auden's.

If we are reading accurately the complex signals of 'In Memory of W. B. Yeats' and 'Musée des Beaux Arts,' then we can conclude that by the end of the decade Auden and MacNeice both would place art in an intermediate role, not directly in the spaces and moments we occupy but aside from and casting their light and shadow on our presence. We can even find passages in MacNeice's poetry that comment indirectly on these two poems by Auden. One passage in MacNeice's masterwork *Autumn Journal*, for example, forms a commentary on Auden's interpretation of Brueghel's Icarus. In Canto XX, amid the pulsations of Trafalgar Square, MacNeice muses on the National Gallery, where 'closed and silent ... in their frames ... like frozen flames' paintings persist in 'other worlds' (*CP*, 141). Vitality and motion seem to belong to the gallery-goers, who voyaging among these stilled lives, 'are anxious ... to land in their own time.' Yet, awakened and completed by imagination, 'these arrogant Old Masters' intrude on our own worlds 'like airmen doing their stunts / Over our private garden.' Ironically, this art from the past assumes the form of present, masterful technology or even of that threatening future of aerial warfare the complacent art-consumers want to ignore. For the imaginative moment, the Old Masters 'Swoop and loop and lance us with a quick / Shadow ...' and 'cast their shadow on us like aspersions' (142). However, MacNeice would agree with Auden that as 'a paradigm / Of life's successions, treacheries, recessions,' these 'slick / Tricks of the airy region' must disappear 'into the green' of the painting with the heliotropic Icarus in Auden's rendering of Brueghel's painting.

While Auden and MacNeice come to share assumptions about poetry's limitations, as well as ambivalences about their audiences, they remain quite different in important respects. However, the importance in their work of asyndeton – taking the form of representative objects set side by side without conjunctions – makes them often appear quite similar. In *Modern Poetry*, MacNeice praises Auden's 'notorious catalogues. His generalities always crystallize into instances and to keep them clearcut he often leaves out the links – the "as ifs", the "for examples"' (107). To illustrate Auden's representational series, each item or action so distinct it forms a snapshot of an epoch's fad or fixation, we need only recall the lines of 'Spain,' too familiar to quote here. Whereas Auden strings together social moments, the classicist MacNeice often turns a word's etymology into a sequence of related thoughts.

For a simple example, consider this series from the opening of *Autumn Journal*, where the anaphoric *and* blurs any real relation between these impressions.

> And August going out to the tin trumpets of nasturtiums
> And the sunflowers' Salvation Army blare of brass
> And the spinster sitting in a deck-chair picking up stitches

From external impressions based on the appearance of these flowers, the poem suggests the sort of summertime Elgar tones that waft from provincial bandstands and, then, with a play on the original meaning of *spinster*, which evokes the feudal base for this Hampshire society, the poem moves into the passing houses' interiors and into the timeless summertime habits of their occupants. Before many lines, the poet confirms that these reflections occur behind the train windows – 'And I am in the train too now and summer is going / South as I go north' – as the poet returns to London from August holidays. Retrospectively, we recognize that the amphimacer, double dactyl, and trochee of the opening line – 'Close and slow, summer is ending in Hampshire' – enact the train's lazy acceleration from an estival inertia.

MacNeice's paratactic series, which can be as dizzying as Auden's spinning collages or displaced cinemagraphic sequences, often find their realistic situation in the viewpoint of a passing train's commuter. Beyond the speed of trains and their importance in the life of MacNeice and of his society, they also suggest for MacNeice – as do escalators and taxis – the intermediacy of poetry. Trains seem particularly appropriate for MacNeice's masterful memoir *Autumn Journal*. Because like other ephemera in this autobiographical poem of 1938 – the brand names, period fashions, headline celebrities of the period – that are also destined to pass nearly with the decade, trains, which will soon be commandeered for troops and then depreciated with coal, succeed in becoming elements in the memoirist's efforts to place himself as an average citizen of a particular world in a particular historical era.

More subtly, in a few poems MacNeice employs trains to represent not just the passing of time but also the poems themselves, carrying us across time and space, as in *metaphor*, but also closed off from the reality on which they nevertheless impinge. In a mysterious poem from 1933, for example, trains are uncharacteristically represented from an outside, non-passenger's viewpoint as 'chains of lighted windows, / A register in an unknown language / For these are the trains in which one never goes.' He continues:

> So listening for the night express coming down the way
> I receive the expected whistle of the engine
> Sharp and straight on the ear like stigmata.

('A Contact,' *McCP*, 21)

On the most literal level, these trains acquire their strangeness because 'one' never goes inside of them; they are mail-trains or other after-commuter-hour trains. Yet, in their 'chains,' their sequences suggest lines or stanzas of poetry, or a 1930s view of language as linear and sequential, that indicate they 'carry across or back' (*register*) a meaning which is folded into their passing but which never unveils itself, as suggested in the rhyming words of the first stanza. In the final stanza, the poet separates himself from the *us* who hear the train's rhythm by listening for the 'expected whistle' which brands ('stigmatizes') him as one who listens for, and presumably sympathizes with, the train's mysterious, undisclosed conveyance. If this conveyance represents the poem, it only brushes against or touches the real world, as the title 'A Contact' suggests.

In 'Train to Dublin' (1934), the poet, enclosed behind the train's window, attempts to depict a world that hurdles past at the train's tempo, marked as if by musical staffs:

> The train's rhythm never relents, the telephone posts
> Go striding backwards like the legs of time to where
> In a Georgian house you turn at the carpet's edge
> Turning a sentence while, outside my window here,
> The smoke makes broken queries in the air.

(*McCP*, 27)

As in 'A Contact,' at the point where the conveyance impinges on reality, this time seen from within, enigmas – 'broken queries' – arise. Set off by glass and speed from the present space and time, the poet nevertheless can convey impressions vividly caught in the passing moment.

A more solipsistic view of the poem is suggested by the eight-line 'Corner Seat,' the last lines of which read:

> – But look again:
> Windows between you and the world
> Keep out the cold, keep out the fright;
> Then why does your reflection seem
> So lonely in the moving night?

(*McCP*, 218)

At least from the time of Wordsworth's lines from *The Prelude* on 'down-bending from the side / Of a slow-moving boat' from which he sees as much the reflected sky and himself as the submarine world, poets have represented the poem as a conveyance that may confuse impressions of the passing world with overlaid reflections of the self. Here, the darkness at the close of the Second World War isolates MacNeice in his own 'moving night.' Usually, however, MacNeice's poem records the journey, both reflective and impressionistic, and he rarely emphasizes destinations which are only stages in an ongoing commute. As he says in the poem placed last in both his *Collected Poems* and in Michael Longley's edition of the *Selected* MacNeice, 'Our end is life. Put out to sea' (*McCP*, 546). In his own life, MacNeice 'put out to sea' on trains which actually conveyed the young man to and from school and, then, university, marking and mixing in memory with beginnings and endings of term, and in the 1930s carrying him between Birmingham and London as well as to and from the boat to Larne or Dun Laoghaire. They enter his poetry, therefore, like the hyphen in his Anglo-Irish experience, transporting him betwixt and between. Occasionally, MacNeice recognizes his own longing for a journey's end or a translation into some transcendent realm. The conclusion of 'Train to Dublin' goes beyond this recognition of the fact of longing to posit a fortunate terminus (or a terminal fortune):

> I would like to give you more but I cannot hold
> This stuff within my hands and the train goes on;
> I know that there are further syntheses to which,
> As you have perhaps, people at last attain
> And find that they are rich and breathing gold.

> (*McCP*, 28)

The same relation of gold to permanence enters a trainless poem, 'The Sunlight on the Garden,' only to be denied: 'We cannot cage the minute / Within its nets of gold' (*McCP*, 84). In the collaborative 'Last Will and Testament,' which Auden and MacNeice place among their *Letters from Iceland*, Louis wishes for his ex-wife Mary, with perhaps a deliberate sentimentality, a golden ever-after: 'And may her hours be gold and without number' (239). In the decade in which Britain finally abandoned gold as the standard of value, MacNeice may have intended some irony in these nostalgic representations of Edenic stasis as golden. In opening his study of Yeats, he comments intelligently on the relation of value to concepts of timeless standards, such as gold, the Good, God the Father, the father, and, according to my argument in Chapter 2, the epic: what Jean-Joseph Goux calls 'general equivalents.' MacNeice writes:

> Idealist philosophers in talking about their Absolutes and Universals have made them vulnerable by hypostatizing them, whereas the only invulnerable Universal is one that is incarnate. We still tend to think that, because a thing is in time, its value can only be explained by an abstraction from the thing of some supposedly timeless qualities.
>
> (vii)

Goux draws out the implications of MacNeice's assertion:

> Plato's archetypal ideas are separated from the world of tangible realities as universal equivalents (gold, father, language) are separated from the world they govern. The *idealist optical illusion* consists in viewing the visible material world as the reflection of general equivalents, whereas general equivalents constitute the focused reflection, the specular image, of the visible world's multiplicity and differentiation.
>
> (94–5)

If MacNeice were fully open to the implication of his statement, he might have created a modernist art less reflective of a recognizable subject and empirical surfaces, even if fluctuant, and more representative of the relativity of value, according to the homology that Goux recognizes between economics and other forms of representation:

> Shortly after Saussure had declared that linguistic values – in contrast to economic values based on a standard – had no foundation in nature, shortly after Wassily Kandinsky and Piet Mondrian had abandoned the search for direct empirical reference in order to espouse pure painting, the economic system dispensed with the gold standard, with the evident result of generalized floating.          (113)

With all of his sense of Heraclitean uncertainties and of the ironic distance between our enclosed selves and nature, MacNeice nevertheless maintains a recognizable poetic voice and projects that voice toward a constructed but recognizably middle-class audience. In *Modern Poetry*, basically an effort to promote Auden and the other *New Signature* poets over Eliot, MacNeice refers to Modernism as the 'Americanization of poetry' (162). With subject matter less esoteric than Eliot's, Auden and Spender represent, MacNeice argues, 'a more vulgar world' through a voice that is personal while avoiding the 'utter individualism' of Yeats. Toward the close of *Modern Poetry* MacNeice characterized the poet in terms that have become well known: 'I would have a poet able-bodied, fond of talking, a reader of the newspapers, capable of pity and laughter, informed in economics,' etcetera (198). Elsewhere, he suggests that this poetic self is a constructed persona. For example, in his book on Yeats, he defends the elder poet's masks and his use of ballads and faux-primitive refrains. Confessing that the poet may be 'many different selves,' he turns to his reader: 'I suggest even that you should study your own personality and consider whether from day to day you have consistently the same moods or even the same ideas – that is, the same self' (166). Whereas Auden would be aware that the *you* he addressees may be many various people, MacNeice seems less questioning about the audience, with whom, he says in *Modern Poetry*, the poet should be collusive: 'A poet should always be "collaborating" with his public, but this public, in the mass, cannot make itself heard and he has to guess at its requirements and its criticisms' (196).[29] Whatever MacNeice's relationship with an uncertain, accelerated world, this collaborative relation between his constructed poetic self and the audience he imagines seems less duplicitous and coy than Auden's ambivalent relationships to his wider audiences and closer in tone than Auden to the Movement poetry, which too uncritically attributed its paternity to Hardy, that will dominate most of the last half-century of British poetry. However, if MacNeice's hyphenated Anglo-Irish intermediacy imbued him with an ironic distance and if he nostalgically retains the self as company in his commutes, he nevertheless rides a modernist trajectory that conveys him apart from the Movement poets and towards a world in which, according to Goux, 'contemporary sociality ... tends to shatter the mirror of representation, opening onto a new modality of the subjective and of subjection, a modality only partially conveyed by the terms *decentering* and *eccentricity*' (120). In this regard, closer to the center than any Irish poet of his generation, MacNeice nevertheless remains eccentric to British 'culture' and poetry shaped by its ideology.

## Some poetic traffic in the 1930s

MacNeice's frequent use of Eliot's poetry as an example of what must be expunged from British poetry establishes his stance toward Eliot as adversarial. Although praise and blame of Eliot usually balance each other in *Modern Poetry* and *The Poetry of W. B. Yeats*, MacNeice's reproaches may well have congealed into one of those anti-blurbs that haunt poets' small hours. In such excerpts from MacNeice's prose, Eliot becomes 'not a great poet...but a very sensitive aesthete...obsessed with the past... a rather pedantic individual...' (*MP*, 59); 'Nostalgia and self-pity are strong in him if under disguise, and also, under disguise, a certain swagger' (*MP*, 84). In his study of Yeats, MacNeice asserts that 'Eliot tends to over-work images with a private significance and to employ figures that come from a private, archaic, and slightly affected mythology...' To those who believe Eliot's aspirations within the world of poetry were as monarchical as his politics, MacNeice may have seemed like Dickens' Trabb's Boy deflating Eliot's 'great expectations': 'Eliot and his early model, Pound, are first and foremost American tourists' (*MP*, 84). And in a more intriguing reminder of Eliot's yankee-ness, he compares Eliot's model of the poetic mind acquiring impressions, stated in 'Tradition and the Individual Talent,' to a Taylorist assembly line: 'Like a motor-car factory where the chassis slides past "impersonally" on its platform until all its body is fitted on to it. Eliot, remember, is an addict to "impersonality" ' (*MP*, 162–3).

For those in professions less grounded on honesty than poetry aspires to be, this must seem not just nipping the hand that feeds you, but more like hand mastication. One need not acknowledge Eliot as 'the Pope of Russell Square' to find something impious in MacNeice's criticism of his elder. Eliot was, after all, MacNeice's editor at Faber & Faber as well as a revisionist essayist and the founding editor of *Criterion* whose influential reviews and lucrative commissions he controlled. Whatever his judicial posture, 'Eliot canonized and excommunicated at will,' in Lindell Gordon's phrase (230).

Fortunately for Eliot and poetry generally, he was attracted to publishing in 1926 by Geoffrey Faber, a lover of literature and a poet himself who had so recently entered the trade through a partnership with Lady Gwyer that he gave Eliot the freedom to develop his own list. Through what would become probably[30] the most distinguished poetry list in the history of English-language publishing, 'he determined the shape of English poetry from the Thirties into the Sixties' (182), in the understatement of Peter Ackroyd.

Beyond MacNeice, Auden, Spender, and Day Lewis, in the 1930s Eliot also published Roy Campbell, Walter de la Mare, Robert Graves, Edwin Muir, Siegfried Sassoon, and Edward Thomas, as well as Pound and Marianne Moore. Ensconced in his small office, formerly a maid's room at 24 Russell Square, Eliot made Faber & Faber his central habitat – a haven from his estranged wife and an epitome of his congenial community. Although Eliot called on assistants to render judgments on poetry, he himself gave the first reading and last judgment to all poetry manuscripts submitted, an average of twenty a week in later decades.[31]

Although Eliot found most submissions 'pure rubbish' (Monteith), neither his standards nor his developing list were narrowly Anglo-centric. For example, through the recommendation of his assistant Richard de la Mare, Eliot published David Jones's richly complex and eccentric *In Parenthesis*, a long prose poem that conveys the immediacy of experiences leading up to the battle of the Somme. Remarkably, this work also suggests the timelessness of such experiences by enacting them on a tessellated bestial floor composed of fragments from Hopkins, folksongs, Surtees, Luke, John, *Henry V*, Blake, Coleridge, the Welsh *Kulhwch ac Olwen* and *Y Gododdin*, the Anglo-Saxon *Battle of Brunanburh*, Malory, the Icelandic *Volospa*, the periodical *Land and Water*, Caesar's *Gallic Wars*, *Chanson de Roland*, Geoffrey of Monmouth, the *Aeneid*, Nehemiah, Skelton, Chaucer, *Richard II*, Tennyson, *Golden Bough*, Carroll's *Hunting of the Snark*, Psalms, Job, Apocalypse, Leviticus, Song of Songs, and Exodus, among other sources to which the work alludes. As different as *In Parenthesis* is from Joyce's work in tone, frequent echoes suggest the Irish novelist's influence on Jones. This description of the moon, for example – 'She drives swift and immaculate out over, free of these obscuring waters; frets their fringes splendid. A silver hurrying to silver this waste...' (34) – suggests Stephen Dedalus's impressions in *A Portrait* after encountering the birdlike girl on the Bull. Or this description of a fog-enshrouded field – 'Biez wood fog pillowed, by low mist isled, a play of hide and seek arboreal for the white diaphane' (60) – may echo Stephen's relections on Sandymount Strand in the 'Proteus' episode. I admit these echoes only to suggest that at Eliot's Faber & Faber there was room for such an outsider to English culture – convertee to Roman Catholicism, devotee to Wales from the periphery of London – because he was an insider to the larger European traditions of Modernism. As Eliot says in his introduction, 'The work of David Jones has some affinity with that of James Joyce (both men seem to me to have the Celtic ear for the music of words), and with the later work of Ezra Pound, and with my own' (vii–viii).

Like the major modernists, Jones can have 'some affinity' with other poets and yet write remarkably distinctive poetry. However, after the general celebration of Hopkins' emergence and the phenomenal popularity of *The Waste Land*, the 1930s in England represents a progressively chilly atmosphere among critics, scholars, and readers for idiosyncratic and even unconventional poetry, especially that which employs the 'mythical method' or is otherwise unhistorical, so that Modernism may be said to end in Britain before it had taken root. Individualist poets such as Jones, Basil Bunting, Hugh MacDiarmid, Austin Clarke, and Patrick Kavanagh who might have been central figures in a literary epoch that celebrated distinctiveness, such as that of the French symbolists or the American modernists, were almost totally ignored in Oxbridge and London. Certainly the assumptions of the decade, that poetry kept the tide charts for history, made Auden's followers and journals such as *New Verse* inattentive to most poetry that seemed outside the path of advancing history. Although Clarke and Kavanagh absorbed international influences, they seem in quite different ways distinctly Irish, non-modernist, and remote from history's flood plains.

Donald Davie stumbled on the poetry of Austin Clarke in the mid-1950s when the Englishman was teaching at Trinity College, Dublin. He found Clarke's poetry so technically advanced that his applications of Irish prosody to poetry in English could, if better known, 'be a momentous innovation in the whole tradition of Anglo-American verse' (Martin, 51). Clarke, however, for most of the 15 years from 1922 to 1937, had lived in the center of London and eddied in certain literary circles without attracting notice from critics with Davie's insight. First, those who might have boosted Clarke into notice inexplicably spurned him. Perhaps because Clarke approached Yeats from the wrong side concerning a possible biography of his great compatriot, raising indelicately questions about Maud Gonne, Yeats omitted Clarke from the *Oxford Book of Modern Poetry* where everyone in Yeats's address book seemed included. While Yeats and A. E. had introduced to the esteemed Macmillan list the Irish writers Lennox Robinson, Padraic Colum, James Stephens, Sean O'Casey, Frank O'Connor, and eventually Patrick Kavanagh, they seem to have remained silent about Clarke.[32] A. E., who lost enthusiasm for Clarke with *The Sword of the West* (1921), had recommended *The Vengeance of Fionn* (1917) to Maunsel, the Dublin publisher who had mishandled Joyce's *Dubliners*, and who was acquired by Allen & Unwin who provided Clarke with a respectable London house for his next five books. Secondly, Clarke himself lacked the map and knack to find any real literary vitality in London. Perhaps because this Dubliner shared with the Georgian poets a touristic attraction to landscape, he confused the Georgian 'Squirearchy' with the mainstream, calling their leader the influential editor J. C. Squire, 'the most powerful literary figure in Fleet Street' (*Penny*, 181).[33]

Yet, in Squire's popular Georgian anthologies of the 1910s, 1920s, and 1930s, and among his circle at the *London Mercury*, very few poets could match Clarke's perfect pitch for assonance and other sound effects. In a 1956 essay Davie identified Clarke's 'use of a device traditional in poetry in Irish, of interlacing assonance and – a corollary of that – rhyming off the beat' (quoted in Martin, 51) as we hear in the late 1930s 'The Straying Student,' a poem that revises the Aisling, the visionary figure of Ireland, to represent the disturbing humanist attraction of the Renaissance. In a note to this poem, Clarke said he was attempting, 'not wholly sucessful[ly],' to reproduce a Gaelic linear pattern of assonance and consonance, ABBAC:

> On a holy day when sails were blowing southward,
>
> A bishop sang the Mass at Inishmore,
>
> Men took one side, their wives were on the other
>
> But I heard the woman coming from the shore:
>
> And wild in despair my parents cried aloud
>
> For they saw the vision draw me to the doorway.

In this opening stanza, according to this marking, lines 1, 2, and 5 might be said to complete the assonantal pattern of ABBAC Clarke mentions, whereas other lines seem to achieve a variation of this pattern. In some cases the pairing of vowels – *bish/Inish; wom/com; pair/ par; they/way; saw/draw* – extends beyond assonance to rhyme or even rhyme riche. Rhyming off the beat, of which Davie speaks, is achieved in *Inishmore/shore*, and perhaps *shore/doorway*.

Even younger poets who have not followed up on Clarke's experiments have granted him a degree of authority for his closer proximity to poetry in Irish. Where Yeats translated heroic models, mythic plots, and a more palpable diction, Clarke carried into English language poetry the pulse and timbre of Irish poetry. By the 1930s Clarke had established his independence from Irish myth and tapped into his own deposit of Irish history, the Celtic Romanesque era of the early independent church in Ireland. Clarke's first novel *The Bright Temptation*, which Yeats admired as 'a charming and humorous defiance of the censorship and its ideals,'[34] may have sown the seed for Yeats's *Supernatural Songs* (1934) in which the hermit Ribh espouses his heterodox views of Christianity.

In spite of his possible influence on Yeats, Clarke might not earn a place among canonical Irish poets of the 1930s, as Jones, the Welsh poet living in London, might not among English. Whereas the eclectic modernist poetry of Jones may never find favor in England, what seemed in the 1930s to be Clarke's misinvolvement in a dying language increasingly seems to be a wise investment in the living, if no longer primary, linguistic basis of Irish poetry.

In light of this, we might consider that an important review of *The Tower* in a March 1928 issue of the *Times Literary Supplement* may have stung Yeats with the plausible assertion that this volume revealed the 'loneliness of mind fallen back upon itself' and showed 'how completely the poet is exiled, in faith though not in art, from his earlier work which had drawn so much upon impersonal belief and upon traditional imagination' (Jeffares, 284). Although Clarke, who was the author of this critique, had earned an authority from his understanding of Irish prosody that Yeats might have envied, we finally cannot know whether envy, ignorance, or, as Clarke would have it, 'enmity'[35] accounts for Yeats's omission of Clarke from *The Oxford Book of Modern Verse*.

About his much more serious exclusion, that of the English 'War Poets,' Yeats left no secret. In his 'Introduction' to *The Oxford Book* he had written: 'I have a distaste for certain poems written in the midst of the great war. . . . passive suffering is not a theme for poetry' (xxxiv). Although Yeats toned down his expression of 'distaste' in a BBC broadcast on 'Modern Poetry' within a few days of the anthology's publication, he had not merely struck a national nerve but disturbed a historical fault line, perhaps one that extends through the western world as well as through Britain. In the trenches of the First World War, soldiers were subjected to horrifying passive suffering that left deep postwar scars and a tortured silence at the dinner tables of returned soldiers. Speaking of the 1930s, Stephen Spender wrote 'of an incommunicable reality which was the truth of history in this decade . . . of there being a terrible reality which was the truth of the time experienced by people in prisons and concentration camps' (11). By the 1960s, the Gulags, the gas chambers, and the atomic bombs had disgorged facts and images that seemed beyond the power of poetry to articulate and that had been ceded to the sloblands of silence, repression, and nightmare beyond poetry's rivers or fountains by Yeats's proscription of silent suffering. Writing in 1964, Ted Hughes broke that silence:

> That moment – the last two years of trench warfare in France, 1916–18 – was so privately English (ignoring what France and Germany made of it) and such a deeply shocking and formative experience for us that it is easy to see some of the reasons why Yeats (as an Irishman) dismissed Owen's verse. . . .                                                              (*HWP*, 42)

The responses of English poets to the Great War and of Irish poets to the Troubles attempt to reclaim this territory for poetry which becomes an important aspect of the exchange of the 1960s.

# 4
# Publishing and Poetry in Ireland and England in the 1960s

## Clarke and the Dolmen Press

Major poets from the 1930s, such as MacNeice and Kavanagh, live on into the 1960s, flare poetically, and flame out, while after *The Sea and the Mirror* the dominant poet Auden quietly assumed a Christian belief which slackened his ambivalence, weakened any exchange between imagination and history, and left him open to only occasional rekindlings of his earlier greatness. Even *Homage to Clio*, which contains poems of permanent value, confirmed for Philip Larkin 'how little the last twenty years have added to Auden's reputation' (Haffenden, 415). Among new poetic luminaries who first appear in the 1950s – Larkin, Hill, Gunn, Hughes, Murphy, Kinsella, and Montague – the most regenerative older poet may have been (even beyond Basil Bunting) Austin Clarke, although his resurgence may finally have been obscured from British readers by his commitment of this new work of the 1960s to an Irish publisher and these readers' slowness to recognize that such existed.

No real Irish publisher of full volumes, certainly after the closing of Maunsel, had existed during the first half-century. Early in Yeats's career, he had told his English publisher T. Fisher Unwin, 'If ever a first rate publishing house arise in Ireland I must needs publish in part with them' (*YCL*, I, 403). Such a publisher, Liam Miller's Dolmen Press, finally emerged in Dublin in 1951. Miller designed and set type for Clarke's two 1950s volumes – *Ancient Lights* (1955) and *Too Great A Vine* (1957) – which were officially published under Clarke's imprint of The Bridge Press. Early in the next decade Dolmen gathered Clarke's poems of the 1950s into *Later Poems* (1961) which also appeared in Britain under 'an arrangement with Oxford University Press whereby they became our general distributors,' in words that reflect the postcolonial pride of Liam

Miller, who continues: 'As well as doing much to establish the Press in a wider field, this book restored Austin Clarke's position in modern poetry...' (Miller, 32). Many of the *Later Poems*, which was the second Dolmen book to be chosen or recommended by the Poetry Book Society in London, focused sharply pointed satires on the collaboration of the Irish state and the Catholic Church, as we can see in the last two of four stanzas of 'The Envy of Poor Lovers':

> Lying in the grass as if it were a sin
> To move, they hold each other's breath, tremble
> Ready to share that ancient dread – kisses begin
> Again – of Ireland keeping company with them.
>
> Think, children, of institutions mured above
> Your ignorance, where every look is veiled,
> State-paid to snatch away the folly of poor lovers
> For whom, it seems, the sacraments have failed.

(CSP, 65)

Sharing 'kisses under a hedge,' the lovers are outlaws of the state, much as eighteenth-century Catholics furtively gathering for hedge schools were outside the Penal Laws. The theocratic institutions, voyeuristic chaperones as Hugh Maxton points out (*CSP*, 221), imprison the lovers as they rise above their ignorance, with the suggestion also that these institutions gain support from and are built *upon* this innocence. Such satires pit Clarke as an adversary of strong constituents of Irish culture, more positive aspects of which enter this poem only in the intricate rhyming – where alternating rhyme *sin* and *begin* are only one consonant away from coupling with the apocopated rhyme *tremble* and *them* – and well-composed assonance, whispers from an older prosody in Irish.

## Kinsella and the Dolmen bond

Among those drawn to the Miller's kitchen by this creative stirring – 'visitors who were pressed into service to set type or pull the press or to cut and fold the sheets' (Miller, 9) – was a yearling in Ireland's Department of Finance, Thomas Kinsella. Within two months of their meeting in January 1952, Miller had printed Kinsella's pamphlet poem *The Starlit Eye*. In 1958 Kinsella's first full volume *Another September* announced the arrival not only of a major poetic talent but also of the

Dolmen Press, as this became the first book printed outside England to be named a 'choice' by the Poetry Book Society of London.

With different degrees of qualification, reviews both in Britain and Ireland applauded this preference. In *The Irish Times* Montague asserted that *Another September* 'could be read beside the best work of the '50s elsewhere; Wilbur, Merwin and Hecht, in America; Gunn, Larkin, and Enright in England' (26 April 1958). In the Belfast journal *Threshold* John Hewitt wrote, 'I do not know any other young Irish poet who shows such a grasp of form...' (2: 2, Summer 1958). A review in the *TLS*, however, begins, 'Since the death of Yeats, English readers have, rightly or wrongly, tended to ignore contemporary Irish poetry' (2 May 1958), and Naomi Lewis in *The Observer* resurrects Arnoldian ethnic terms: 'Sometimes, as you might expect, Mr Kinsella shows off by being wilfully mad, deliberately obscure. But when a poem succeeds, the effect is magical' (22 June 1958).

The *TLS* and Hewitt specify 'A Lady of Quality' and Lewis names 'Midsummer' as poems that particularly reveal their debt to Auden, the latter mentioning 'the Audenesque six-line stanza.' For example, 'A Lady of Quality' employs exactly Auden's stanza from 'Out on the lawn I lie in bed' which rhymes AABCCB and truncates the third and sixth lines whereas 'Midsummer' uses the same stanza with the third and sixth lines shortened to four syllables. Lewis quotes the stanza from 'Midsummer' –

> Something that for this long year
> Had hid and halted like a deer
> Turned marvellous,
> Parted the tragic grasses, tame,
> Lifted its perfect head and came
> To welcome us.

> (*KCP*, 7)

– which echoes the mysterious ending of Auden's 'Who stands crux left...': 'But seldom this. Near you, taller than grass, / Ears poise before decision, scenting danger.' More obviously, 'Baggot Street Deserta' duplicates the speaker's position as midnight's windowside *flaneur* found in Auden's 'Now from my window-sill I watch the night' which continues: 'The church clock's yellow face, the green pier light / Burn for a new imprudent year' (*EA*, 115). Kinsella's speaker enters a similar scene explicitly as occupant of 'my attic' and implicitly as nerve-center for a psychologized landscape:

> . . . the window is wide
> On a crawling arch of stars, and the night
> Reacts faintly to the mathematic
> Passion of a cello suite
> Plotting the quiet of my attic.

(KCP, 13)

Autobiographical, even confessional, poetry might have been the natural mode for a writer who wishes to 'look for the past in myself' ('Irish Writer', 625). Because of a natural reticence and a deepening psychological intention, however, Kinsella, like Auden, cloaks his linear narrative of the self in a version of that 'language of indirection' we discussed in Chapter 3.

In a recent and rare reading at Emory University in the autumn of 1997,[1] Kinsella spoke of Auden's early influence and said he 'left the ghost of Auden in the distance' in the course of translating *The Táin*. Through this labor of some years, he learned that 'daily matter could connect with the older tradition' and that he might bridge the gap within 'the inheritance [which] is mine, but only at two enormous removes – across a century's silence, and through an exchange of worlds,' as he said in a well-known speech delivered in the US at the Modern Language Association meeting in the closing days of 1966. This translation of Ireland's major epic not only reached back for 'the past in myself' but also participated in a version of every modern, especially post-holocaust, writer's necessity. As he told the MLA, in words frequently recited:

> Every writer in the modern world . . . is the inheritor of a gapped, discontinuous, polyglot tradition. Nevertheless, if the function of tradition is to link us living with the significant past, this is done as well by a broken tradition as by a whole one – however painful it may be humanly speaking.　　　　　('The Irish Writer,' 629)

All writers, then, at least all that Kinsella might recognize, are translators, of various sorts and to different degrees.

This remarkable change in Kinsella's poetry, first fully evident in *Notes from the Land of the Dead*, published by Cuala Press in 1972, and *New Poems*, published in 1973 by Dolmen and Oxford, can be traced in correspondence between Kinsella and Miller, beginning in 1967 when the poet taught at Southern Illinois University. As he prepared texts for the chapbook *Nightwalker* (April 1967) and the full volume *Nightwalker and Other Poems* (March 1968), he vacillated about the long love poem 'Phoenix Park': 'I've had my nth change of heart about it, even reaching a decision to leave it out at one time. . . . It won't fit in any later, as I think I am off on a new tack. It will be another sore thumb like "Downstream" ' (23 May 1967).[2] Three days later, he wrote, 'I beg your patience on "Phoenix Park", but maybe it isn't too bad.' Within two months, he has broken through and found the setting for 'Phoenix Park' which he wants to shift to the end of the 1968 volume:

> This is for plot reasons – it makes more sense to have the total involvement first, then the ritual of departure, then the departure – but even more because I have just had all kinds of lovely ideas for me next book: I plan to open it with a continuation of the movement at the end of 'Phoenix Park,' i.e. the delicate distinct flesh will continue to form, and lead off into all sorts of goodies.          (11 July 1967)

His enthusiasm spills over into news of his rapid progress in translating *The Táin* which may after all be the source of his enthusiasm above.

With only the poetry to account for the reinstatement of 'Phoenix Park,' the dismissal of the silver-tongued poet, and this sense of a new disjunctive structure for his work, we can recognize that the spatialized dialectic of this concluding poem of the 1968 volume –

> The orders of stars fixed in abstract darkness,
> Darkness of worlds sheltering in their light;
> World darkness harbouring orders of cities,
> Whose light at midnight harbours human darkness;
> The human dark pierced by solitary fires . . .

> (*KCP*, 93)

– finds its equivalent in the endless temporal sequence of conquest or assimilation and loss and reconquest, etcetera, which, based on the twelfth-century text *The Book of Invasions*, will become the 'plot' of much of Kinsella's subsequent work. Of how or when *The Book of Invasions* (or *Lebor Gabála Erinn*) became a framing text for this work the letters say not a word.

Although Kinsella has acknowledged that the radical change in his work arose from the process of translating *The Táin*, he does not specify how his labors on the national epic affected, some critics said wrecked,[3] his own poetry so radically. He does recount some of his choices and his objectives. Of the three sources of the Ulster Cycle, the expression of an Irish society at the time of Christ – the twelfth-century Book of the Dun Cow, the fourteenth-century Yellow Book of Lecan, and the twelfth-century Book of Leinster – the latter is the most complete and florid of the texts and the host text for most of the Victorian translations. Kinsella, however, returned to the fragmented Book of the Dun Cow which he describes in his 'Introduction' to *The Táin* as

> ...the work of many hands and in places...little more than the mangled remains of miscellaneous scribal activities. There are major inconsistencies and repetitions among the incidents. On occasion the narrative withers away into cryptic notes and summaries. Extraneous matter is added, varying from simple glosses and comments to wholesale indiscriminate interpolations from other sources, in some cases over erased passages of the original.... (xi)

Kinsella undertook to extract 'a reasonably coherent narrative...with a little reorganization' but with no 'interference of the text as it stands....' Blending voices arising here and there from the original oral tale, emendations of scribes and other monkish redactors, and his own voice, Kinsella achieved a coherent linear narrative with occasional inconsistencies which convey only the fleeting taste of a society fascinatingly other than our own.

As the translator must have recognized the simultaneity of these contending voicings and scratchings described above, so the poet, questing 'for the past in myself,' freed his narratives from dependence on merely one time, such as events from his childhood or a stage in the invasion myth. Consequently, in most poems from the sequence *Notes from the Land of the Dead*, the poetry resonates with autobiography, myth, and emblems of the psychic journey.

The shift from a more linear narrative to this blending of temporal references becomes most evident in two versions of the much anthologized 'Hen Woman.' In this second poem in the volume, the poet recalls the child watching a neighbor rush from her house, seize a hen about to lay an egg, fumble the emerging egg, and then comment wryly when the egg breaks. The events offer a basis in memory and historical time for stages of a psychic descent recounted in the opening poem. Brian John has called attention to this earlier version which in April of 1968 was published in David Marcus's 'New Irish Writing' page of the *Irish Press*. In this earlier version, the opening 24 lines, of which John

quotes 18, contain six pronoun references to the poet that are removed
in the final version. The boy's age and the season of the year are removed,
as is Mrs Delany's name, so that she becomes the title-character and
a member of the coven of old women, or *cailleachs*, that people these
poems.[4]

To represent the severity of Kinsella's pruning in which the original
130 lines become 85, I will quote the entire 24 lines of the poem's second
section:

> I don't know how long
>   this pause may have continued
> when, <u>at my feet,</u> thus becalmed,
>   a single <u>tiny movement</u> caught my attention,
> <u>tiny and mechanical.</u>
>   <u>A beetle like a bronze leaf</u>
> was grappling something, <u>inching</u> over
>   a wide, stony waste
> – backwards, it suddenly appeared:
>   <u>clasping</u> and rolling <u>with its small tarsi</u>
> <u>a ball of dung much bigger than its body.</u>
>   I saw its back, as though magnified,
> as a squat shield
>   with a head like a vizor of pure will
> clamped at the rim. Now <u>the serrated brow</u>
>   <u>pressed humbly</u> with its horny processes
> against <u>the ground</u>, now <u>lifted in a short stare</u>
>   as the toothed tibiae took the strain.
> Neatly fashioned, though fraying a little
>   in that shifting grasp,
> the precious globe <u>advanced</u>
>   offering to the light and dark, as it turned
> dry <u>fragments, specks of staleness</u>
>   <u>and freshness</u>, the fruitfulness to come.

(Dolmen Archive Box 120A.3)

With the addition of a very few words, the underlined portions of these
24 lines become the eleven lines of the revision. In addition to some
awkward phrasing (as when his feet threaten to become 'thus becalmed'
or the technically correct but awkward 'horny processes'), he also removes
reference to the beetle's 'vizor of pure will,' which blurs with Darwinian

phrasing the beetle's mythic significance. Kinsella also deletes, and thus secretes, suggestions of the dungball's cache of eggs in the phrases 'precious globe' and 'fruitfulness to come,' but he also removes the direction 'backwards' which works against the allusion to Khephera, the beetle-like form of the Egyptian sun-god Ra assumes at dawn, pushing *forward* its future generations concealed within its excreta from the past.[5] As I suggested elsewhere, the scarab, which symbolized for the Egyptians 'the renewal of life and the idea of eternal existence,' also becomes a comic analogue to the Sisyphean poet and a serious emblem for his task of carrying the past into the future.

This radical reduction of the passage renders the narrative so succinct that it can be grasped in an elongated moment. Whereas all printed literature can be viewed as a spatialization of oral and therefore temporal art, the passage from 'The Hen Woman' printed above might look especially like a spatial structure after demolition, with the underlining representing the remaining partial ruin of certain of Kinsella's poems or even of 'the gapped, discontinuous . . . tradition' to which he is heir. To observe this structure, we no longer enter by the ground floor and follow our guide through corridors and landings. With walls partially removed and with those turns of the landing – *when, now . . . , now . . .* – blown out, it can be viewed from the outside with the activities of separate floors witnessed, various voices heard, and parallel lives viewed, simultaneously. As in *The Táin*, the voice of the ancient charioteer, the monkish redactor, and the poet all emerge into the present.

Such spatialization must have been enforced for Kinsella during *The Táin*'s creation by two other influences. First, Kinsella was a proponent and skillful teacher of Pound's modernist forms. Secondly, the pen and ink drawings of Louis Le Brocquy, adapted from Picasso's Don Quixote series, can represent a paragraph of battle narrative in a glimpse. For example, at the close of chapter thirteen, before the final battle, Mac Roth marvels to Fergus concerning the size of the Ulster assemblage of warriors: 'My eye travelled from Ferdia's Ford to Slemain Midi and fell on men and horse instead of hills and slopes.' Fergus answers, 'You have certainly seen a man of some following.' We turn the page onto a spread of ingeniously shaped ink blots representing graphically the host of Ulster (236). These are literally the 'black riders' of McGann's study of the material conditions of printed books, which we discussed in Chapter 1. The collaboration with Miller and LeBrocquy must have enforced for Kinsella this sense of their final text as a spatial artifact. Furthermore, the high level of such collaboration must have kept Kinsella content[6] with Irish publication.

In spite of a loyal and very sympathetic representation of Kinsella in Britain by OUP's John Bell and Jon Stallworthy, Kinsella remains aloof from poetic institutions in England. Although honored by the Poetry Book Society in 1968, he resisted having his 'best book yet to be labelled a runner-up to anyone,' which he believed would be the effect of a PBS Recommendation, although Miller finally convinced Kinsella to accept this recognition. In a BBC interview several years later with Edward Blishen for 'The World of Books,' Kinsella seems doubtful or even indifferent about winning an English readership. 'I do regard my centre of operations as being in Ireland,' he said, but added that he was much more concerned about an American than an English readership: 'It seems to me that there is a greater volume of notable poetry by a greater number of real poets being written in the United States at the moment, and for say a generation past than actually I can detect in Britain. There are one or two, of course, exceptions.'[7]

Ironically, the changes in Kinsella's poetic enterprise, which emerge during the period of his collaboration with Liam Miller, sweep him away from his English readership which has considerably diminished by the decade's close.[8] For related but somewhat different reasons, John Montague, too, became isolated by his partnership with Liam Miller which developed over this same decade.

## Montague's publishers in the 1960s and his British readership

If we, today, are witnessing a second poetic renaissance in Ireland, it began with the emergence in the 1950s of Kinsella, John Montague, and Richard Murphy and with the appearance of some of their strongest volumes in the 1960s. Montague's '1960s' might be charted between a reading at the Hibernia Hotel with Richard Murphy and Tom Kinsella in 1961 and a dramatization of *The Rough Field* at the Round House in London in 1973. The following account of his creative relationship with Tim O'Keeffe and Liam Miller, who were his close friends[9] and his British and Irish publishers, respectively, can shed some light on the growing separation between poets from the Irish Republic and British publishers and readers. Yet finally, posterity will judge his success during this expandable 'decade' by his four major poetic works – *Poisoned Lands* (1961), *A Chosen Light* (1967), *Tides* (1970), and *The Rough Field* (1972) – and by his volume of short stories *The Death of a Chieftain* (1964).

Around Montague's five islands of achievement surges a remarkable creative activity which may be distinguished from the equally impressive creative productivity of Kinsella or Murphy by its insistent collaborativeness.

Even the grouping of this triad of writers as the emerging generation or, indeed, the 'second renaissance' is, in fact, Montague's dream, a frequent and exhortative assertion that distinguishes Montague's correspondence during this period from Murphy's or Kinsella's. The Hibernia Hotel reading in 1961, organized by Liam Miller; the *Dolmen Miscellany* – a collaboration of Kinsella, Montague, and Miller, published in 1962; the Dolmen Editions readings in Dublin organized by Miller and Montague; advisory work with Tim O'Keeffe to bring into print for MacGibbon & Kee selections of Patrick Kavanagh, fiction of Francis Stuart, and poems of John Hewitt; *A Tribute to Austin Clarke on His Seventieth Birthday* – essays and poems solicited and edited by Montague and Miller; the Claddagh Records series of recorded readings by poets, including Clarke, Kavanagh, Kinsella, Heaney, Graves, and MacDiarmid – founded by Garech Browne with Montague's initiation and guidance and with the first record sleeve designed by Miller; the 1970 reading tour in Northern Ireland with John Hewitt – billed as 'The Planter and the Gael' – repeated in 1971; and the dramatic reading of *The Rough Field* in The Round House, featuring the music of the Chieftains: we might expect such collaborations from a composer or a film director but hardly or rarely from a practitioner of the eremitic art of poetry.

In his efforts to form an editorial team or poetry's flying column, Montague conformed to a colonial or postcolonial Irish practice, begun in the nineteenth century, of poets pooling their efforts and mutually supporting each other. Of such collectivisms, Seamus Deane has said,

> This structural organization of Irish writing was to persist into the twentieth century, with the Irish Revival and the northern poets as the dominant groups and the consequent marginalization of those who did not wholly or properly belong.[10]

Paradoxically, the collectivist aspect of Northern poets from the 1960s forward, such as Jimmy Simmons, Longley, Mahon, Heaney, Ciaran Carson, Muldoon, and McGuckian, springs from their unwillingness to be co-opted by any sectarian cause and their generally unspoken agreement to represent their situations in independent poetic terms. We can observe this individualist solidarity, which owes something initially to the policies of Jimmy Simmons' journal *The Honest Ulsterman*, in their almost uniform denial that the informal workshops with the Glasgow poet Philip Hobsbaum made them a Group. Ironically, the collectivist aspirations of Montague and John Hewitt to speak for their respective tribes tilted them toward isolation both in Britain and, to a lesser extent, in Ireland.

Montague's relationships with his two publishers in the 1960s, Liam Miller and Tim O'Keeffe, reflect two different approaches to belonging – collectivist and individualist. With Miller, Montague hoped to bring the new Irish writers to the attention of the literary establishment, whom he usually conceived of as English, whereas with O'Keeffe he is more the individual Irish poet, trying to crack the establishment and win the attention of the wider British readership. Nearly self-evidently, these contrasting self-representations arise from Montague's different publishing relations with these two editors. For most of this 'decade,' Tim O'Keeffe as editor for the London firm MacGibbon & Kee remains Montague's primary publisher with whom Montague entrusts *Poisoned Lands, A Chosen Light*, and *Death of a Chieftain*. Until Dolmen Press's publication of *Tides* in 1970, Liam Miller serves both as Montague's secondary publisher of chapbooks, which would become sections of larger works, and as co-midwife to the new renaissance.

Soon after his 1956 return to Ireland from his three years of studying and writing poetry in the States, Montague met Miller. While editing and writing for the Irish Tourist Board, adapting to marriage, and working toward a PhD at University College, Dublin, Montague nevertheless found time in 1958 to gather his first poetry publication entitled *Forms of Exile*, twenty or so poems written over the decade. Although this chapbook was handsomely designed by Miller and published by Dolmen, Montague withheld his first full volume *Poisoned Lands* for publication in 1961 from London by MacGibbon & Kee. Whatever his feelings might have been about the relative advantages of British or Irish publication, Montague believed Kinsella was already installed as Dolmen's central poet and Miller's literary advisor.[11] The Poetry Book Society's naming of *Another September* as their 'Choice' seemed only to confirm Kinsella's advantages. Consequently in 1959, when Tim O'Keeffe, having successfully published Montague's friend Brendan Behan for Hutchinson, came scouting for writers in Dublin, Montague had signed a contract with O'Keeffe's new firm MacGibbon & Kee. Montague received a healthy advance of £75 for a book of poetry and £200 for short-stories[12] and began to fill the sort of role as reader and advisor for O'Keeffe that Kinsella performed for Miller.

Whereas Montague's secondary collaboration with Miller must have begun in 1960, Montague's move to Paris just after New Year in 1961 to become correspondent for the *Irish Times* provides a written record of both these relationships in the steady exchange of letters. The assertion that Miller and Montague are agents of the new Irish renaissance becomes an insistent drumbeat in correspondence between Montague and Miller.

Soon after his arrival in Paris, Montague lists the possible contents of a new occasional journal, including fiction by Brian Moore, Aidan Higgins, John MacGahern, and James Plunkett, and poetry by Kinsella, Valentine Iremonger, John Jordan, and Montague. With the title of *The Dolmen Miscellany*[13] Montague intended to 'challenge certain British trends to modishness and reassert Dublin as intellectual capital of England and also (gently) advertise the genius of its editor . . . ,' and, he added later, 'More the idea of presenting a generation, really.'[14]

In his correspondence with his Irish collaborator Miller, Montague nominates Kinsella as poetry editor and himself as fiction editor, with the sign-off 'The Young Ireland Movement (Paris Branch),' as a year later he would close with 'We are a great generation.'[15] In that same letter, Montague offers a draft of his introduction to the *Dolmen Miscellany* which begins:

> In recent years a new generation of writers has begun to emerge in Ireland, probably the most interesting since the realists of the 1930s. While not forming any sort of movement, they do reflect a general change of sensibility, and this Miscellany is an attempt to provide them with a platform.

Even if this is slightly understated as manifestos go, Montague nevertheless exposes his obstetrical intention for the new generation. In the necessary foreshortening of correspondence, the brevity of the gap between the peaks of expectation – 'the first blow in the 2nd Anglo-Irish Renaissance!' – and the salt flats of disappointment – 'Did you find out what happened to the *Miscellany* in England? The only two reviews were the ones I arranged. Oxford [the distributor in Britain] *must* be to blame?' – is painful.[16]

So many of Montague's collaborations in the 1960s follow this same downhill trajectory from boyishly enthusiastic beginnings to a disappointingly weak British reception that this stage of his career might be entitled *Great Expectations*. Beyond the development of his own stories, which would be published by MacGibbon & Kee in 1964, and the gestation of his next book of poetry, the collaboration that preoccupied him next concerned the poetry of Patrick Kavanagh which he selected and edited for publication by Tim O'Keeffe in 1964 as *The Collected Poems*. This too would end in a slough of despond, although in this case for reasons aside from its British reception. Although Montague had expended real effort on Kavanagh's behalf, he came to question Kavanagh's value relative to other contemporaries, such as MacDiarmid and, especially,

Austin Clarke, of whom Montague wrote, his 'new collection, due from Dolmen/Oxford in the Autumn or Winter, will put the skids on K. It is an astonishingly lecherous, anti-clerical work, and marks Clarke's full blossoming as the first Irish Catholic poet.'[17]

In 1964, when Montague was teaching at the University of California at Berkeley, he published his collection of stories *Death of a Chieftain* with Tim O'Keeffe's house and collaborated with Liam Miller on the publication of sections of his forthcoming books as collectors' chapbooks. From the autumn of 1965, with the departure of Kinsella for Southern Illinois University, Montague's collaboration with Miller intensified, and their correspondence became more confidential, as we see from an exchange in late November of 1965. Montague proposes a 'fleadh for poetry' including 'an evening of Austin (called *Gloomy Sunday* [after Billy Holliday] . . .' 'Strikes me that what one needs, and what we partly find in each other, is a kind of passionate "sounding board." I have only managed to use about 2/5 of my energy yet and partly feel that this is due to the lack of a small audience' (presumably the 'fit though few' that Milton and Yeats also coveted).

Six days later, after hearing of Miller's successful trip to Oxford University Press and to London where he saw Tim O'Keeffe, Montague makes a prescient proposal:

> What about another big DE [Dolmen Editions] readings in the Spring? Some kind of general programme in which (at the time of publication) I could read ALO [All Legendary Obstacles], Liddy and the locals could perform (Austin's record could be launched) and Seamus Heaney's fare down could be paid (we must try and enlist this colt, before we have a Rival Renaissance going full blast in Belfast, with both sides *doomed* to failure. I mean this: we must contact the Belfast group at its apex, which does seem to be Heaney).[18]

Although Heaney did not publish his first book *Death of a Naturalist* with Faber & Faber until 1966, Miller held inside knowledge of Heaney's poetry. On 16 September 1964, Dolmen received a submission from Heaney entitled *Advancements of Learning*, a book returned on 2 March 1965, apparently at Heaney's request.[19] According to Montague's recollection, his suggestion prompted Heaney's first Dublin reading, at the Lantern Theatre in a Dolmen-sponsored festival in the spring of 1966. In November of 1966, Montague again suggests Heaney among other Ulster poets – Mahon, Longley, and Hewitt – for a large festival to coincide with the opening of the Peacock Theatre.[20]

As consistently as with Kinsella and Ted Hughes, Montague refers to Heaney throughout this decade's correspondence only in respectful tones. Only in retrospect does one 1965 comment – 'Heaney's success is fascinating. The Bertie Rodgers of the late Sixties?', made at a time when even Heaney's mother could not envision his future Olympian achievements – seem mildly derogatory.[21] When Tim O'Keeffe attributes the success of *Death of a Naturalist* to Heaney's 'very forceful sister in law' and says he found him to be 'an ox,' Montague turns the insult ninety or so degrees to say that if Heaney is an ox, he 'is one that has taken a course in bull-fighting.'[22] While Montague remains respectful of Heaney's talent, he became annoyed at his promotion relative to himself, eventually complaining that his own distribution was much less adequate than Heaney's. In 1969, comparing his own sales to those of Heaney, Mahon, Murphy, and Kinsella, he confesses to O'Keeffe grimly, 'It does not leave one mad keen to produce more, to disappear like snow off a rope.'[23]

Yet, in the more hopeful period of 1965 and of 1966, the fiftieth anniversary of the Easter Rising, Montague engages in his most fruitful collaboration with Liam Miller. First, they invite contributions to and edit *A Tribute to Austin Clarke on His Seventieth Birthday*. In his own tribute, Montague praises Clarke as 'the first completely Irish poet to write in English' and one who 'has helped us to learn how to write English poetry, with an Irish accent.'[24] When the *TLS* reviewer attacks the *Tribute* early in 1967, it is Montague who responds, commenting to Tim O'Keeffe, '"The life of a wit is a warfare on earth" seems more true now than in the 18th century!'[25]

The most serious of the Montague–Miller collaborations – the handsomely designed Dolmen Editions chapbooks that contained sections of future MacGibbon & Kee publications – began with *Forms of Exile* in 1958 but picked up in a steady sequence from February 1966. *All Legendary Obstacles* contained poems that would comprise the first section of *A Chosen Light* (MacGibbon & Kee, 1967). In an unpublished commentary on these poems, Montague wrote:

> Liam was responsible for many little changes in the text, and gave especial care to the planning of the book. . . . This manuscript is associated in my mind with a change of style, after the tightness of *Poisoned Lands*, and the writing of *Death of a Chieftain*. It begins as early as '62, with 'That Room' which appeared in *Poetry Ireland*. . . .

By October of 1965, these extensive revisions were complete: 'Yes, *All Legendary Obstacles* seems much better, the most integrated group of poems to yet come from my . . . pen. . . .'[26]

One specific revision, which occurs in two poems, may be a key to an underlying disposition in all of Montague's poetry in the '1960s.' In three versions of 'Loving Reflections,' the opening lines alter from 'I hold your neat pear / Shaped face in the hollow / Of my hand . . .' to 'I hold the ash pale / Face. . . .' Remarkably, the same word *pale* enters into the final line of 'the Grugach' although Montague says in a letter to Miller that 'I cannot get the last adjective. . . .' What originally had been 'Bare ribs of rock' becomes finally 'Pale ribs of rock.' Much later in the 1990s, when the poet's *Collected Poems* were in preparation, the Canadian writer and editor Barry Callaghan warned his friend Montague that the word *pale* appeared at an epidemic proportion in his poetry. As a consequence, *pale* in these two poems reverted to '*ashen* face' and to '*Bleached* ribs of rock.' Symptomatically, Montague could not alter his most celebrated usages of *pale* in 'All Legendary Obstacles' – 'At midnight you came, pale / Above the negro porter's lamp' – where the word contrasts sharply with the darkness of the porter's skin and of midnight. In contributing to the lover's secondary role as Eurydice, *pale* designates her proximity to death from which she has returned. Whether displaced onto the land or associated with the poet or his lover, Montague's *pale* derives from the pale horse of *Revelations* by way of the Romantics, Keats's 'palely loitering' or Benjamin West's painting 'Death on the Pale Horse,' the viewing of which was the occasion for Keats's letter concerning 'Negative Capability.' For Montague, *pale* is not the whiteness of nothingness as of the snow in 'Courtyard in Winter' but the living shade that most approximates death and reminds us of what has been or will be taken.[27] This expression of melancholy conforms to Montague's sense in the 1960s, everywhere suggested but nowhere stated until the 1980s, that poetry born out of loss – the mother who fostered out her son – must inevitably return to that loss.

Eventually, this melancholic, individualist theme of the lost mother will find more overt expression in the maternal landscape of *A Slow Dance* and more specifically in the narratives of *The Great Cloak* and *The Dead Kingdom*. In the 1960s, however, the collaborative and tribal ambitions achieve a certain success. In what appears to be a note to Miller in the Southern Illinois Archive, Montague praises the design and production of *All Legendary Obstacles*: 'First the format is exceedingly handsome, a thing to clutch in one's hand as protection against evil spirits, or to use at Sunday High Mass if the gospel book gets lost. . . .' This Dolmen Editions collaboration leads next to the placement of the Derricke woodcuts, from the Elizabethan work *The Image of Irelande* (1581), in *The Patriotic Suite* and to subsequent designs, using various artists, of *Home*

*Again*, *Hymn to the New Omagh Road*, *The Bread God*, and *The New Siege*, all enforcing Montague's sense of the poem as an object in space, perhaps first suggested to him by American poetry. Ultimately, of course, this collaboration culminates in the 1972 publication of Montague's masterwork (if not necessarily his best book of poetry) *The Rough Field*. Although poems in this volume were written as early as 1960, Montague credits Miller with the idea of strong poetic sections. In a letter to O'Keeffe dated 27 August 1968 and accompanying the Dolmen Edition of *The New Omagh Road*, Montague wrote:

> I find Liam's format rather old-fashioned but it has given me the idea of producing the long poem in sections, like (what modesty!) the CANTOS. That way I don't have to forcibly end it but can leave it open for future developments. So THE BREAD GOD will appear for Christmas. . . .                                   (Tulsa Archive)

Two other collaborative efforts in the 1960s may have shaped Montague's conception of his own poetry. With Garech Browne, he planned and undertook the impressive Claddagh Records series that included readings by Clarke, Kavanagh, Kinsella, Heaney, Montague, Graves, and MacDiarmid. This would eventually lead to a dramatic reading of *The Rough Field* in Dublin, broadcast by Radio Eireann, and in London at the Camden Town Roundhouse in 1973. Although a recording was made that emphasized the temporal sequences and aural aspects of this sequence, heavily spatialized and visual in its Dolmen design, it was never produced commercially.

Later in the '1960s,' in the autumns of 1970 and 1971, as a cross-sectarian gesture in the dangerous period after Burntollet and the onset of the Troubles, Montague teamed with the older Northern Protestant poet John Hewitt to undertake a reading tour, sponsored by the Northern Ireland Arts Council, of a number of towns in the North. Earlier in the decade, Montague had brought Hewitt to the attention of Tim O'Keeffe who published his *Collected Poems 1932–1967* for MacGibbon & Kee. In these readings, according to the Arts Council program, 'each poet explores his experience of Ulster, the background in which he grew up and the tradition which has shaped his work. John Montague defines the culture of the Gael, John Hewitt that of the Planter.'[28] To whatever extent this 'programme of poems' created sympathy across sectarian lines, it may also have strengthened Montague's sense that in *The Rough Field* he could speak for his tribe.[29]

Although, ultimately, Montague's success in the '1960s' will be judged by third-millennial retrospection, during this decade Montague himself turned to the contemporary court of the British establishment and the index of sales. From the beginning he took as representative of British poetic opinion the Poetry Book Society which four times each year has sent its members a 'Choice,' a book selected as the best of those about to be published in the British Isles. The PBS also named a few 'Recommendations' each quarter, but the Choice had the strong advantage of boosting sales according to the number of members, six to seven hundred in the 1950s to nearly two thousand in the 1990s.[30]

From the beginning of his publishing career, Montague frequently encouraged O'Keeffe to submit his books to the PBS selection committee.[31] As disappointment at not being chosen gave way to annoyance at the '"stunted children" of the ancient Movement' (19 June), he pondered: 'It might just be that we are introducing a new thing which the rather "thin" establishment of the 50's cannot see. . . . As you can see my influence in England is practically nil, though, since Ted Hughes wants to put me in an anthology, it will begin to grow' (10 July). In 1963, when Clarke's *Flight to Africa* received only a Recommendation, Montague wrote to Liam Miller about the PBS: 'My already low opinion of them sinks to zero: have they ever crowned anything dangerous?'[32] Three years later, as the launching date for *A Chosen Light* approaches, Montague's concern for PBS recognition returns.[33] When the Choice goes to Thom Gunn, he writes in disappointment: 'The English just don't like me; and . . . poems like "All Legendary Obstacles" and "The Cage" can't open their conditioned eyelids. . . . My wife suggests that I should . . . buy a motor cycle but I think they would not be deceived' (29 October 1967). By 2 November, his conclusion has hardened into a denunciation: 'My conviction grows that the whole English literary structure is rotten except for a few individuals, like Ted Hughes and – who else? They just can't recognise feeling in verse any more. Tricksters to the last. . . .'

Earlier in that year, anticipating another rejection from the PBS, Montague enquired of Liam Miller: 'Perhaps you will explain to me why the Poetry Book Society does not like my work; there is something very odd happening in that direction. . . .'[34] When Miller responded several months later, his answer – perhaps founded on his close working friendship with John Bell and Jon Stallworthy of Oxford University Press – reflected none of Montague's mistrust of English institutions:

> I do not understand the remark about the Poetry Book Society as I have always found Eric White in favour of your work and feel

that the whole thing is an affair of timing, and selection – like backing horses, one must study the form of the field and the obtaining
prices.[35]

Although, subsequently, three of Montague's Dolmen titles would be
recommended (*Tides* (1970), *A Slow Dance* (1975), and *The Dead Kingdom*
(1984)), Montague's frustration at being among the unchosen would
emerge much later – perhaps riding Miller's punter's metaphor – in his
comments in the *Poetry Book Society Bulletin*:

> I am grateful to the Poetry Book Society, about which I am beginning
> to feel like Gordon Richards and the Derby; this is my third Recom-
> mendation! But *The Rough Field* was an also-ran, so my speed over
> the distance is improving.[36]

Between the founding of the PBS in 1954 and 1993, when Stephen
E. Smith listed the Choices and Recommendations, the PBS chose 156
books, 21 of which were by poets from the North or the Republic of
Ireland. During this period, the PBS chose one book each by Irish poets
Austin Clarke, Paul Durcan, Patrick Kavanagh, Michael Longley, Hugh
Maxton, Richard Murphy, Tom Paulin, and Matthew Sweeney, and more
than one book each by Eavan Boland (2), Seamus Heaney (4), Thomas
Kinsella (2), Louis MacNeice (2), Derek Mahon (2), Paul Muldoon (2), and
Frank Ormsby (2).[37] For Christmas of 1972 and Spring of 1978, Stewart
Conn's *An Ear to the Ground* and Peter Porter's *The Cost of Seriousness*,
respectively, were chosen while Montague's *The Rough Field* (1972) and
*The Great Cloak* (1978) were not even recommended. In light of this
list and such neglect of major works, the omission of Montague seems
inexplicable.[38]

Because negative choices are never defended, we can only generalize
feebly about the PBS's neglect of Montague. According to the influential
poet and editor Blake Morrison, in a preface to an anthology of poems
from PBS Choices and statements about the PBS, this society remains
deeply conservative:

> T. S. Eliot was one of the first directors of the Poetry Book Society. . . .
> The Georgianism he was supposed to have banished . . . had never
> really gone away. . . . Georgianism in its best sense – downbeat, socially
> realistic, local, anecdotal, metrically accomplished – can be found
> throughout this anthology; the dissenting wild men (George Barker
> and Michael Hastings prominent among them) can be counted on

one hand. Is this conservatism of the PBS or of the times? Hard to say. . . .[39]

Although we can point out that Montague – inheritor of poisoned lands and declarer that, after *The Rough Field*, 'there will be no more space for rural picturesqueness'[40] – was anti-Georgian, so too, in their way, were Kinsella, Clarke, and even Heaney. We could also recognize that the PBS is a national institution, as declared by Eliot in comments that have been called the 'imprimatur' of the PBS: 'I have always held firmly that a nation which ceases to produce poetry will in the long run cease to be able to enjoy and even understand the great poetry of its past.'[41] However, although Irish poetry in English emanates from quite different sources from those of English poetry, the PBS had chosen, as we have seen, Irish poets such as Clarke and Kinsella who are radically different from English poets. It seems more likely that Montague's American sources and influences, in the work of poets such as Williams and Duncan, distanced him from English taste more than did his Irish sources.[42]

Whatever the causes, Montague's neglect by English critics cost him potential readers. Montague once wrote, in anticipation of the publication of *A Chosen Light*:

> God, I hope the book does well. These half-successes are like thunder without lightning. Not money, but the sensation that the book has got through, is being read by the people one would have wanted to read it.[43]

In the light of such reasonable aspirations, the event in 1973 that closes Montague's '1960s,' as we have defined them, seems particularly poignant. Although neglected by the Poetry Book Society, *The Rough Field* had appeared in 1972 to the acclaim of important reviewers, both in Britain and Ireland. Late in that year Liam Miller organized a reading in the Peacock Theatre in Dublin, with music by the Chieftains, which was broadcast by Radio Éireann.[44] On the heels of this successful dramatization, a dramatic reading was scheduled for the Round House on the western edge of Camden Town in London for July of 1973, to be filmed by Radio Telefís Eireann and recorded by Claddagh Records. Readers were Heaney, Benedict Kiely, Pat McGee, Tom McGurk, and Montague himself, with music by the Chieftains. Six weeks in advance, according to Montague's recollection, he sent notice to Carol Buckroyd, then poetry editor with his British publisher OUP, concerning the need for books at the reading. When he came to London the day before the reading and went directly into rehearsal, he noticed the absence of books and telephoned Oxford at the first break. He was told that because of the weekend, the oversight could not be corrected, and consequently 1500 listeners sat through the reading without the script these books would have supplied.[45]

From the publication of *A Slow Dance* by Wake Forest in 1976 and of *Mount Eagle* by the Gallery Press in 1988, Montague has found most of his readers in North America and Ireland, rather than in England. The neglect of Montague in Britain, willfully maintained in a recent Penguin anthology of contemporary poetry edited by Simon Armitage and Robert Crawford,[46] may no longer have seemed to Montague a final judgment by the last tribunal, as he shifted between the Distinguished Professorship at the Writer's Institute of New York State at Albany from which he had just retired and the first Irish Professorship of Poetry, shared by Queens University, Trinity College, Dublin, and University College, Dublin.

## 'It could only happen in England': Larkin, Betjeman, and Eliot

Certain poems of Larkin's remind us by their references that between 1950 and 1955 he lived in Northern Ireland, working as an assistant librarian at Queen's University in Belfast, and by their rhetoric that he was devoted to Yeats. However, we need his letters to learn that only a better job at Hull won him away from Belfast, and we may even speculate that he otherwise might have stayed on as an elder in the 'Northern Ireland renaissance,' if partially to avoid marriage to Monica Jones and full maintenance of his mother.

Larkin arrived in Belfast with some reputation as a budding novelist who also wrote poetry, having published his second novel *A Girl in Winter* in 1947 with the prestigious Faber & Faber. In 1948 the same firm had rejected his second volume of poetry *In the Grip of Light* which exposed too easily its Yeatsian influence. For just one example from that volume, 'Night-Music' concludes:

> And in their blazing solitude
> The stars sang in their sockets through the night:
> 'Blow bright, blow bright
> The coal of this unquickened world.'

(*LCP*, 300)

The cosmic animism, imperatives of the musical spheres, the broadcast of desire (if not the singing eyes) offer evidence of Larkin's devotion to Yeats which seems particularly evident from his twentieth to his twenty-fourth year when, according to his own disputed claim, through the discovery of Hardy he underwent an 'undramatic, complete and permanent' reaction against the Irish poet (*RW*, 29). In a 1968 broadcast for Radio 4, he explained his allegiance to Hardy:

> What I like about him primarily is his temperament and the way he sees life. He's not a transcendental writer, he's not a Yeats, he's not an Eliot; his subjects are men, the life of men, time and the passing of time, love and the fading of love.                      (*RW*, 175)

Four years earlier he decried the sort of hieratic function associated with Yeats: 'The days when one could claim to be the priest of a mystery are gone: today mystery means either ignorance or hokum, neither fashionable qualities' (*RW*, 83–4). Over the five years in Belfast, Larkin completed the turn from novelist and Yeatsian poet toward an occasionally Audenesque but more frequently Hardyean poet whose debt to Yeats was hidden.

In February of 1954, he accepted an invitation from Donald Davie to take the train down from Belfast to lecture at Trinity College, Dublin. In October, Larkin was reinvited by Davie for a Fellowship dinner at Trinity and for a lunch with Liam Miller of the Dolmen Press who was considering Larkin's volume of poetry *The Less Deceived* for publication. In his letters, Larkin expresses disappointment that the two Irish members of 'the triumvirate selection board' with whom he lunched turned down the book (229). With three years of experience and little more than a dozen books, Miller may have been guided by a local instinct, if not a stated nationalist policy, to stay home and publish Irish writers. If our speculation about Larkin's possibilities for an alternative life in Ireland are 'sweet / And meaningless, and not to come again' (*LCP*, 21),[47] we might recognize that the 1960s separatist tendency of Irish poets and publishers, recorded earlier in this chapter, emerges here.

Whatever caused the Dolmen failure to recognize the universal appeal of poems such as 'Lines on a Young Lady's Photograph Album,' 'Church Going,' and, especially, 'Poetry of Departures,' this volume reveals Larkin's own turning back toward a special relation to his English audience, a reliance on place names and topical references, and other attributes – recognizable if sometimes elusive – that will come to be called Larkin's

'Englishness.' Later, in the preface to his *Oxford Book of Twentieth-Century Verse*, Larkin will recognize 'an English tradition coming from the nineteenth century with people like Hardy' and excluding Yeats and Eliot. The wider tradition that includes Pope's 'Windsor Forest,' Gray, Cowper, Wordsworth, Arnold, and the Georgian poets shares a nostalgic, if not nationalist, formal rendering of landscape and specific places, but the narrower, more recent subtradition from Hardy must be seen as empirical: a belief in the material world and it laws of operation, in the senses' ability to perceive this world, and in science's capacity to determine and confirm these laws and to correct our perceptions and our longing for transcendence. In the present century, in a true protestant fashion England's materialist belief might be seen as dividing over the nature of the observing self into Marxist, Christian humanist, and Liberal agnostic camps. Although the division among the three is deep, they all may act like religions at times, expressing a love for the transient world in which they are even more ephemeral.

Very frequently in Larkin's poetry, details of the world we fade from can embody a poignant sweetness, as in 'Cut Grass' where the passing of the recognizably English summer offers the readers a collective sense of their own generational passing:

> It dies in the white hours
> Of young-leafed June
> With chestnut flowers,
> With hedges snowlike strewn,
>
> White lilac bowed,
> Lost lanes of Queen Anne's lace,
> And that high-builded cloud
> Moving at summer's pace.

(LCP, 183)

Larkin's poems observe the injunction of the speaker in Shakespeare's Sonnet 73 'to love that well which thou must leave ere long' or even Arnold's plea in 'Dover Beach' '...let us be true / To one another...,' yet he goes beyond love of an individual, 'Ah, love...,' to seem to fulfill a trust, in Wordsworth's sense of a 'formal engagement,' which offers the readership something like an agnostic religion (*religare*, to bind together) or a belief. Scientists, who maintain an authoritative relationship with the material world, cannot, almost by definition of their objective function, infuse into or educe from that relationship 'care, desire, love,' synonyms at the Indo-European root of be + *lief*. That role is left to Hardy, Housman, Owen, Larkin, and other poets of that post-Darwinian persuasion and perhaps some novelists.

During our decade of the 1960s, the poems Larkin published in *The Whitsun Weddings* (1964) and in journals or newspapers (most of *High Windows*) establish this association with Englishness. As Donald Davie wrote in his decisive study *Thomas Hardy and British Poetry* in 1972:

> We recognize in Larkin's poems the seasons of present-day England, but we recognize also the seasons of an English soul.... The congested England that we have inhabited day by day is Larkin's England.... There is to be no historical perspective, no measuring of present against past. (64–5)

Since Davie's canon-constructing study, critics such as Stan Smith, Steve Clark, and Andrew Swarbrick have recognized that Larkin's temporal perspective is more complicated than Davie assumes and has been so since the opening poem of *The Less Deceived*. 'Lines on a Young Lady's Photograph Album' offers photography, which 'Faithful and disappointing... / ... / will not censor blemishes / Like washing-lines, and Hall's Distemper boards,' as a metaphor for Larkin's art. As does Larkin's 'realism,' photography 'overwhelming persuades / That this is a real girl in a real place / / In every sense empirically true! / Or is it just *the past*?' (*LCP*, 72). This poem raises not only phenomenological questions about the relation of the poetic object and the observing subject but also questions both about the estheticizing eye as predator and about the Lockean 'I' who renders other subjects as objects necessarily projected into a past. 'The gap from eye to page' of the photograph album becomes the gap between the absent object of desire and the embalming fluency of the poet. 'In every sense empirically true' resonates with ambiguities concerning English epistemology.

This alliance of poetry with photography, also suggested in poems such as 'Whatever Happened?,' 'Essential Beauty,' 'Wild Oats,' and 'Sunny Prestatyn,' Larkin extends to cinematography in fleeting images, rather than entire poems. For example, in the brilliant 'Days' 'the priest and the doctor / In their long coats / Running over the fields' evokes a death scene in a French, perhaps a Renoir, film. Larkin's preference for photography over painting and cinematography over theatre as a means of focusing questions of esthetics aligns his concerns, paradoxically, with controversial issues of the English left of that era, raised in Antonioni's

London film 'Blow Up,' as well as in other films, and in theoretical writing within the journal *Screen*.

Larkin's clear poetic statements, his attractive forms, his vivid rendering of familiar images, his wit, and his sexual frankness won readers to trust him, even when his underlying truth, as in 'Lines on ... Album,' is that poetry must falsify. Establishing this relation of trust with his reader Larkin frequently asserts should be one of the objectives of the poet, along with recording an event out of one's life and the accompanying emotion. On the basis of these poetic objectives he elevates the author of nostalgic antiquarian poetry John Betjeman to the front ranks of English poetry. In the view of most readers of modern poetry this judgment is incomprehensible, but it is so important to an understanding of Larkin's place in the poetic economy that we must digress into a discussion of Larkin, Betjeman, Eliot, and culture as a background to Larkin's poetry.

In two essays on Betjeman, a review of his verse autobiography 'The Blending of Betjeman,' and an introduction to his collected poems entitled 'It Could Only Happen in England,' Larkin locates Betjeman's straightforward poetry as the polar opposite of the 'difficult,' modernist poetry Eliot espouses and writes. Through an 'imaginative and precise evocation' of the poet's and his readers' recent past, served by 'an astonishing command of detail' (*RW*, 132), Betjeman manages to 'prove ... that a direct relation with the reading public could be established by anyone prepared to be moving and memorable' (*RW*, 129). Finally, in sharp contrast to *tone* in Irish poetry, as we have discussed it in Chapter 2, Betjeman addresses his reader with 'a sincerity as unselfconscious as it is absolute' (*RW*, 132).

Because of their very local nature, Betjeman's details must often baffle readers from Ireland or America. The cult of Englishness, the Belfast critic Edna Longley has said, 'is a cosy tribal ritual which bewilders outsiders' (1986, 118). We can only suppose that lines such as the following from Betjeman's blank-verse autobiography *Summoned by Bells* can have a strong appeal to those English readers whose long-term memory is intact:

> In late September, in the conker time,
> When Poperinghe and Zillebeke and Mons
> Boomed with five-nines, large sepia gravures
> Of French, Smith-Dorrien and Haig were given
> Gratis with each half-pound of Brooke Bond's tea.[48]

When Betjeman tries to move his topophilic verse beyond his own locality, however, as in 'Ireland's Own,' his poem about Thomas Moore, he descends into Bord Failté clichés and waltzing anapests in place of Irish measures:

> No! the lough and the mountain, the ruins and rain
> And purple-blue distances bound your desmesne,
> For the tunes to the elegant measures you trod
> Have chords of deep longing for Ireland and God.

> (*Collected Poems*, 313)

Larkin concludes the second essay on Betjeman by shifting from Eliot the poet to Eliot the nurturer of English culture. In his *Notes toward the Definition of Culture*, Eliot writes:

> The reader must remind himself, as the author has constantly to do, of how much is here embraced by the term *culture*. It includes all the characteristic activities and interests of a people: Derby Day, Henley Regatta, Cowes, the twelfth of August, a cup final, the dog races, the pin table, the dart board, Wensleydale cheese, boiled cabbage cut into sections, beetroot in vinegar, nineteenth-century Gothic churches and the music of Elgar. The reader can make his own list.      (30)

Larkin introduces this catalogue, beginning with 'Derby Day,' with the question 'And what is this "whole way of life" that a poet should (presumably) concern himself with expressing?', and then after quoting Eliot's list he adds, 'Now if this passage reminds us of anyone's poetry, it is Betjeman's rather than Eliot's or anyone else's' (218). Larkin not only promotes Betjeman as culture captain but also returns poetry to that role in the center of culture to which Newbolt and then Leavis assigned it but which Eliot reserves for religion and family. Only in an appendix to his *Notes* does Eliot designate writers, but not specifically poets, as central to culture: 'My last appeal is to the men of letters of Europe, who have a special responsibility for the preservation and transmission of our common culture' (128). When Larkin next asks the question, 'Can it be that, as Eliot dominated the first half of the twentieth century, the second half will derive from Betjeman?,' we answer with a resounding 'No!' or we understand that Larkin is employing Betjeman as a wooly mascot for the tradition others would come to call 'Larkinesque.'

By the 1960s, Larkin was recognized by many critics as the last poet standing of a group of writers heralded as 'the Movement' in an article in the *Spectator* in 1954 and represented in Robert Conquest's *New Lines* anthology in 1956. The *Spectator* essayist Anthony Hartley defined these writers in terms of what they opposed as 'anti-phoney...anti-wet; sceptical, robust, ironic, prepared to be as comfortable as possible in a wicked, commercial, threatened world...,'[49] mostly young unproven writers fed up with the orotundity of Dylan Thomas, Vernon Watkins, and advocates of the New Romanticism. Poets such as Thom Gunn and Donald Davie, who were listed on the Movement's rosters, attacked the principles of this group and followed their own independent interests. Although Larkin remained the only poet of real merit still recognizable by these reactionary terms, his attraction to a middle-class English reader nostalgic for a familiar England was so powerful that the Movement persists to the century's end and, embodied in the new poet laureate Andrew Motion, perhaps beyond.

Among Larkin's poems that serve especially in the 'preservation and transmission' of English culture, perhaps all readers would identify – along with 'The Whitsun Weddings,' 'MCMXIV,' 'Show Saturday,' and 'The Trees' – 'The Explosion,' which Motion tells us was inspired by 'a television documentary about the mining industry that he watched... during Christmas 1969' (394–5). Although Lawrence's novels, film adaptations *Sons and Lovers* (1960) and *Women in Love* (1969), and other films such as *This Sporting Life* (1963) and the earlier film *The Brave Don't Cry* (1952) had romanticized coal miners as working-class heroes struggling in a lost cause, 'The Explosion' represents, as Neil Corcoran says, a 'fantas[y] of an impossibly idealised community' (94).[50] This idealization, however, reflects the national aura that surrounds the subject of the poem, not coal mines but coal-mining disasters, those periods in history when the entire nation set aside the class controversy concerning the mines, remained riveted by BBC reports of rescue attempts, and contributed to relief funds as an act of national grieving.[51] The poem can be read casually as redemptive, offering solace to survivors or even transcendence to the victims. For example, Terry Whalen writes, '*High Windows* closes with "The Explosion", a poem which manages to move from an ironic mining-disaster to a vision of transcendence which makes it one of the most compelling religious poems of our day' (7).

The poem does open ominously –

> On the day of the explosion
> Shadows pointed towards the pithead:
> In the sun the slagheap slept

– positing signs to be read. The compressed lethal energy of the third line – the overloaded alliteration, the dormant power – evoke a collective memory of the Welsh disaster in 1966 where a slagheap 'awoke' and avalanched down on the village of Aberfan, killing 116 children at play in the schoolyard and 28 adults. The second line, suggesting a Homeric underworld, represents a collective projection based on more distant memories such as that of the worst of Britain's mine disasters which occurred in 1913 at Senghenydd in Wales where 439 died (Duckham, 208). The poem continues:

> Down the lane came men in pitboots
> Coughing oath-edged talk and pipe-smoke,
> Shouldering off the freshened silence.
>
> One chased after rabbits; lost them;
> Came back with a nest of lark's eggs;
> Showed them; lodged them in the grasses.

We can only presume that these stanzas carry us beyond the quietly closed doors of the homes and out of view of the families. The fifth stanza breaks from the trochaic triplet with its unstressed line endings, which critics trace implausibly to Longfellow:[52]

> At noon, there came a tremor; cows
> Stopped chewing for a second; sun,
> Scarfed as in a heat-haze, dimmed.

The three stressed endings (reading *dimmed* as a single syllable), which gain emphasis by the absence of final stresses in all but four other lines, are further set off by the caesurae. As a consequence, we have a remote but palpable suggestion of a mythic duality, consistent with pointing shadows, where the Greek earth's surface of *sun* and *cows* can be dimmed by its chthonic counterpart.

The consoling voice of the preacher then introduces the poem's last ten lines:

> The dead go on before us, they
> *Are sitting in God's house in comfort,*
> *We shall see them face to face –*

> Plain as lettering in the chapels
> It was said, and for a second
> Wives saw men of the explosion
>
> Larger than in life they managed –
> Gold as on a coin, or walking
> Somehow from the sun towards them,
>
> One showing the eggs unbroken.
>
> (*LCP*, 175)

Almost all critics comment on the eggs and the 'epiphany' of the last line. Andrew Swarbrick offers a cautionary word: 'The poem is careful not to be seduced by the wives' understandable need to see an after-life. They see only "for a second", and it is their vision, not the poem's' (150). Yet, when the larking miner 'came back with a nest of lark's eggs; / Showed them; lodged them in the grasses,' the wives of course were not among the pit-bound miners. The vision of the eggs, therefore, must be vouchsafed to the wives by the poem itself, as Swarbrick seems to concede:

> As the man took care of these eggs, so the poem with the men. It shows them, and lodges them in their community, amongst their nameless wives and families. The poem makes them 'Larger than in life they managed.' (151)

If the poem is complicit in the vision, the vision, surely, is qualified. The miner's intention – neither to fry up the eggs nor to hatch them – is esthetic: to show off the eggs in their miniature perfection. His esthetic aim undermines regenerative possibilities, as a scolding member of the Royal Society for the Protection of Birds would have told him. Recalling a similar act of stealth, Wordsworth of *The Prelude* acknowledges that he was a 'plunderer' of the mother bird's 'lodge' and his theft of eggs he confesses was 'mean / . . . and inglorious' (I, 328–9). As a verb *lodged* has as strange a resonance as does the noun *lodge* in Wordsworth, suggesting a removal from circulation into memory, as into 'a mansion for all lovely forms.' In this sense, the gold coin (if it is not an obal to pay Charon) and the cinemagraphic 'walking / Somehow from the sun towards them' – by which camera-angle the individual, 'face to face' identities are lost in the glare – both remove the men from circulation and render them as a keepsake. The poem is not only complicit in but also subtly confessional about its estheticizing of the men's afterlives.

## Hill and Larkin

Within its limits, the ending of 'The Explosion' is 'moving and memorable,' virtues of Betjeman's poetry according to Larkin. We cannot extend to Larkin, however, as he did to Betjeman, the assertion that he addresses his reader with 'a sincerity as unselfconscious as it is absolute' (*RW*, 129, 132). The poem's rhetorical flourish goes beyond Hardy's empirical acknowledgments in the 'Poems 1912–13' that humans long for an afterlife or Yeats's equally dramatic conclusions, as in 'Dialogue of Self and Soul' that 'Everything we look upon is blessed,' which must be understood as part of a dialectic.

Knowing compromises with the readership, such as that in 'The Explosion,' must contribute to Geoffrey Hill's condemnation of Larkin at the conclusion of a 1996 essay 'Dividing Legacies' in which Hill deplores Eliot's decline from the intense 'pitch' of his early poetry into the 'tone' of 'generous common humanity' in *The Four Quartets*. This softening of poetry as a commodity for 'culture' Hill sees extended into the poetry of Larkin. Hill writes:

> What Larkin represents is an assumption, a narrow English possessiveness, with regard to 'good sense' and 'generous common humanity.' 'Good sense', so propertied, so keen to admit others, at a price, to its properties, strikes me as a deplorable kind of *bienséance*. During his lifetime Larkin was granted endless credit by the bank of Opinion and the rage which in some quarters greeted his posthumously published *Letters* was that of people who consider themselves betrayed by one of their own kind. In fact Larkin betrayed no-one, least of all himself. What he is seen to be in the letters he was and is in the poems.
>
> ('Dividing Legacies,' 27)

Although Larkin's puerile misogyny, his racism, and anti-semitism outraged many readers of the letters, Hill condemns his withering from an apparent 'generous common humanity' to 'a narrow English possessiveness,' a shift we might deduce from the 'gold coin' offered but unredeemable at the close of 'The Explosion.'

Among Hill's several objectives in 'Divided Legacies' was a gentle chiding of his colleague Christopher Ricks for praising Larkin. In *The Force of Poetry* Ricks had claimed that Larkin possessed a reactionary virtue that 'turns even "his greatest soft sell" (279) into an awareness of "destination" which in turn "itself arrives as one of Larkin's greatest destinations, the end of 'The Whitsun Weddings'"' (279–80, in Ricks, 27).

Among the most quoted lines in Larkin, and therefore among contemporary verse, this final stanza closes as the train enters London by collecting the observing and sometimes condescending 'I,' the honeymooning 'they,' and the increasingly frequent 'we' into a representation of the contemporary, specifically English, collective journey of life:

> this frail
> Travelling coincidence; and what it held
> Stood ready to be loosed with all the power
> That being changed can give. We slowed again,
> And as the tightened brakes took hold, there swelled
> A sense of falling, like an arrow-shower
> Sent out of sight, somewhere becoming rain.

> (*LCP*, 116)

Although the association in 'this swelling scene' of arrow-showers with honeymoons might recall some pre-teens' primer-film on human sexuality, Tom Paulin acutely identifies the source of a peculiarly English association:

> Most daringly, the 'sense of falling' in 'The Whitsun Weddings' becomes an 'arrow-shower' like the clothyard arrows in Olivier's film of *Henry V*. The poem summons both the play's patriotism and that of the film (it was made during the Second World War). . . .

> (Regan, 162)

. . . but not that of history or a real historical moment, we might add ('for Larkin, indeed this seems to be one of the rules of the game,' Davie says; 'there is to be no historical perspective, no measuring of present against past' (65)). That Larkin should represent this moment on the threshold of collective regeneration in terms of this patriotic summons to self-sacrifice – 'Once more unto the breech' – seems ironically appropriate to the author of selfish or timorous poems – prophylactic against marriage – such as 'Self's the Man,' 'Dockery and Son,' and 'This Be The Verse.'

Hill's difference from Larkin, proclaimed in 'Dividing Legacies,' emerges clearly from a comparison of this close of 'The Whitsun Weddings' with Hill's own poems about the more divided era of Henry VI and the War of the Roses, the eight-poem sonnet sequence 'Funeral Music.' Although specific battle images appear here, the poems are set after the Yorkist victory at Towton on Palm Sunday of 1461 in some reflective zone between history and the otherness of a moment brought back into the present tense. He captures that in-betweenness particularly in the frozen aftermath of the slaughter, in which sound and touch return memory to the body:

> Recall the cold
> Of Towton on Palm Sunday before dawn,
> Wakefield, Tewkesbury: fastidious trumpets
> Shrilling into the ruck; some trampled
> Acres, parched, sodden or blanched by sleet,
> Stuck with strange-postured dead. Recall the wind's
> Flurrying, darkness over the human mire.

('Funeral Music,' 2: *HN&CP*, 59)

Some attention is given to the cause of such slaughter, 26 000 dead in this small space – 'They bespoke doomsday and they meant it by / God ...' ('Funeral Music,' 3) and

> 'Prowess, vanity, mutual regard,
> It seemed I stared at them, they at me.
> That was the gorgon's true and mortal gaze:
> Averted conscience turned against itself,'
> A hawk and a hawk-shadow.

('Funeral Music,' 7)

and

> Once
> Every five hundred years a comet's
> Over-riding stillness might reveal men
> In such array, livid and featureless,
> With England crouched beastwise beneath it all.

('Funeral Music,' 3)

but the causes – human nature, the stars, England having become its own dragon – are mutually cancelling, and we are left with the fact of slaughter. In an essay appended to *King Log*, Hill wrote:

The battle of Towton itself commands one's belated witness. In the accounts of the contemporary chroniclers it was a holocaust.... A. H. Burne...reckons that over twenty-six thousand men died at Towton and remarks that 'the scene must have beggared description ....' (68)

Although Hill's line from above, 'Every five hundred years...,' indicates that the First World War is on his mind, he treats it neither mythically as the occasion of lost innocence (as in Larkin's 'MCMXIV') nor historically as the tidal shift in England's imperial destiny (as in Hughes's *Wolfwatching* poems). In his interview with Haffenden, Hill said:

There are...good political and sociological reasons for the floating of nostalgia: there's been an elegiac tinge to the air of this country every since the end of the Great War. To be accused of exhibiting a symptom when...I'm offering a diagnosis appears to be one of the numerous injustices which one must suffer.... (93)

Nostalgia takes different forms, as sonnet 6 indicates:

> Some parch for what they were; others are made
> Blind to all but one vision, their necessity
> To be reconciled. I believe in my
> Abandonment, since it is what I have.

Ultimately, Hill's subject is theology or negative theology, the acknowledgment of an absent center, rather than history. His examination of nation and self occurs 'set apart in timeless colloquy,' in an 'exemplary cave,' appropriate to the three neo-Platonic martyrs to whom 'Funeral Music' is dedicated. In one startling sonnet, the site of intellectual examination is not the shadowy cave but a marble hall which, like Yeats's cold heaven,' is 'riddled with light':

> Averroes, old heathen,
> If only you had been right, if Intellect
> Itself were absolute law, sufficient grace
> Our lives could be a myth of captivity
> Which we might enter: an unpeopled region
> Of ever new-fallen snow, a palace blazing
> With perpetual silence as with torches.

In his conversation with Haffenden, Hill glosses this poem:

> Averroism was the doctrine ... that there's only one single Intellect ... for the whole of humanity, and it seemed to me at first sight a most comforting doctrine ... but afterwards I felt it was not a doctrine to be embraced at all; it seemed to be the archetype of the totalitarian state. ... The attraction of what I came to see as its specious comfort and also of its coldness is captured in that metaphor ... an image of beautiful coldness and desolation. (98)

The dreamlike beauty adheres to the poem's music, as in the assonance of the first line's 'Averroes, old heathen' (*o* ... *e o* ... *e*) or of the fifth line's 'unpeopled region' (*un* ... *e, e* ... *ion*) or the sixth line's brightening *a*s in 'a palace blazing.'

The 'beautiful coldness and desolation' of Hill's passage might be compared to the sort of desolation Larkin evokes in lines from 'The Old Fools':

> or sometimes only  
> The rooms themselves, chairs and a fire burning,  
> The blown bush at the window, or the sun's  
> Faint friendliness on the wall some lonely  
> Rain-ceased midsummer evening. That is where they live:

(*LCP*, 196–7)

This penultimate stanza of the poem begins: 'Perhaps being old is having lighted rooms / Inside your head, and people in them, acting. / People you know, yet can't quite name ...,' and then, with 'or sometimes only,' these shadowy presences yield to an 'unpeopled region' with a central, vegetative consciousness. The lines locate us in a season and an English upper-middle class but not in history. Readers who have studied old-timers, watched for the onset of Alzheimer's, or imagined death's advance can recognize where the poem gathers us. In that act of recognition, shared memory humanizes, or returns selfhood to, the act of Lockean perception. The light animism of fire, bush, sun, and evening invites readers to wrap themselves in their common humanity against the shiver of *timor mortis*.

While fire and sun still provide light and comfort to the fading consciousness of Larkin's 'old fools,' in Hill's poem this more-closely-fitting-than-metaphor for reason, Light, which fueled western philosophy and

the Enlightenment photology, burns coldly for humanity. In this monologue about soul and reason, in which intellect is discredited, reason
performs the sorting and parsing that allows for this 'image of a beautiful coldness and desolation' (98). Both poets direct us toward final
things: Larkin through recognition, Hill through the struggle of mind and
imagination. More readers participate in Larkin's poems, for which the
initiation is easier. The initiation into Hill's poetry is more stringent and
dearer, for which some believe the value returned is considerably greater.

## Hughes and the Celtic exchange

Hill's poetry advances book by book into the 1990s and therefore into
Chapter 5, but it never enters into a serious exchange with Irish poetry.
Hill and Kinsella share a rich and rewarding complexity, the power to
evoke the past not as it might have occurred but in a productive relation to the present, and an interest in etymology and the exact phrase,
but Hill has not read Kinsella's poetry beyond the 1960s, and Kinsella
has not found time for Hill's poetry.[53] Remarkably, Larkin too has few
adherents among Irish poets. The wit, clean lines, and Movement-like
formality of Derek Mahon's and Michael Longley's poetry derive in part
from classical models; Mahon's wit is much more dependent on his rich
vocabulary and turns of phrasing than is Larkin's.

Hughes, however, distances himself from English Georgian poetry
and aligns himself with Yeats and with ideas of a feminine principle in
nature, and, perhaps as a consequence of that, he has influenced both
Montague and Heaney and won adherents among other Irish poets.
Hughes's career was launched precipitously in the 1950s. When his wife
Sylvia Plath completed her Fulbright studies at Cambridge in the spring
of 1957, she and Hughes sailed to New York, much as Auden and Isherwood had twenty years earlier. A few months before his arrival, his poetic
career had begun in New York, and Auden had played a significant role
in that take-off. With Stephen Spender and Marianne Moore, he had
selected Hughes's first volume, neatly typed and submitted by Plath
from Cambridge, as the winner of the first YMHA's poetry prize for best
first poetic volume. The prize led to the publication of *The Hawk in the
Rain* that spring by Harper and in the autumn, with T. S. Eliot's blessing,
by Faber & Faber in London.

For a young man from a modestly educated family from the relatively
remote region of the West Riding of Yorkshire, the story of Hughes's
debut includes a familiar cast of writers who figure significantly in this
story. He was first drawn to poetry by Yeats, inspired by teachers at

Cambridge, including Leavis, selected by Auden and Spender, and published by Eliot. In the remarkably original *Hawk in the Rain* we can nevertheless observe, more fully than in subsequent volumes of this increasingly original poet, how fully Hughes had drawn on the economy of British and Irish poetry which he characterized, in its wider sense of a culture's myths and rhythms, as 'a shared bank account of the group wealth' (*HWP*, 310). Whereas the inimitable Hughes will influence his contemporaries John Montague and Richard Murphy, as well as Seamus Heaney, Plath, and perhaps younger poets such as Simon Armitage, in a representative poem from *The Hawk* such as 'The Horses,' we can observe traces of Hughes's own progenitors, such as Wordsworth, Hopkins, Lawrence, and Yeats.

Before looking closely at 'The Horses,' we need to know how Yeats stands behind the rhythm of that poem and indeed behind Hughes's rich awareness of rhythm. In an account of his earliest influences, Hughes tells of first being drawn to poetry by rhymes and rhythms, and later by myths, which led him on a private quest for satisfying poems. He recalls:

> One of the richest mines of folk tales, legends and myths in the world is the Irish. I fell under the powerful spell of these Irish tales. At the height of this craze, I came across ... 'The Wanderings of Oisin,' ... by W. B. Yeats, an Irish legend of the most magical sort, and the third part of Yeats's telling of it is written in the kind of metre I could respond to.                                    (*HWP*, 6)

Yeats's tale, we may recall, adapts the Pre-Raphaelite's woven, enameled, and bejeweled world of art and the poetic imagination and drives it 'on a horse with bridle of findrinny' into the Irish otherworld, that variant temporal zone coincident with this world. Hughes summarizes this account of discovering poetry:

> The magic door in metre and rhyme was opening to let me through into the underworld of strange goings on that we call poetic imagination. Everybody who gets into that underworld has to find their own way.                                                        (*HWP*, 6)

We recognize that his spatial metaphors invert Yeats's Irish Otherworld into the verticality often associated with the unconscious.

Indeed, 'The Horses' concerns cultural repression and the near emergence of forms from an ancient English culture. 'The kind of metre' to which Yeats shifted in the third part of 'The Wandering of Oisin' attracted Hughes probably because it offered release from a strict meter of insistent rising rhythms, the iambs and anapests of the first two parts of Yeats's poem and, indeed, of the dominant English poetic meter since the Renaissance. Although this section of Yeats's poem struggles in and out of iambic meter, its extended, 16-syllable lines occasionally, as in the third section's opening line ('Fled foam underneath us, and round us, a wondering and milky smoke'), suggest a more stress-oriented rhythm that escapes strict accentual-syllabic meter, one which Hughes associated with Hopkins' sprung rhythm and an older rhythm indigenous to English culture. Hughes makes his case for this non-metrical rhythm in terms of a political struggle that dates from the Reformation or even earlier. He asserts that up through Chaucer's time 'The King's Court still regarded itself... as an army of occupation, racially distinct,... still maintaining a primary allegiance to French and Continental culture, and still, most important of all, speaking the language of superior status...' (*HWP*, 366). He continues somewhat hyperbolically:

> On the one hand, the class which inherited and constantly reasserted the Military Occupation's governing role, and with it that speech code of superior status, also constantly re-enforced the rule of strict metrical forms, which went on evolving as a poetic tradition rooted in the court-centred 'high' culture. On the other hand, ... the innate music of its 'sprung rhythm' survived and multiplied, underground, like a nationalist army of guerrillas, in the regional dialects of common speech. (*HWP*, 367–8)

He then makes an alliance with not only Yeats but also all Welsh, Scots, and Irish poets: 'For various reasons, the Celtic presence is usually to be found supporting the old English, and as time passes becomes less and less separable from it' (*HWP*, 369).

In a long essay first published in *Winter Pollen*, Hughes suggests that 'The Horses' is written in the unorthodox rhythm associated with that older suppressed tradition. Free of orthodox metrical requirements, the lines plunge and rear the reader from stress to stress without regard for unstressed syllables, sometimes 'distributing' one stress between two adjacent words where consecutive, balanced stresses might return the line to more regular meter. Hughes offers his last lines as examples:

Between the streams and the red clouds, hearing curlews,
Hearing the horizons endure.

This scansion combines two offered by Hughes where his prosody becomes necessarily imprecise because he is trying to garner for the modern English poetic line an older musical quality. Of the unorthodox quonset roofs that span two syllables, he says, in reference to the final line: the fourth stress 'falls mainly on – "ons" but . . . extends itself over "en-", "distributing itself in some manner" over both.' The effect is of a musical note held:

> The final four stresses heap up one from behind the other, all pro-longed and all at different levels, until the last one, '-ure,' is held into the blue distance, like the recession of horizons behind horizons on the Pennine moorland being described.                      (365)

Hughes also hears 'red clouds' bound together in one distributed stress by which, I believe, he means that the duration of that distributed stress approximates the time of other stresses. We can find another instance in the poem's fifth line – 'Where my breath left tortuous statues in the iron light' – where Hughes's 'governing principle' of five stresses is main-tained if we read the near-rhyme *breath/left* as a prolonged syllable or a distributed stress.

Hughes employs this older accentual rhythm as the appropriate vehicle for the poem's subject which is some prehistoric form just emerging into the modern consciousness. 'The Horses' begins:

> I climbed through woods in the hour-before-dawn dark
> Evil air, a frost-making stillness,
>
> Not a leaf, not a bird, –
> A world cast in frost. I came out above the wood
>
> Where my breath left tortuous statues in the iron light.
> But the valleys were draining the darkness
>
> Till the moorline – blackening dregs of the brightening grey –
> Halved the sky ahead. And I saw the horses:
>
> Huge in the dense grey – ten together –
> Megalith-still. They breathed, making no move,
>
> With draped manes and tilted hind-hooves,
> Making no sound.

(lines 1–12)

As the valleys are 'draining the darkness,' the statuesque horses, 'Mega-lith-still,' emerge from the 'blackening dregs' – that Old English term for *dark* but also for the 'undesirable remainder' – on the margins of consciousness just above, but tethered by, the moorline.[54] Within this simple narrative in which the speaker climbs in the Pennines beyond these silent horses toward the sunrise and then descends to re-encounter them thawing in the morning light, the poem pays tribute to other poets who share Hughes's respect for the ancient British culture suggested by 'megalith-still':

> I listened in emptiness on the moor-ridge
> The curlew's tear turned its edge on the silence.
>
> Slowly detail leafed from the darkness. Then the sun
> Orange, red, red erupted.
>
> Silently, and splitting to its core tore and flung cloud,
> Shook the gulf open, showed blue,
>
> And the big planets hanging –

(lines 16–22)

These lines reveal their relation to Hopkins's 'azurous hung hills . . . / . . . as a stallion stalwart . . .' which 'hurls for him, O half hurls earth for him . . .' ('Hurrahing in Harvest'). We see further kinship with Hopkins in lines 6 and 7, quoted above, which reverse themselves rhythmically: the anapests of 'But the valleys were draining the darkness / Till the moorline' flip over to the dactyls of '– blackening dregs of the brightening grey' in a manner very reminiscent of Hopkins's counterpoint.[55] Whereas in line 20, quoted above, it is the sun whose 'core tore and flung cloud,' nevertheless, the curlew of line 17, whose 'tear turned its edge on the silence,' may initiate this solar birth. The Janus-faced noun *tear* – aubade or rending of dawn's birthsack – seems to contribute to 'core tore,' with an echo of Yeats's 'A Memory of Youth' in which 'the cry / Of a most ridiculous little bird / Tore from the clouds his marvellous moon.' As a number of critics have observed, the conclusion evokes Wordsworth. Keith Sagar says, '"Resolution and Independence" is its model,' and suggests that Hughes's ending – 'In din of the crowded streets, going among the years, the faces, / May I still meet my memory in so lonely a place' is 'almost as banal' as Wordsworth's final reference to the Leech-gatherer (Sagar, 1978, 19). Surely, Hughes's lines also echo 'Tintern Abbey' – 'But oft, in lonely rooms, and mid the din / Of towns and cities, I have owed to these' – and perhaps even Yeats's ending to 'Innisfree' where he too will 'stand on the roadway, or on the pavements gray' and recall his moment in nature.

Hughes's poem too will have its shadowy afterlife in 'The Good Night' section of Montague's *The Rough Field* and in Plath's 'Sheep in Fog.'[56] However, the mythic center of the poem, the emergence into half-light of something from our past or unconscious, more frequently recurs in Hughes's own poetry and prose. For example, in 'Myth and Education' (1976), Hughes suggests that the pre-Socratic philosophers were more integrated with nature and the unconscious:

> Plato was preceded in Greece by more shadowy figures. . . . Nothing is more striking about their ideas than the strange, visionary atmosphere from which they emerge. Plato . . . invented that careful, logical step-by-step style of investigation . . . which . . . ; evolved finally into the scientific method itself. But his predecessors stand in a different world. By comparison they seem like mythical figures, living in myth, dreaming mythical dreams. . . . Their vast powerful notions are emerging, like figures in half-relief, from the human/animal darkness of early Greece.                                                    (*HWP*, 137)

As the poet approaches the horses, 'stumbling in the fever of a dream, down towards / The dark woods, from the kindling top,' he seeks some aspect of himself in nature and the past from which humanity is estranged.

## The trenches, the Holocaust, and the bomb in the 1960s

With many English intellectuals across the political spectrum from Raymond Williams to T. S. Eliot, Hughes shares the need, perhaps consistent with the English elegiac mode, to fix the date of the nation's fall into the modern. In the passage above, Plato turns away from the pre-Socratic and initiates the move toward science. In others of Hughes's essays, the Reformation accelerated man's scientific control and dominance of nature. Most often, the descent into England's terminal corridor occurred in the First World War, and Hughes's most acclaimed volume *Crow*, written in the 1960s and published in 1970, can be read as profitably in the twilight of that war as of the nuclear conclusion of the Second World War. 'A Disaster' suggests the latter war and the bomb:

> It could digest nothing but people.
> So there it shrank, wrinkling weaker,

Puddling
Like a collapsing mushroom.
Finally, a drying salty lake.
Its era was over.
All that remained of it a brittle desert
Dazzling with the bones of earth's people

Where Crow walked and mused.

(33)

Yet, more frequently, *Crow* reflects images from his essays and later poems concerning the first war, as in this passage from 'Crow Alights':

There was this coat, in the dark cupboard,
                in the silent room, in the silent house.
There was this face, smoking its cigarette between the dusk
                window and the fire's embers.

Near the face, this hand, motionless.
Near the hand, this cup.

(21)

When we are told that Crow 'stared at the evidence. / Nothing escaped him. (Nothing could escape),' we recognize Hughes as a small boy, the witness of his father's post-First World War trauma, who dons the mask of Crow. Two decades later in the volume *Wolfwatching*, as if surfacing into meaning, the boy's 'inescapable evidence' emerges into full consciousness:

I looked at your face, your cigarette
Like a dial-finger. And my mind
Stopped with numbness.
Your day-silence was the coma
Out of which your night-dreams rose shouting.

('For the Duration,' 27)

In 'Dust As We Are,' he writes that attendance on his father, who was 'killed but alive,' was 'after mother's milk ... the soul's food' (13). In 1990, in the *Weekend Telegraph*, he wrote of the Great War, that

from the point of view of the son of an infantryman . . . it was virtually the Creation Story, and such a shattering, all-inclusive, grievous
catastrophe that it was felt as a national *defeat*, though victory had
somehow been pinned on to it as a consolation medal.

(*Rain-Charm* . . . , 58)

This characterization of the Great War's legacy as Hughes's 'Creation
Story' sheds light on *Crow*, which has been called a creation myth, as
a cognate nightmare. Earlier, in a 1964 review of Wilfred Owen's poetry,
he had spoken of this wound to the national psyche in political terms,
as well. 'The real enemy is the Public Monster of Warmongering' (*HWP*,
43) by 'those who remained in England. These were the politicians,
financiers, businessmen . . .' (42). He went on to write, 'The Great War was,
in fact, a kind of civil war, (still unfinished – which helps to explain its
meaning for modern England, its hold on our feelings . . .' (43). In 1965,
he wrote again that 'the First World War goes on getting stronger – our
number one national ghost. It's still everywhere, molesting everybody.
It's still politically alive, too, in an underground way' (*HWP*, 70).

Other major writers supported Hughes's assessment that the effect of
the Great War is ongoing. For example, Geoffrey Hill said, in an interview
with John Haffenden, 'There are, however, good political and sociological
reasons for the floating of nostalgia: there has been an elegiac tinge to
the air of this country ever since the end of the Great War' (quoted by
Gervais, 222). Author of 'MCMXIV', Larkin nevertheless has much less
to say about the war of 1914–18. In a 1963 review of Owen's poetry,
Larkin judged the period of England's trauma to be much briefer, two
decades in fact: 'The conviction [that early death and maiming are 'what
is terrible about war'] was to permeate the entire national consciousness
during the next twenty years' (*Required Writing*, 161). In the same review
he wrote, 'But in the end Owen's war is . . . all war, not particular suffering
but all suffering; not particular waste but all waste.'

# 5
# Toward the Present of English and Irish Poetry

In the recent history of the concept of *culture* within the English and Irish poetic exchange, the year 1916 must be the watershed. As stewards of *culture* in England, English poets mourn the death in nightmarish, mechanized battles such as the Somme and Ypres of individual poets, of the rural model of society, and of the nonindustrialized individual Englishman. Irish poets, on the other hand, turn away progressively from the violent nationalistic model of the 1916 Rising toward a distinct poetic language – syntax, diction, rhythm – and Irish myth and narrative. In the 1930s, however, neither English nor Irish poets seemed engaged with *culture* in the ways defined above. The left-leaning English poets were too preoccupied with international politics to write elegiac or nostalgic poetry; the Irish poets were too disenchanted by the Irish theocracy, which employed the Irish language as a means of punitive discrimination, to embrace the old culture. By the end of the 1960s, however, England's humiliation from loss of Empire and from a yea-saying, complementary role in Vietnam had found expression in irony, restraint, and the anti-exuberance of the Movement. In Ireland, the return of the Troubles and a more meaningful recovery of the matter of Ireland, as in Kinsella's translation of *The Táin*, turned the poets away from sectarian politics and toward their 'gapped, discontinuous, polyglot tradition' in Kinsella's famous phrasing. By the end of the century, a majority, but not all, English poets seemed bound by their commitment to culture and, therefore, to persist after all in their attachment to the central experience of loss and its locus in the First World War, while Irish poets had found an authority in the Irish matter which seemed no longer at 'a great remove' from, but just under the surface of, their language and poetic expression, in which translation functions as a regular dimension of poetic creativity.

## Translation and recent Irish poetry

One of the most certifiable and important differences between post-Second World War English and Irish poets concerns their facility with secondary or tertiary languages, the Irish being relatively polyglot compared to the English. Although we can name famous translators among the English poets, such as Michael Hamburger, Michael Hofmann, and Stephen Romer, most grew up insular and appear to be relatively content with their one superior language. With the same laggardness with which we recover English polyglots, we scroll for Irish poets with only one language. The bilingual English-Irish education in the Republic and among many Catholics in the North partially accounts for the Irish facility. Yet, even Protestant poets, such as Michael Longley and Derek Mahon, and poets who otherwise had little access to Irish such as Eavan Boland, perhaps because they sensed their mother tongue being threatened by the hyphen of Hiberno-English, made other languages, especially Latin and French, central to their studies and their writing. Generally, Irish poets were more self-conscious about their language and more aware of the relativity of language.

Still, the topic of translation concerns all poets, English and Irish, if we employ the broad sense of the word which is enjoying some currency under the heading of 'translation theory.' According to this wider sense, Edmund Leach can characterize the anthropologist as one who solves 'problem[s] of translation, of finding categories in his own ways of thought which can be fitted to the complex of observed facts that he records' (53; cited in Brodzki, 213). Where we might expect a narrow definition, in the work of Robert Welch, a pioneering scholar on the relation of Anglo-Irish to Irish poetry, we find the doors flung open:

> All legitimate intellectual enquiry is translation of one kind or another: it takes a text, a phase of history, an event, . . . and proceeds to understand it by reliving it in the process of re-creating it. In doing so it renews the unpredictability of the event or text by subjecting it once again to the challenges and opportunities of contingency.
>
> (*Changing States* (1993), xi, cited in Cronin, 168)

Both because Welch does not recognize that 'the challenges and opportunities of contingency' are more likely to belong to the present moment than to the irrecoverable moment of the past and because his definition is open to non-verbal communication, it may be too broad to be helpful.

For an inclusive definition of translation, Wordsworth's statement about language as a referent for passion might be the most helpful:

> As it is impossible for the Poet to produce upon all occasions language as exquisitely fitted for the passion as that which the real passion itself suggests, it is proper that he should consider himself as in the situation of a translator, who does not scruple to substitute excellencies of another kind for those which are unattainable by him.
>
> ('Preface' to the *Lyrical Ballads,* in *Selected Prose,* 290)

Because this addresses the limitations and license of poetry, it allows us to detain English poets on stage while we discuss the relation within Irish poetry of the two languages. The fruits of this exchange, however – the incorporation of elements of Irish tradition within the poetry of most Irish poets and the translation of Irish poetry into English – rarely enter into the exchange between English and Irish poets.

Over the century that has followed the creation of the Gaelic League, the relation in Ireland between the two linguistic, literary traditions has altered significantly. Critic/translators such as Robert Welch, Míchaél Ó hAodha, and Bernard O'Donoghue, for example, have argued that Yeats and other Irish poets crawled out of late Victorianism through distinctively Irish syntax, rhythm, and sound effects they found in the translations from Irish of Edward Walsh, Samuel Ferguson, Douglas Hyde, and others. For example, the editor of a new edition of the *Love Songs of Connacht* asserts that Hyde's translations, which first appeared in 1893, 'marked a turning-point in the Irish Literary Revival and revealed a new source for the development of a distinctive Irish mode in verse and poetic prose' (v, cited in Cronin, 135). In confirming Hyde's primacy as a translator from popular poetry in Irish, Yeats could accept this new influence of Hiberno-English as a gift without having, himself, to return to the Irish language.[1] Declan Kiberd has pointed out that Hyde's success undercut efforts to recover the language as a creative medium (197), as it also confirmed the position Yeats took as early as 1892 in favor of translation over the original language.

Over the first four decades of this century, some knowledge of Irish gave a foundation to the Hiberno-English of Joyce, Clarke, Beckett, Flann O'Brien, and others, and it served as a basis for translation, but not until the 1940s did Irish re-emerge as a truly creative medium in the poetry of Máirtín Ó Direáin, Seán Ó Ríordáin, and, in the next decade, Máire Mhac an tSaoi. Although these poets remained to different degrees marginalized, they influenced individual poets who wrote in English such

as Montague, Ní Chuilleanáin, and Thomas McCarthy, and they began
the creative interchange that would lead to bilingual anthologies and
bilingual editions of poets such as Ní Dhomhnaill, Michael Hartnett,
Michael Davitt, and Cathal Ó Searcaigh, to the willingness of English
language journals such as *Poetry Ireland* and *Cyphers* to print some poems
in Irish, and to macaronic impulses in poets such as Carson and Muldoon
to turn over words and even lines of their poems to Irish. The enterprise
of translating one's friend or fellow-poet from Irish has created a new
collaborativeness in the 1990s. *Pharaoh's Daughter*, Ní Dhomhnaill's
selected poems translated by 13 other poets is the most celebrated case,
but Cathal Ó Searcaigh and Michael Davitt have also attracted a broad
band of translators from among Irish poets writing in English.[2]

As the relation between Irish and English poetry has grown more intimate in Ireland, so have notions about translation become more complex
and self-reflexive. The passage from Joyce's *A Portrait*, discussed at length
in Chapter 2, where Stephen debates language with the Dean of Studies,
remains the classic text on colonial ambivalence, yet this linguistic condition is inherited by Anglo-Irish Protestants as well as Catholics in the
North, as Edna Longley reminds us with regard to Northern poetry:

> It exploits the full hybrid inheritance of Ulster English, whose vocabu-
> lary, structures and idioms have been influenced by Gaelic and Scots.
> It also places in the foreground the fact that we have a problem with
> language.                                                   (*The Living Stream*, 62)

Concerning specifically translation, Michael Cronin says, 'The experience
of a colonial rather than imperial past should make Irish translators
more conscious of the need to protect diversity and promote heterogen-
eity' (197). Perhaps only those translators of Ní Dhomhnaill who do
not command Irish[3] would support a thorough accommodation to the
target language, making the poem read like other English poems, consistent with the Enlightenment model of translation characterized by
David Lloyd: 'The ground for equivalence is ... located in the original
pre-linguistic experience, which the process of translation seeks to repeat
in order to establish, as it were, a common origin of source and target
texts' (1987, 105). On the other hand, poets who have acquired the
language with the belief that 'it contains within it a spirit, an essence,
a mind-set that is fundamentally different from English' and that 'is
defined, in a sense, by its untranslatability,' avoid the separatist implications of this belief, voiced most compellingly by Biddy Jenkinson in

1991 in the *Irish University Review*. This highly respected poet in Irish wrote in 'A Letter to An Editor': 'I prefer not to be translated into English in Ireland. It is a small rude gesture to those who think that everything can be harvested and stored without loss in an English-speaking Ireland' (34).

Contemporary translators negotiate between these poles, recognizing the untranslatable otherness of Irish literature, yet willing to compromise to make some shadow of it available to all readers in Ireland. Three decades ago, Kinsella manifested a degree of this ambivalence. In translating *The Táin*, he tried to create 'a living version of the story, leaving as few obstacles as possible between the original and the reader' (vii), and he acknowledged that 'no attempt has been made to preserve the actual texture of the Irish narrative' (xi). No doubt he recognized the necessary attrition of distinctive Irish qualities that reside in that texture, so he problematizes the translation by retaining monkish redactors and misogynist commentators in narrative asides.

Paul Muldoon acknowledges the otherness of Irish not by striving for Irish effects in English so much as by leaving evidence that the translation distorts, as it attempts to convey, certain distinctively Irish characteristics. Because Nuala Ní Dhomhnaill offers her translators cribs, line by line English versions of her poems, some comparison of these cribs with Muldoon's translations of Ní Dhomhnaill's volume *The Astrakhan Cloak* can illustrate how a very good contemporary translator negotiates between the source and the target languages. In two cases in 'The Lay of Loughadoon,' he casts the light on himself and loses his transparency as a translator. In a list of game-birds he adds to Ní Dhomhnaill's *capercaillie* the adjective *acrostical*, thereby sending us back to his own volume *Madoc* to discover that his own poem 'Capercaillie' offers an acrostical jibe at poetry selections for *The New Yorker*. In a second instance, he refers to a motif that runs throughout *Madoc*.[4]

For the most part, however, Muldoon follows the spirit of the original and sometimes the exact phrasing of the crib, but he regularly forces himself into alternative phrasing to conform to a rhyme pattern, not present in the original, rhyme thereby becoming a feature of an English-language passport. The headnote to the crib reads, 'This is a mock Fenian Lay in the appropriate metre,' in which the family's recreational walk associates myth and legend with landscape. Muldoon's off-rhyme – in which *art* can rhyme with *riot* – seems appropriately playful or even parodic and consistent with Ní Dhomhnaill's own playfulness. This long poem draws to a close, following 'while below us, from the valley-mouth,' in the crib with

> We can hear dogs barking and the cries of men
> Where herds of sheep are being brought home
> By the herders or hornless does
> Are being hunted by the Fianna.

Muldoon's translation –

> come hound voices and the view-halloo
> not of shepherds, no,
> but Fionn and the Fianna hunting high and low
> for that elusive, hornless doe.

– asserts over a mundane pastoral alternative the primacy of the legend of Fionn and the Fianna on an eternal, ghostly hunt. Through an allusion to Yeats's poem 'Hound Voice,' he extends Ní Dhomhnaill's poem or makes it more nearly explicit, so that Yeats's poem is reaved into the tradition of the Fenian lay, perhaps like Ní Dhomhnaill's, playfully or even parodically.[5]

This is not the only instance when Muldoon draws to the surface a submerged connection to Irish myth or tradition or widens such a reference. Toward the end of 'First Communion' where the author echoes the still-popular seventeenth-century love poem 'Úna bhán,' Muldoon alters this somewhat to offer the English-language equivalent, a slightly more remote echo of Yeats's 'Red Hanrahan's Song about Ireland,' which he renders as 'comelier than golden candlesticks at Mother Mary's feet' (33). In extending the echo to Yeats, Muldoon associates the major Anglo-Irish poet with the popular nationalist link between Mary and the high queens of Ireland (*banríona*).[6]

As with much traditional literature, so much of Ní Dhomhnaill's poetry concerns journeys, often lifelong and through psychologized landscapes. As the volume ends with a 14-part 'Voyage,' so 'First Communion' closes with the life-journey of her daughter which her crib renders: 'how can I tell her about all that lies before her, / of the darkness she will have to walk through / alone, over my dead body, and against my will?' Muldoon renders this with a characteristic succinctness – 'what can I tell her of the vast / void / through which she must wander alone, over my dead body?' – where the black hole of his penultimate line sucks in so many words of the original.

Muldoon's tendency to draw toward the surface of the translation mythic references more submerged in the Irish poem may be best illustrated by 'First Fall' where even the title contains a pun on fall/autumn

not available in the Irish *Titim i nGrá*. In Ní Dhomhnaill's crib, the
poem opens:

> I fall in love every year, in the Fall
> with the raindrops milling against the dashboard of the car,
> the unhealthily delicate poetic light going down
> behind the edges of the hills at the horizon before my eyes.

Beyond adding effective onomatopoeia in the second line here, the
translation makes a subtle but important spatial alteration:

> I fall in love, in the fall of every year,
> with the smattering of rain on my windshield
> and the pale and wan light toppling over the sheer
> edge of my field
> of vision, with leaves strewn in my way

One can read the poet's crib or, presumably, her original poem as a psychological confession about her link between death and decay, on the
one hand, and, on the other, love and investment in the transient. The
translator links this Keatsian theme to one of Keats's mythic extensions
with the 'pale and wan' of 'La Belle Dame Sans Merci.' He extends the
possiblity of a demonic lover with the enjambed fourth line, where
momentarily the speaker's perspective becomes a farm-field bound by
a sheer drop which in the final quatrain we might come to see as just
the sort of crime scene where Hades abducts his lover. The second stanza,
quite close in the translation and the crib, says in the latter: 'the seeds
of corn safe asleep underground / I fall in love, a little, with my death.'
The poem itself concludes in the translation:

> how I throw off the snowy sheet and icy quilt
> made of feathers from some flock
> of Otherworldly birds, how readily I am beguiled
> by a sunny smile, how he offers me a wing.

We may not notice the sinister eye-rhyme of 'and icy quilt' and 'I am
beguiled,' extended by assonance to *smile*, all flashing death's presence.
In the crib, the speaker is seduced by the sun ('once more led astray by
the sun's broad smirk and the heat') whereas the referent for *he* in the
translation must be 'death itself' or, if we have followed the poem to the

sheer fall at the edge of the field, the lord of the underground courting his Persephone.

## Muldoon's 'imarrhage' and 'pied' writing

Here, the relationship between the autumnal eroticism of Ní Dhomhnaill's speaker and the rape of Persephone by Hades can barely be glimpsed in the surface of Muldoon's translation and only intuited in the original. Perhaps, Muldoon himself offers the aptest characterization of this sort of reference, when he speaks in the Bateson lecture of a 'bleeding image' or 'imarrhage' (113) and in the Clarendon lectures of 'the tendency for one event or character to blur and bleed into another, what I've called elsewhere an "imarrhage"' (74). Without adopting Muldoon's neologism (why not 'conte-twosion'?), we can see the need to characterize this emergence of one image or story or character in the surface of another, as blood surfaces in a bruise. Muldoon illustrates this slightly differently in the opening of his Bateson lecture when he offers discrete images that 'imarrhage': 'the image of the horse standing with its back to the wind and rain. The image of the hole in the plaster wall showing the strands of horsehair.... One has the other under its skin' (109). Or, as Ciaran Carson says in *Fishing for Amber*, 'Behind the story that we tell today another story lies' (75). Throughout the century Irish literature has sought metaphors, such as Joyce's 'cracked lookingglass of a servant,' that distinguish itself from the mirror of British empiricism or from any assumption that we can reflect clearly a reality external to ourselves. Irish art, these metaphors suggest, reflects different contending representations or reveals different levels of individual and collective imagination, between which the poet plies as a type of Hermes in Muldoon's frequent self-characterization – no Apollonian agent of beauty but simply the functioning go-between conveying truth.[7]

In *The Annals of Chile* (1994), Muldoon's 'Incantata,' his celebrated elegy for his friend and lover the artist Mary Farl Powers who died of cancer in 1992, incorporates a variety of these metaphors for art. The poem opens: 'I thought of you tonight, *a leanbh*, lying there in your long barrow / colder and dumber than a fish by Francisco de Herrera.'[8] Her barrow locates her fixedly determined death from which, according to her own fatalistic opinion, she had no right to escape. The poet, however, converts the absoluteness of her death into the phrase from Yeats's 'All Things Can Tempt Me' that characterizes the romanticized poem in terms of its mask – that coldness that holds down passion. He translates that image of the poem, in turn, back into her own medium

of painting, demonstrating art's power to transform. As her necessary place, the barrow appears later as the ditch, where she lay with a friend of the poet, and then is transformed into a vapor trail, and 'the furrows from which we can no more deviate' in her grim determinism, her view that 'nothing's random, nothing arbitrary' (20). He writes, 'The fact that you were determined to cut yourself off in your prime / because it was *pre*-determined has my eyes abrim':
The representational function of art –

> There's nothing, you'd say, nothing over
> and above the sky itself, nothing but cloud-cover
> reflected in a thousand lakes; it seems that Minne-
> sota itself means 'sky-tinted water'...

(20)

– is dispersed among countless surfaces which, beautiful though they may be, mirror 'nothing.' The rhyme-scheme moves toward a sort of mirroring, beginning with paired or approximately paired rhymes – AABB – to CDDC in which image/reflection of two worlds, such as art and remembered reality, touch, are transformed by entering the other realm or not, and move apart:

> where the salmon breaks through the either/or neither/nor nether
> reaches despite the temple veil
> of itself being rent and the penny left out overnight on the rail
> is a sheet of copper when the mail-train has passed over.

(21)

The de Herrera fish, which comes alive as it enters the ethereal spaces it cannot survive in (neither/nor), passes through 'the temple veil.' This separation between one world and the other Muldoon calls in *To Ireland, I* 'the *feth fiada* or *ceo sidhe*, the magic mist or veil, a kind of world-scrim that hangs about them...' (*To Ireland*, I, 7). As the other-world bleeds through these images of the Minnesota landscape, we recognize that behind Muldoon's word *imarrhage* we glimpse *immram*, the name for those tales of travel between this world and the other.

The guide and agent for such travel, as throughout Muldoon's career, remains Hermes, who is identified with the poet and the agency of poetic form and language, as well as the artist Mary Powers. In translating from one realm to the other, Hermetic language necessarily transforms, as this couplet suggests: 'of the many moons of glasses on a tray, / of the brewery-carts drawn by moon-booted drays.' In the repetition of *moons/moon-*, the same word that measures time by lunar cycles, still scattering moonlight among images of plenitude, also invests labor with radiance, transforming the draft horses even as drafts of their load will brighten the night for others. Finally, the poet's language must transform that which it reflects, just as the poet's 'verse,' recalling its etymological origins, transforms as it mirrors Mary's grimly determined furrows.

Tim Kendall has pointed out that the 'catalogue aria' (217), which begins with stanza 24 and recalls the shared moments of poet and artist, is effaced by the quiddity of art that survives the artist. The 'quoquoquo' of Power's potato-mouth lithographs are 'all that's left' of the recalled events, but as the list proceeds, that phrase 'all that's left' drops out 'and the only reminder that these various items are being reduced rather than eulogized is the tiny word "of."'[9] The effect is that of a reflection without its material reflector on referent.

The poem's ending offers another version of the same effect, in which we are told that we can 'no more deviate' from the determined furrows 'than that' she can be retrieved from death. Again, the agent for this retrieval is 'the Irish Hermes, / Lugh. . . .' Whereas in the opening of the poem, Mary is compared to Lugh by the length of her arms and, thereby, her ability to gain distance from her work, at the conclusion, Hermes/Lugh becomes the poet who would offer her as antidote 'this *Incantata*.' Moving away from repetition of the phrase 'we can no more deviate,' the poet assumes the Hermetic function of the psychopomp to draw her from her determined death, inviting her to 'look up from your plate of copper or zinc / on which you've etched' for a momentary reunion. For this moment, we picture the artist herself pausing in her work, but we correct that to see the artist looking out of the mirroring surface of her own work, from which she reaches out. In the mirroring chiasmus their hands touch and close together: 'that you might reach out, arrah, / and take in your ink-stained hands my own hands stained with ink.'

This ending, which reviewers and other readers have praised, I find incantatory and transformative. The poet as psychopomp thus recovers her from the work of art as object, which we recall is an engraved negative etched by corrosives from which only simulacra can be restruck, to the work of art as labor, that which stains her hands, and his, and unites them in this common sign of labor. Reinforced by a memorable earlier passage in which she merges with her handiwork –

I saw you again tonight, in your jump-suit, thin as a rake,
your hand moving in such a deliberate arc
as you ground a lithographic stone
that your hand and the stone blurred to one

(16)

– the poem closes with the artist 'embodied' in her work: 'that you
might reach out, arrah, / and take in your ink-stained hands my own hands
stained with ink.' Those last six words offer a visible representation of
that most secret labor, as the poem returns to a suggestion of Yeats's 'All
Things Can Tempt Me' of the poet / dramatist's actual labor: 'Now nothing but comes readier to the hand / Than this accustomed toil. . . .' The
poetic work transforms experience, employing poetic language and form
to move a real place or person or moment into the reader's imagination.
In the 'Incantata,' the poet's stained hands not only recover a beloved but
also bear witness to the very human labor required for such a recovery.

## *Údar*: the authority of the absent in Irish poetry

As features or images from one level of consciousness 'imarrhage' or
bleed through to another level, their passage may defy meaning or interpretation, so the relationship in this reference may become obscured
because the source of the deeper, and often older, reference is lost or
purposefully secreted. In his Clarendon lectures, Muldoon offers as one
of four distinctive characteristics of Irish literature 'an urge towards the
cryptic, the encoded, the runic, the virtually unintelligible' (4) which,
borrowing from Robert Graves, he calls 'pied.' Beyond Muldoon's two
terms or the concept discussed in Chapter 3 of *fiduciary* poetry, which
elicits the reader's trust at moments when personal disclosures are withheld, I find particularly helpful the term *údar* because it refers both to the
willfully suppressed elements Muldoon calls 'pied' and to the accidental
loss of a reference over time, and because it includes an extra-dimensional
resonance or authority that Irish literature accrues from such omissions.
I would adapt the term from Hugh Shields who employs it to characterize songs that withhold or fail to supply their contexts. Shields applies
the term to the original occasion for the poem, the fuller narrative. He
identifies as the traditional *údar* the authority for the poem, saying,
'Those who listen to songs know that certain things occurred which were
the occasion of the songs, even if they do not know what things they
were.'[10] The term might be compared to the fiduciary trust between

early Auden and his readers, but in this case the unstated referent resides in the foundation of Irish culture rather than in merely private sources. If we extend the term *údar* to recent Irish poetry, Shields's statement can characterize our response to poems by Kinsella, in which *The Book of Invasions* is the unstated context; by Muldoon, in which the Otherworld or voyage myths – *immra* or *echtrae* – supply the background; unstated references to tribal secrets throughout the poetry of Ní Chuilleanáin; or what McGuckian calls *reserve* when she complains that 'too many poems are all meaning and no reserve.'[11]

If the Wordsworthian contract between English poets and their readers requires, or at least prefers, a Larkinesque clarity, with no references to what Larkin calls the 'myth-kitty,' for several reasons Irish readers prefer, or at least respect, this authority of the unspoken and unspecified context. First, secrecy is warranted and rewarded under the dual aspects of Irish colonialism. As the Irish language and even Hiberno-English regionalisms permit an Irish community to conduct its intimate conversation without surveillance or exploitation from the colonizing stranger, so the Irish poet may invite certain initiates into a secret space within the poem or simply imply that such space exists. This tendency toward secrecy is reinforced by Counter-Reformational tendencies within the Catholic Church toward secrecy or equivocation, so that poems may have their spiritual secrets, equivalents of priests' holes, secret rooms in the homes of English or Irish recusants where instruments of the mass or even priests were hidden. Finally, out of a vast storehouse of shared stories and songs, the exact reference may be lost even while the reader or auditor retains a general sense of the context. The Irish *údar* differs from the Modernist esoteric reference in being communal or insular, knowing, and linguistic rather than international, learned, and permeable with keys from psychology, anthropology, or comparative mythology.

The concept of *údar* can provide a helpful distinction between English and almost all Irish poetry, but it also distinguishes, and discriminates along a scale among Irish poets, some who were raised with the Irish language and some who inherited a Hiberno-English dialect but all of whom 'fretted in the shadow' of high English and received pronunciation. The term, then, will be more helpful in discussing poetry in Irish or in bilingual form or that of Ní Chuilleanáin, Carson, Hartnett, Muldoon, Kinsella, and Montague (to suggest one part of our own scale).

Ní Chuilleanáin's 'Daniel Grose,' for example, both illustrates this notion of *údar* and indirectly comments on it. The poem's secrets are only temporarily lodged in the title character who is a recoverable figure of art history. The draughtsman Daniel Grose assumed the authorship of *Antiquities of Ireland* (1792) at the death of his more famous uncle, the Englishman Francis Grose, providing most of the etchings of picturesque ruins that filled this book.[12] The poem seems to offer his perspective, trained like a marksman's:

> Now the military draughtsman
> Is training his eye
> On the upright of the tower,
> Noting the doors that open on treetops;
> He catches the light in the elder branches
> Rooted in the parapet, captures
> The way the pierced loop keeps exactly
> The dimensions of the first wounding,
> Holding in the same spasm the same long view
> Of field and river, cottage and rock
> All the way to the deconsecrated
> Abbey of the Five Wounds.

His actual drawings, which include such famous ruins as 'Kells Church and Tower,' 'Mellifont Abbey,' and 'Boyle Abbey,' are parodied here in the 'Abbey of the Five Wounds,' his vanishing point. Nowhere explicit in Grose's text, Christ's passion echoes in the words – *catches, captures, pierced, the first wounding, spasm* – associated with the destruction of these buildings and their societies, which began during the Reformation's confiscation of church properties: 'Then silence for three centuries / While a taste for ruins develops.' In the picturesque panorama presented by the poem, history is omitted: 'No crowds engaged in rape or killing, / No marshalling of boy soldiers, / No cutting the hair of novices.'[13] The poem contrasts two perspectives, the geometric, scientifically endorsed perspectives and the communal history they repress, reminding us that, as W. J. T. Mitchell writes, 'Perspective is a figure for what we would call ideology – a historical, cultural formation that masquerades as a universal, natural code.'[14]

Responding to one of the strongest ekphrastic attractions, the poet then temporalizes space, opening this picturesque effect to its historical causes:

> Where is the human figure
> He needs to show the scale
> And all the time that's passed
> And how different things are now?

The response is startling, even uncanny:

> The old woman by the oak tree
> Can be pressed into service
> To occupy the foreground.
> Her feet are warmed by drifting leaves.

This final line recalls the association of autumnal life and a repressed past in Shakespeare's indirect reference – 'bare ruined choirs' – to ruins of the 'Old Church' (Sonnet 73). The aged woman, standing druidically beside the oak, is the *cailleach*, that mysterious abandoned figure of Irish society and legend, a persona assumed sometimes by Eithne Strong and Nuala Ní Dhomhnaill in their poetries and by Ní Chuilleanáin herself in a recent essay subtitled 'The *Cailleach* Writes about the Renaissance.' She also suggests the *spéirbhean*, the sky-woman appearing here in her third emanation as the hag,[15] and therefore a figure of colonial repression, employed to enforce the Anglo-Irish draughtsman's perspective but otherwise ignored:

> He stands too far away
> To hear what she is saying,
> How she routinely measures
> The verse called the midwife's curse
> On all that catches her eye, naming
> The scholar's index finger, the piper's hunch,
> The squint, the rub, the itch of every trade.

Contending with the draftsman's eye trained to reduce the scene to rational perspective, the *cailleach* subdues 'all that catches her eye' to a measured poetry that gives her an ancient, practical power of the curse. The hag represents the poet herself as the return of the repressed, a baroque *extravagance*, who, literally, 'takes us beyond' the framed or bound space of the engraving, aside from the geometric perspective, beyond spatial into poetic measure and, thereby, into unrepresentable time.[16]

A poem from her earlier volume *The Magdalene Sermon*, 'A Voice' (27), achieves the displaced or dream-like effect that the suppression of the *údar* often gives to traditional songs. The poem begins:

> Having come this far, in response
> To a woman's voice, a distant wailing,
> Now he thinks he can distinguish words:
>> *You may come in –*
>> *You are already in.*

The singer, he finds, is a skeleton, but he reasserts his reason and 'takes account' of stones and walls to disperse this voice. Nevertheless, with the woman now lying 'in the bed of the stream,' the voice returns, singing from her 'Gravegoods of horsehair and an ebony peg.' The poem concludes: '"What sort of ornament is this? / What sort of mutilation? Where's / The muscle that called up the sound / The tug of hair and the turned cheek?" The sign persists, in the ridged fingerbone. // And he hears her voice, a wail of strings.' The context that gave rise to this poem is sufficiently removed that we can only guess at it; the distance our speculation travels becomes, in a sense, the point of the poem. We can speculate that it alludes to a ballad – 'Two Sisters' – in which one jealous sister drowns another to marry the widower and then makes of her sister's 'little finger bones' a fiddle-peg and of her hair the fiddle strings that can only play a song that reveals her murder to the husband.[17] Consequently, the body of fact which would have validated a song rendition, the *údar*, must here itself be a traditional song – Child Ballad 10 long ago adapted into Donegal Irish – rather than any account of the original murder.

Here, we must pause in our discussion of Ní Chuilleanáin's indirect use of ballads, to which we will return, to say that this use of uncited ballads or popular tales frequently and traditionally entails radical revision or even deconstruction of the original folk reference. For example, Merriman's 'Midnight Court' gains force by substituting for the beautiful vision of Ireland in the *aisling* affrontive spokeswomen for real Irish females. In the 'Sirens' episode of *Ulysses*, Bloom punctures a ballad session in the Grand Ormond Hotel that revolves about '*Love and War . . .* God be with old times' (220) with a silent affirmation of the present moment: 'Who fears to speak of nineteen four? Time to be shoving' (234). Perhaps the most thorough deconstruction of the Otherworld, which Ciaran Carson remaps to include all utopias, the ideal republic of the French philosophes, United Ireland, the Union, narcotic or alcoholic stupors, heaven, all places for which we are asked to sacrifice the present moment, occurs in his volume of 77 long-lined sonnets in *The Twelfth of Never* (1998), a volume which concludes with this sestet:

> Of maidens, soldiers, presidents and plants I've sung;
> Of fairies, fishes, horses, and of headless men;
> Of beings from the lowest to the highest rung –
>
> With their long ladder propped against the gates of Heaven,
> They're queued up to be rewarded for their grand endeavour,
> And receive their campaign haloes on the Twelfth of Never.

('Envoy,' 89)

In *The Brazen Serpent*, Ní Chuilleanáin adapts the complex poem 'Following' from 'She Moved through the Fair,' already a thorough revision by Padraic Colum of a traditional song 'Our Wedding Day.' In Colum's song, the woman's love-pledge and then her jilting of her lover achieve a mystery that is heightened by her return in a dream – 'So softly she entered, her feet made no din.' Two poems after *'Following her coffin in a dream . . . ,'* 'Following' echoes some of Colum's second stanza – 'She stepped away from me and she moved through the fair, / And fondly I watched her go here and go there' – but in this case the *aisling* is her father whom the woman tracks through a masculinized landscape:

> So she follows the trail of her father's coat through the fair
> Shouldering past beasts packed solid as books,
> And the dealing men nearly as slow to give way –
> A block of a belly, a back like a mountain,
> A shifting elbow like a plumber's bend –

She traces her father's 'light footsteps' through a bog into an otherworld so haunted by its past – 'gesturing trunks,' 'Hands of women' shroud-sewers – that, when she overtakes her father, patriarchal in his fine clothes and amid his orderly library, we are prepared for the return of the repressed, in which something like her own nature, incorporated into these books and this setting, breaks out, through progressively energetic enjambments, from its confinement:

> The smooth foxed leaf has been hidden
> In a forest of fine shufflings,
> The square of white linen
> That held three drops
> Of her heart's blood is shelved

> Between the gatherings
> That go to make a book –
> The crushed flowers among the pages crack
> The spine open, push the bindings apart.
>
> (32)

The last two lines echo the awakening of Galatea in 'Pygmalion's Image,' the important opening poem of *The Magdalene Sermon* and itself a revision of Patrick Kavanagh's 'Pygmalion.' In transforming Colum's slow air, Ní Chuilleanáin reassigns gender roles and gains a haunting, unconventional third-person voice, but she also suggests, paradoxically, that when she, like Galatea, sprouts 'her green leaf of language,' she gestures toward the 'Real,' toward something of bestial and human nature beyond the margins of the father's books and order.

In the dark heart of *The Brazen Serpent*, Ní Chuilleanáin, probably writing out of that de-shelled fragility that follows deaths of loved ones, touches on another margin of language and *the Real*: the relation of language to the inexpressibly atrocious, traumatic, or unspeakable events that are encountered or glimpsed but never assimilated into consciousness. 'Passing Over in Silence,'[18] first entitled *Praeteritio* (a rhetorical term meaning I will not speak of something about which I cannot remain silent), begins:

> She never told what she saw in the wood;
> There were no words for the stench,
> The floated offal, the burnt patches.
> She kept the secret of the woman lying
> In darkness breathing hard,
> A hooked foot holding her down.
> And held her peace about the man who waited
> Beside the lettered slab. He sang:

These particularly disturbing glimpses of this first stanza, which suggest murder and rape, insinuate cancer. As John Kerrigan says:

> Once we gather, from other poems, that the 'hooked foot' is cancer, it can only intensify our awareness that secrecy is part of the poem's subject, as well as its characteristic means, because it deals with the poet's sense of guilt that she cannot but be too transparent a reporter of what she saw.
>
> (92)

We are not permitted to read the lettered slab, but we hear the man's song concerning a barmaid who wept silently for 'the pierced head, / The tears our Saviour shed' and thereby, according to the terms of some *geasa*, extended forgiveness to the man. Bound by her own reticence, the principal 'she' of the poem, nevertheless, records the benefits of bearing witness to suffering.

'Vierge Ouvrante' undertakes a similar indirect commentary on the inexpressibility of human suffering. Here, we enter another architectural structure, perhaps an enlargement of a reliquary, representing the Virgin's body and meant to harbor bones of martyrs or saints. Instead, we glimpse photographs of violated corpses, as we move through increasingly darker rooms to view the body of the Virgin herself, or her violated successors, restrained by ropes or routines from even writing. She can only 'commit / To the long band of memory' until she unwinds withershins as she discharges this memory of violation and fills this space 'full of the stuff, sticky / White as a blue-bleached sheet in the sun' (*Brazen Serpent*, 37). This shining, seminal 'blank chronicle of thread' overexposes and blots out any clear representations of this dark history, women's suffering which must remain secreted within the body represented by the Virgin's icon.

## The body in Irish and English poetry

Discussion of the body in Irish and English poetry returns us to the seventeenth-century history that divides the two islands. Ní Chuilleanáin invokes the Counter-Reformation in Europe when she recalls her own discovery of the body in art. In her twentieth year, she was viewing the paintings in Berlin's Dahlem Gemäldegalerie when she stepped through a door out of the darkness of Lowlands art into the dazzle of Correggio's *Leda*, 'full of blue and white, narrative space, and perversity' ('Acts...,' 576). Ní Chuilleanáin sharpens the contrast between what she calls 'Brownish Rembrandts' from the Calvinist Netherlands and this Mediterranean nude:

> Here was the body at the centre of a story, female and pleased in all its dimensions. I was suddenly back in a world before the upheaval of the Reformation, before the Protestant war on icons of the body, rituals, and material ceremonies.

Correggio's painting helped Ní Chuilleanáin discover the importance of what she calls 'the life of the body,' not only to history but also to 'the way we apprehend language or visible beauty.' It also must have drawn her soon after to Correggio's great ceiling mural in the Duomo of Parma which becomes the subject of 'Fireman's Lift,' the opening poem in *The Brazen Serpent* (1995). Recently, Ní Chuilleanáin said of this poem, 'When I found myself compelled to write about Correggio's *Assumption of the Virgin*, . . . I could only concentrate on one aspect, the way it shows bodily effort and the body's weight' ('Acts . . . ,' 575, 578).

In this massive mural on the cupola of the Duomo in Parma, which Cecil Gould praises as 'perhaps the greatest *tour de force* in Italian art' (114), saints and angels are depicted merging into a vortex of torsos and faces, legs and arms, lifting the Virgin toward heaven and a waiting Christ. In the mass of her body, the angels' efforts, and the colposcopic view of the cervical cupola, the painting could be said to reflect and celebrate the feminine body. Of course at the height of the camera/cervix, Christ waits, as if he were Irigaray's *kore* – a diminished man or the gyneco-logical philosopher's reflected pupil – preoccupying Mary's space.[19] On the other hand, the figure of Christ, diminished, slightly off-center, and embryonic, seems more swaddler than savior, an about-to-be-reborn Christ, still a resident of his mother's assumed body.

In 'Fireman's Lift' (*Brazen Serpent*, 10–11), the dome added to a Roman-esque church in Parma participates gymnastically in the Assumption of the Virgin. The spiraling, ascending interaction of art and architecture, characteristic of Baroque buildings, was first suggested by the work of Michaelangelo, according to art critics Bearden and Holty:

> In the passionate and often unfinished volumes of his last sculptures, in the restless and flamelike action of his frescoes (especially such works as *The Brazen Serpent*...) were born the mannerisms of the baroque style. (129)

By widespread consensus, however, the true proto-Baroque painter was Correggio: 'the most precocious of the great masters of the High Renais-sance, who seems to us today to have been in reality a Baroque painter born a hundred years too soon...' 'More than any other painter, Correg-gio prefigures the Baroque.'[20] Ní Chuilleanáin's enjambed lines, alliterat-ive pauses, and internal rhyme or assonantal chimes project the sound incrementally and thereby imitate this energetic collective heaving up of Mary's carnality, which becomes a 'fireman's lift' of 'teams of angelic arms,' a Baroque collusion of paint, plaster, parapet and squinch, arch and architrave:

The back making itself a roof
The legs a bridge, the hands
A crane and a cradle.

Their heads bowed over to reflect on her
Fair face and hair so like their own
As she passed through their hands. We saw them
Lifting her, the pillars of their arms

(Her face a capital leaning into an arch)
As the muscles clung and shifted
For a final purchase together
Under her weight as she came to the edge of the cloud.

When we recognize that this depiction of a joyful boosterism by which Mary reaches heaven complements as it contrasts with contemporary paintings of the rescue-squad deposition of Christ's body, then we see how the poem elevates the feminine side of Catholicism as well as woman's body. This recognition becomes enforced by the point of view. As has been noted, frequently Ní Chuilleanáin's poems maintain their secrets of plot by dispersing point of view. In this poem, the poet follows Correggio:

> The whole of the zone of the Duomo cupola containing the angels is tilted in the direction of the spectator advancing east from the nave, and this introduces a new and dynamic principle. . . . The idea of forceful communion between the spectator and the figures in the painting . . . is now applied to murals.[21]

Similarly, Ní Chuilleanáin invites the reader immediately into the poem: 'I was standing beside you looking up / Through the big tree of the cupola.' Later, when 'we stepped / / Back, as the painter longed to / . . . / We saw the work entire . . . ,' the point of view shifts out of an authorial perspective fixed in space and time. We enter, in fact, the perspective of memory ('This is what love sees, that angle') as the dates – 1962, when the student poet visited Parma with her mother, and 1994, when her mother died and she wrote this poem to her – indicate to us. Now we can recognize that the opening *you* must be primarily her mother for whom, amid an uncertainty that the title and joking tone suggest, the poet hopes, desires, and composes an equally loving assumption. In the words *purchase* and *weight*, in the adhesive *u* syllables – *usc*, *ung, urch, und, oud* – and in the drawn-out closing hectasyllabic, the closing lines emphasize that body goes with soul in this final hoist toward the terminal bourn: 'As the muscles clung and shifted / For a final purchase together / Under her weight as she came to the edge of the cloud.'

In a manner analogous to Correggio's, and later Bernini's, 'conflation of painting and stucco with real and simulated architecture' where 'the eye was meant to be deceived and to accept the illusionist convention that the architecture merged into the painted or half-painted heaven of the ceiling,'[22] Ní Chuilleanáin's poetry resists containment, within the literal or physical or domestic, as she wanders beyond borders and margins and walls of structures. She often represents such traversing of thresholds and boundaries in relation to architecture. In 'The Architectural Metaphor,' we tour a convent which was founded 'Here, a good mile on the safe side of the border / Before the border was changed' (*Brazen Serpent*, 14–15). This feminine space contains secret recesses that sequester versions of the self or deliver qualified rebirths. Speaking of such spaces, Ní Chuilleanáin has described her 'dreams about houses . . . in which you particularly find there's an extra room. . . . I was interested in those before I ever read Freud on the interpretation of dreams . . . the house and the body both come into that.'[23]

Whether this greater interest in the body is a distinctive feature of Irish poetry or, simply, of interest to Ní Chuilleanáin as woman and Catholic, we nevertheless can trace this emphasis back to the seventeeth century, to the Counter-Reformation and the Baroque period in art. Martin Jay identifies a way of seeing which – limited neither by gender nor sect – he calls 'Baroque vision.' His terse characterization of philosophical manifestations of the Baroque may be usefully related to Ní Chuilleanáin's shifting perspectives and her sudden, strange exposures of the sacred:

In philosophical terms, although no one system can be seen as its correlate, Leibniz's pluralism of monadic viewpoints, Pascal's meditations on paradox, and the Counter Reformation mystics' submission to vertiginous experiences of rapture might all be seen as related to baroque vision. Moreover, the philosophy it favored self-consciously eschewed the model of intellectual clarity expressed in a literal language purified of ambiguity. Instead, it recognized the inextricability of rhetoric and vision, which meant that images were signs and that concepts always contained an irreducibly imagistic component.

Citing the contemporary French writer Christine Buci-Glucksman, Jay argues that 'the baroque self-consciously revels in the contradictions between surface and depth, disparaging as a result any attempt to reduce the multiplicity of visual spaces into any one coherent essence' and thereby opposes 'the absolute ocularcentrism of its Cartesian perspectivalist rival.' Jay cites Buci-Glucksman because he supports her argument that Baroque perspective and classical Albertian perspectives continue to the present as antithetical esthetics: 'It is precisely the explosive power of baroque vision that is seen as the most significant alternative to the hegemonic visual style we have called Cartesian perspectivalism' (16).

Whether Protestant or Catholic, the Irish poet dwells near the unreformed precincts where body and spirit cohabit and within memory of the Oath of Adjuration, the passage from the Penal Laws that granted identity and privilege for those who would forswear in an *ab*juration that

> in the sacrament of the Lord's-supper, there is not any transubstantiation of the elements of bread and wine into the body and blood of Christ, at or after the consecration … and that the adoration of the Virgin Mary … and the sacrifice of the mass, as they are now used in the church of Rome, are superstititious and idolatrous.[24]

Unlike rhetorical language, poetic language entertains negations, so that, for example, when the Wordsworthian sonnet says, 'That neither present time, nor years unborn / Could to my sight that heavenly face restore,' that image of his daughter remains uneffaced in the poetic imagination. The energy generated by an ideology's denial of image must contribute to image-building in the poet, a notion implicit in Derek Mahon's 'Consolations of Philosophy' which, in the manner of Ní Chuilleanáin, begins with the body's envelope:

> When we start breaking up in the wet darkness
> And the rotten boards fall from us, and the ribs
> Crack under the constriction of tree-roots
> And the seasons slip from the fields unknown to us,
>
> Of, then there will be the querulous complaining
> From citizens who had never dreamt of this –
> Who, shaken to the bone in their stout boxes
> By the latest bright cars, will not inspect them

And, kept awake by the tremors of new building,
Will not be there to comment. When the broken
Wreath bowls are speckled with rain-water
And the grass grows wild for want of a caretaker,

There will be time to live through in the mind
The lives we might have lived, and get them right;
To lie in silence listening to the wind
Mourn for the living through the livelong night.

(42)

The wry tone questions both a disembodied afterlife and the resurrection of the body, but the poet 'can [only] embody truth,' to paraphrase Yeats's last letter.[25]

Although the Anglican creed affirms 'the resurrection of the body,' as a child in Belfast Michael Longley would not have encountered representations of Christ's assumption within his own church. Whereas he would have been offered an empty cross as icon, to emphasize Christ's resurrection, in 'The Linen Workers' he comes to represent Christ's assumption with its gritty bodily excrescences and to transpose that empty spot into a cavity:

Christ's teeth ascended with him into heaven:
Through a cavity in one of his molars
The wind whistles: he is fastened for ever
By his exposed canines to a wintry sky.

A more recent poem represents poetic invention weighing against the 'terrible yawn' of a dying mother-in-law. The second and third of three stanzas read:

Your mouth has opened so wide you appear to scream.
We will need something to close your terrible yawn.
I hoke around in my childhood for objects without
Sharp edges and recover the oval mustard tin.

A daughter strokes your forehead and says 'There. There.'
A daughter holds your hand and says 'I'm sorry.'
I focus on the mustard tin propping your jaw,
On the total absence of the oval mustard tin.

('The Mustard Tin,' *The Weather in Japan*)

This poem has remarkable charm, the source of which is not quickly evident. Brought to the bedside of the dying, the poem knows this is what it's thought to be hired for. The almost flaccid twelve-syllable lines suggest the awkward impotence of a conscientious, protocol-less visitor to the dying. The second quatrain opens with a shocking report, complete and end-stopped, to which the poet responds with a point-less, second-person assessment: 'We will need something. . . .' Confronting this unsociable gape of death, he is reduced to a child-like action of *hoking*, a child's term that blends *poking* and *hacking* to return with the image of the mustard tin, so improbable and ordinary it startles: 'I focus on the mustard tin propping your jaw, / On the total absence of the oval mustard tin.' For one line the poetic image performs its work of palliating before, finally, relenting and going out of focus. The poem is remarkable, and particularly Irish, not because of its ambivalence concerning death but because of the rude intrusion of the body in the opening stanza – 'your eyes stay open and it doesn't seem to hurt' – and again in the fifth line: 'Your mouth has opened so wide you appear to scream.'

For contrast with this embodied poem, we might look at Simon Armitage's 'A Glory' as a contemporary successor to Hardy's representation of the body as a shadow on a stone. This Yorkshire poet, not yet middle-aged, has been called 'the first English poet of serious artistic intent since Philip Larkin to have achieved wide popularity.'[26] In part, his popularity springs from his irreverent, 'ludic' quality derived initially from Muldoon's influence. Whether or not Muldoon is 'the most charismatic poet now writing in Britain and Ireland,' as reviewers have said,[27] he must be the most imitated, certainly so among certain young poets such as Mick Imlah, Alan Jenkins, Ruth Padel, Ian Duhig, and Simon Armitage (the phrase *Muldoids* would be disrespectful for such interesting poets who bear the marks of his influence). To open 'The Dead Sea Poems,' the title poem of his 1995 volume, Simon Armitage writes, 'And I was travelling lightly, barefoot / over bedrock, then through lands that were stitched / with breadplant and camomile. Or was it / burdock. . . .' The beginning *in medias res* and the finicky self-correction ('Or was it . . .') imitates Muldoon in emphasizing the poem's fictionality, as if, as John Bayley says, 'putting poetry . . . in inverted commas.'[28] The poem's self-reflexiveness – here, the poet discovering in ancient caskets within a cave the poems he is about to write – is a characteristic of most of the poets from Northern Ireland, as Christopher Ricks has demonstrated (1985, 51). In *Moon Country* Armitage has written that 'all writing comes from the past, from childhood or innocence or naivety, and from loss, lost lives and lives gone by . . .' (43), or, in 'The Dead Sea Poems' from excavations of his own burials that become the foundation of his poetic scriptures. If Armitage's most personal myth, reflected in this poem and others such as 'The White Hart,' 'Five Eleven Ninety Nine,' 'A Glory,' and the verse-play 'Eclipse,' concerns creation out of nothing or out of the unconscious, the source of this myth remains, of course, inaccessible. In 'The White Hart,' a sequence of prose poems set in Iceland, he begins: 'It comes to me first against the green of the trees, a kind of vacancy, not the creature itself but a whiteness in the image of the creature. As if it had sensed me and moved on, leaving a pure emptiness in its place.'[29]

In his recent volume *CloudCuckooLand*, Armitage risks writing every teenage-poet's snow-angel poem and revises this notion of absence-as-presence in 'A Glory.' Following the usual procedures for snow-angel-making, the 'you' in the poem, presumably a woman, 'Sprang clear of the print / and the angel remained, fixed, countersunk, / open wide, hosting the whole of the sky.' At once an angel, holy spirit, the absent lover, desire, nothing, and the decasyllabic form of the poem itself, 'On ground where snow has given up the ghost / it lies on its own, spread-eagled, embossed, / commending itself, star of its own cause.' The poem ends, 'Angel, / from under the shade and shelter of trees / I keep watch, wait for the dawn to take you, / raise you, imperceptibly, by degree' (3). Because the spilt religion on the snow is acknowledged in the renewed cliché 'given up the ghost' and the blatant but precise balancing of *imperceptibly* and the pun *by degrees*, the poem cancels any ascension or relegates the body to abstractions beyond perception.

## Hughes and Heaney: laureate prose

Writing in the summer of 1970, Ted Hughes attributed certain prevailing attitudes toward the body and nature to the rise of Protestantism: 'The fundamental guiding ideas of our Western Civilization are against Conservation. They derive from Reformed Christianity and from Old Testament Puritanism' (*HWP*, 129). This essay, to which I'll return later, is published in *Winter Pollen*, which with *Shakespeare and the Goddess of Complete Being* comprises his most copious, and perhaps most important, writing in the 1990s. Because this writing helps us to characterize and assess Hughes's career, and because his death and Heaney's Nobel Prize are the most important news for English and Irish poetry in the 1990s, we will give some attention to the prose of these two poets and to their relationship generally.

In early reviews, it was a commonplace to point out Heaney's indebt-edness to Hughes, and Heaney himself acknowledged this, though he has not written often about Hughes. After the enormous success of *North* from 1975 and the cooling reception of Hughes's work after *Crow*, the two poets were often compared on their own terms, but after about 1984, when Hughes became Poet Laureate, Heaney's ascent and Hughes's apparent decline made comparisons rare. Currently, many readers would find more to contrast than compare in the escalation and deescalation of their poetic careers, and current comparisons may have more to do with politics than with poetry. For example, those who applauded Heaney's 1983 'An Open Letter,' his poetic protest against being included in Blake Morrison and Andrew Motion's anthology bearing the title . . . *British Poetry*, probably had also enjoyed this anthology's declaration that Heaney was the 'most important new poet of the last fifteen years.' Morrison and Motion had praised Heaney for being central to this anthol-ogy in which six of the 20 poets anthologized were Irish. In his, by now, familiar rejoinder Heaney wrote, 'My passport's green. / No glass of ours was ever raised / To toast *The Queen*. / / No harm to her nor you who deign / To *God Bless* her as sovereign, / Except that from the start her reign / Of crown and rose / Defied, displaced, would not combine / What I'd espouse.'[30]

In contrast, in this postcolonial era when the House of Lords has been reduced to its Rump, Hughes's more Laureate celebrations of the mon-archy sounded somewhat reactionary and quaint. In a birthday poem for the Queen Mother, he wrote, 'When Britain wins, I feel that I have won. / Whatever Britain does, I feel I have done. / I know my life comes somehow from the sun. / / I hardly understand what I can mean / When I say Britain's Queens and Kings are mine. / How am I all these millions, yet alone?' (*Duchy*, 30). In an explanatory note published first in the *Weekend Telegraph* on the Queen Mother's birthday in 1990, Hughes wrote that a nation gains 'biological resilience' necessary to survive 'the ultimate trial' through a 'sacred myth':

> In Britain's case, when the trial came with the Second World War, our sacred myth, the living symbol of a hidden unity . . . turned out to be the Crown. As it happened . . . the mantle of this palladium settled on the Queen Mother, who was then Queen. . . . For those who fought in and survived the First World War, . . . she was the generation of their wives, and for those who fought in the Second and expected the Third, she was the generation of their mothers.
>
> (*Duchy*, 60)

These apparently antithetical positions of the English Monarchist and the Irish Republican emerge from their occasional poetry and especially from their prose into which the two poets have poured much of their labor over the last decade and which help define each poet for their reading public. In Heaney's case, these essays and lectures must have contributed significantly to his selection by the Nobel committee. Whereas Heaney's four collections of essays and lectures have been spaced over the last 15 years, Hughes published his first book of prose – aside from a very good primer on the making of poems – only in 1992. In that year, his *Shakespeare and the Goddess of Complete Being* appeared as a 500-page elaboration of the idea, which Hughes first expressed in 1971, that 14 of Shakespeare's mature plays conceal the same basic myth, what he calls the 'DNA' of Shakespeare's 'poetic organism' 'which in turn reflected, even in a sense embodied, a daemonic, decisive crisis in the history of England,' as Hughes says in the Foreword to his book (xii). In 1995, Hughes collected his occasional prose – prefaces to others' books, reviews, interviews, and essays, some previously unpublished – under the title *Winter Pollen*. Here, again, that original myth ascribed to Shakespeare and to England in time of crisis, to which we will return, appears in enough guises to suggest it is deeply buried also in Hughes's own psyche.

Heaney's publication of prose has been more progressive and, I believe, deliberate. In 1980, Heaney published *Preoccupations* which characterizes his own poetry and defines his poetic ancestry, including especially Wordsworth, Hopkins, Yeats, and Kavanagh. Heaney also reacts as a colonial subject, aware of the binaries that shape the identity of Irish poetry. In the essay 'Yeats As An Example?,' he writes, 'When, as a young poet, he [Yeats] sought a badge of identity for his own culture, . . . he found this distinctive and sympathetic thing in the magical world view of the country people. It was a conscious counter-culture act against the rationalism and materialism of late Victorian England' (101), a point Heaney repeats in another essay (135). In an essay on Hughes, Larkin, and Hill, Heaney writes, 'The poets of the mother culture, I feel, are now possessed of that defensive love of their territory which was once shared only by those poets whom we might call colonial . . .' (150–1).

In *The Government of the Tongue* (1988), Heaney expanded his poetic horizons to include Chekhov, the Mandelstams, Miroslav Holob, Zbigniew Herbert, Czeslaw Milosz, and Elizabeth Bishop, among others, and he widened his concerns to the function and efficacy of poetry in the face of crisis. *The Place of Poetry*, the shorter Ellmann lectures at Emory University, cleared the way for his Oxford lectures by acknowledging his debt to Irish poets. In his most recent book, *The Redress of Poetry*, the Oxford Lectures, he returns, for the most part, to poetry of the British Isles – Merriman, Clare, Wilde, MacDiarmid, Dylan Thomas – to stake out the strategies and virtues of English dissident poetry or poetry from the Celtic fringe, before driving his stake, if not through the heart of English poetry then through the heart of the modern English poetic canon.

The central essay in the book 'Joy or Night' compares the attitudes toward death expressed in the poetry of Yeats and Larkin, and thus returns to an English poet central to his other two major prose collections. In *Preoccupations*, he had asserted that in Larkin's poetry we hear 'a stripped standard English voice' that leads back to medieval England 'when the Middle Ages are turning secular' and echoes, in turn, *Everyman*, Skelton, Cavalier poetry, Augustan verse, Tennyson, Hopkins, and Hardy. He is 'urban modern man, the insular Englishman, responding to the tones of his own clan, ill at ease when out of his environment. He is a poet, indeed, of composed and tempered English nationalism . . .' (167). In *The Government of the Tongue* Heaney writes that Larkin's 'collected poems would fit happily under the title *Englanders*' (19). Yet, he recalls that Larkin's early attachment to Yeats, before he gravitated toward Hardy's ironic disillusionment, still manifests itself in an 'appetite for sweetness flowing into the breast, for the sensation of revelation, which never deserted him' (16). However, in *The Redress of Poetry*, Heaney argues that the Yeats of 'The Cold Heaven' and 'The Man and the Echo' opposed the sort of nihilism Larkin expressed in his line from 'Aubade': 'Death is no different whined at than withstood' (157). Heaney says of 'Aubade': 'This, for me, is the definitive post-Christian English poem, one that abolishes the soul's traditional pretension to immortality and denies the Deity's immemorial attribute of infinite personal concern' (156). Heaney offers no other explicit examples of this class that Larkin's poem defines, but he raises a host of opponents, those who do not follow Larkin to the bottom of British empiricism.[31] Principally, Heaney employs the Polish poet and Nobel Laureate Czeslaw Milosz as ensign-bearer, coming before and after Heaney's denunciation of this poem with the supportive statements. Heaney writes, 'As Czeslaw Milosz has observed, no intelligent contemporary is spared the pressure exerted in our world by the void, the absurd, the anti-meaning . . . Poetry, Milosz pleads, must not make this concession but maintain instead its centuries-old hostility to reason, science and a science-inspired philosophy' (153). This sounds remarkably like Yeats, in his lifelong tilting with Arnold's 'On the Study of Celtic Literature,' but with a Polish accent.

For example, in the preface to a study of Berkeley, quoted earlier in Chapter 2, Yeats wrote:

> It is customary to praise English empirical genius, English sense of reality, and yet throughout the eighteenth century when her Indian Empire was founded England lived for certain great constructions that were true only in relation to the will.                    (Hone, xix)

By the mid-1930s, in lines quoted earlier in this book, Yeats has reduced Newtonian and Lockean thought to 'the mechanical theory':

> I am convinced that in two or three generations it will become generally known that the mechanical theory has no reality, that the natural and supernatural are knit together, that to escape a dangerous fanaticism we must study a new science.                    (*YE&I*, 518)

This is the Yeats that Larkin's proponents, such as Blake Morrison, assumed had been drubbed and chased from the premises. In 1989 Morrison wrote that English poets had lost interest in Yeats who 'is perceived as marginalized or "not British"....as alien, too, because of his theosophy, because of fairies, *A Vision*.'[32] However, if Morrison glances out the back door, Yeats is back, supported in Heaney's essay by a small army of opponents of the English atheist poem – the Czech poet Miroslav Holob, Wallace Stevens, surprisingly, Hardy ('but not the Hardy to whom Larkin was converted after the strong enchantments of Yeats had failed for him' (152)), Shakespeare, Emily Dickinson, Beckett, Karl Barth, Mozart, and, of course, Milosz and Heaney. Heaney has enlarged what Arnold called the Celtic 'reaction against the despotism of fact' into an alliance of European Catholicism and new-world agnosticism, encircling 'to ring right out' this dour form of English empiricism.

So skillful is Heaney in attaining the higher ground and maintaining his international credentials, that even the most respected English nationalist poet, and critic, Donald Davie – shortly before his death in 1995 – responded to *The Redress of Poetry* with an admiration approaching obeisance:

> In the world of English language poetry Seamus Heaney has...a position of unchallenged authority. And that is a boon for all of us who inhabit that world; one shudders to think how it would have been for the rest of us if that authority, earned by solid accomplishment, had been vested in a person less generous and less prudent....It is

a main part of Heaney's claim upon us that he has offered that romantic role, refused the privileges that it offered him. He has consistently refused, in the face of tempting offers, to be either outlandish or partisan.　　　　　　　　　　　　　　　　　(*Poetry Review*, 38)

Of course by his very position as an Ulster Catholic, Heaney is 'outlandish' *and* 'partisan,' but Davie praises him for his restraint and makes Heaney's authority dependent on this discretion.

It is part of Heaney's discretion that he repudiates Larkin's poem as representative of a narrow category rather than as an expression of the dominant school of English poetry which it may still be. Heaney exempts Hughes from this school when he says, in a 1979 interview, quoted in *Winter Pollen*:

> It's a voice that has no truck with irony because his dialect is not like that . . . I mean, the voice of a generation – the Larkin voice, the Movement voice, even the Eliot voice, the Auden voice – the manners of that speech . . . are those of literate English middle-class culture, and I think Hughes's great cry and call and bawl is that English language and English poetry is longer and deeper and rougher than that.
>
> (Haffenden, 73–4)

Hughes, we know, was one of Heaney's influences, and their poetic exchanges have probably profited both of them. For example, in his inaugural lecture from the Oxford Chair of Poetry in 1989, when Heaney seeks emblems for poetry's function of *redressing* – to rebalance wrongs and to bring the society back to its rightful course, he writes that 'the poet stands like an embodiment of both the loaded scales and the trembling pointer needle' (McDonald, 188). In 1992, Hughes offered an explanation for his Laureate poem 'The Unicorn': 'The germ of this whole composition was the idea of a magnetized needle . . . searching out and pointing to North. . . .' He then converts the horn of the Unicorn, the ancient symbol of England, into the 'balancing finger of the needle, . . . the pillar of a pair of scales' (61). Beyond observing what looks like Hughes's borrowing from Heaney, we might notice how each laureate adapts his emblems to his laureateship: Hughes to the position he must fill as nationalist poet; Heaney to the international laureateship for which the universalizing of these images prepares and qualifies him.

As representative of a more important exchange, in a 1976 lecture in *Preoccupations*, Heaney speaks of the Northern vigor of Hughes's poetry which 'has much to do with this matter of consonants that take the measure of his vowels like calipers, or stud the line with rivets' (154). In this simple statement, which Heaney has borrowed from Hughes's 1967 poem 'Thistles,' we glimpse the distinctions that Heaney was developing in *Wintering Out* and *North* between the Irish language – feminine, vowel-dominated, and liquid – and Saxon English – masculine, consonantal, and stony. In an early essay, 'Feeling Into Words,' Heaney extends such associations into the myths that underlie cultures:

> There is an indigenous territorial numen, a tutelar of the whole island, call her Mother Ireland, Kathleen Ní Houlihan, the poor old woman, the Shan Van Vocht, whatever; and her sovereignty has been temporarily usurped or infringed by a new male cult whose founding fathers were Cromwell, William of Orange and Edward Carson, and whose godhead is incarnate in a rex or caesar resident in a palace in London. *(Preoccupations, 57)*

By association, Heaney enrolls the consonantal Hughes in the masculine, imperial power when he writes, 'His consonants are the Norsemen, the Normans, the Roundheads in the world of his vocables, hacking and hedging and hammering down the abundance and luxury and possible lasciviousness of the vowels' (154).

In this 1976 summary, Heaney characterizes Hughes's idea of a nation, spiritually divided from itself, in which the masculine principle subdues and represses the feminine principle. This repression is manifest in the structures and conventions that govern the nation, in the structure and conventions of its language, and in the psyches of individuals. Heaney's summary about warrior consonants hammering down 'luxury and possible lasciviousness of the vowels' suggests this dissociation of sensibility as Hughes had found it in Shakespeare's narrative poems and plays, as expressed by Hughes in a 1971 preface to Shakespearean lyrics. Hughes derives from 'Venus and Adonis' and 'The Rape of Lucrece' the following pattern found in the plays: one part of nature – in the form of the rigorously chaste hero Adonis – separates himself from another aspect – the goddess of love – and is gored to death by the lustful boar who springs from Persephone who represents this rejection and repression. This dissociation completes itself in the next narrative poem when the puritanical governor erupts as the rapist. Hughes argues that Shakespeare employs this myth of repression repeatedly because he finds it driving the English Reformation, the Puritan Revolt, the ascension of science, and eventually the Industrial Revolution that creates modern England. In fetchingly amateurish scholarship – repetitive, undocumented, enthusiastic – Hughes explores this theory for the 517 pages of *Shakespeare and the Goddess of Complete Being.*

As a consequence, Hughes has become the most outspoken devotee of the Goddess, although Heaney, like Montague, Graves, and others, has been her priest or acolyte. For Heaney, in the poems and prose of the mid-1970s, this feminine principle was the nationalist *aisling*-victim in 'Feeling into Words,' the lay of the land in 'Bone Dreams,' or a northern earth-goddess Nerthus in the sacrifice poems in *North.* Perhaps because of criticism from Boland, Cullingford, and others against what may be seen as projections of male desire, explicit references to the Goddess have nearly vanished from Heaney's poetry in the 1980s and 1990s.

If Heaney has actually become, as Donald Davie says, *prudent,* Hughes seems both imprudent and parochial in his association of the Goddess with the national bard and in his identification of patriotism with the matriarchal, in the person of the Queen Mother. Yet, behind Hughes's local application rests a more universal and ancient faith. In that 1970 review with which we began this section, he wrote:

> The subtly apotheosized misogyny of Reformed Christianity is pro-
> portionate to the fanatic rejection of Nature, and the result has been
> to exile man from Mother Nature – from both inner and outer nature.
> The story of the mind exiled from Nature is the story of Western
> Man. . . .                                                    (*HWP*, 129)

Hughes's ecological beliefs, as straightforward as they seem, could be confused with other critiques of capitalism's violation of nature. For example, Jean Joseph Goux summarized a contemporary Marxist materialism:

> Law, reason, order, form, controlling power are not preexisting tran-
> scendent principles, constituting a logic or logos to be conceived out-
> side of or apart from matter in movement; the existence of a dialectic
> of nature means, in other words, that matter and its organizational
> laws are one. Hence thought, consciousness, and mind again become
> functions of nature, products of matter when it is organized in a
> certain way.                                                      (235)

Goux goes on to assert, 'To think of material organizational potency as including the production of concepts, to make mind the offspring of organized matter, is to explode the *paterialist barrier* between concept and materiality' (236).

Yet, Hughes would not replace conceptualization with a concept but rather with a living in nature in order to recover a creaturely instinct and appreciation. If this sounds as *utopian* as Goux's formulation, at least it does not take place in *no place*. Hughes would return us to the local, the parochial, and the particular places of this world. The detachment from nature is a detachment from place, as we see in the zoo-bound creature of Hughes's title-poem 'Wolfwatching,' a wolf who represents man's 'fanatic rejection of nature,' a creature who, no more than man, has been divorced from 'both inner and outer nature':

> He's hanging
> Upside down on the wire
> Of non-participation.
> He's a tarot-card, and he knows it.
> He can howl at night
> And dawn will pick up the same card
> And see him painted on it, with eyes
> Like doorframes in a desert
> Between nothing and nothing.

(Wolfwatching)

In representing such placelessness as the basis for nihilism, Hughes's poem could be read as a rebuke or, perhaps, an anatomy of Larkin's nihilistic anxiety. It may also serve as a cautionary reminder, which Heaney may not need, that there's a world of difference between this wolf's nothing of rootlessness and the nothing of imagination grounded in memory of nature and home, what Heaney himself calls, in referring to his mother's absence, 'a space / Utterly empty, utterly a source'[33] ('Clearances').

## Recent poetry and publishing in England and Ireland

Aside from the poetic market's 'spike' of Heaney's 1995 Nobel Prize, as seen from England the poetic news of the 1990s must be Hughes. Of course, Hughes and Heaney frequently emerged together before the public eye, as in the 1997 launching of *The School Bag*, which they co-edited, or resided there together in the tandem of their aspirated *H*s as the chthonic Northern presences *Hughes* & *Heaney*. Further kept in public view by his tactful negotiation between his private life and public role as the English Laureate, Hughes advanced in the public's appraisal by the publication of *Birthday Letters* in 1998 and by his death in the autumn of that year from a cancer whose intimacy with his body had been kept secret from the public.

Hughes's standing relative to the best English poets of this age was enhanced by the self-portrayal of loutishness in Larkin's *Selected Letters*, published in 1992, and Hill's dour self-isolation and condescension expressed somewhat in his *Canaan* (1996) but especially in *The Triumph of Love* (1998), both works otherwise admirable. Probably for a combination of reasons, Hughes's readership, always impressive, enlarged considerably, so that in the year of his death, according to Whitaker's *Book Track's Book Sales Yearbook*, his sales led all authors in the 'Literature and Poetry' category, grossing over one and a quarter million pounds. His translation of Ovid, along with several other editions, contributed to the success of that classical writer as the second top-selling poet in the UK. In a list that also includes Heaney as seventh largest grossing author, Betjeman as 11th, and Plath and Eliot as 17th and 19th, Hughes reappears in the 14th position as editor of selections of Shakespeare's (1971; rev. 1991) and Coleridge's (1996) verse, *The School Bag*, and presumably Plath's *Collected Poems* (1981).

The surge in Hughes's sales contributed to a general growth in the UK of interest in poetry that began with the 1990s. Up until the beginning of that decade, poetry production had grown incrementally from about 500 titles in 1955[34] to 707 in 1975 to 975 in 1990. By 1995 the number of new titles had more than doubled to 1944, and by 1998 that number had reached 2496 new titles, with the first half of 1999 running only a little behind the year of *Birthday Letters*.[35] Although these figures would have included new titles by Northern Irish publishers such as Blackstaff, the great majority of these new books would have come from England, from major literary publishers such as Faber & Faber and Penguin, but also from predominantly or exclusively publishers of poetry such as Bloodaxe and Carcanet. In light of this evidence, the decision by Oxford late in 1998 to terminate their venerable but steadily vitiated poetry list should be seen as a kind of geriatricide that does not reflect on the general health of English poetry publishing.

Of course, any declaration of poetry's health based merely on publishing activity and new titles must be qualified in several ways. The sensational and controversial aspects of the relationship of Hughes and Plath as well as Hughes's previous reticence and his dignity must account as much as poetic virtue in the success of *Birthday Letters*. More importantly, 1998 is merely the culmination of promotional efforts to renew or broaden the English tradition of poetry, efforts which themselves contribute to a promotional tradition going back to the 1930s and employing *New* in the title of anthologies or journals. More recently, the energetic pitch of Morrison and Motion's *Penguin Book of Contemporary British Poetry* (1982), which in part extended the Movement tradition, was countered by *The New Poetry* (Bloodaxe, 1993) whose editors promoted Bloodaxe's pluralistic, decentralizing ambitions in part by presenting among 55 poets 15 published by Bloodaxe, while representing no poets from the Faber list and only two from Oxford University Press.

In spite of its evident biases, *The New Poetry* may have contributed to the idea for the 1994 major campaign promoting the 'New Generation Poets,' 20 under-forty poets selected by a panel of judges, announced with fanfare in *Vogue* and major journals and newspapers, and presented in a series of readings in numerous venues throughout the month of May. In an edition of *Poetry Review* promoting 'the New Generation,' the editor Peter Forbes concluded from answers these poets gave to a questionnaire that 'the only unifying feature of their responses was their relative disdain for English poetry of the 20th century and their enthusiasm for American and European poetry' (4). Forbes sees these younger poets as opposed to those poet/critic/editors who had extended the English poetic establishment, standing independently apart from the 'clear line from the Movement, through Ian Hamilton's Neo-Movement of the '70s to Blake Morrison, Andrew Motion and Craig Raine in the '80s' (6).

Forbes ascribes to Bloodaxe a special role in fostering the New Generation:

> Only one key institution has played a significant role in the rise of the New Generation (besides this magazine, of course): Bloodaxe Books. Without such an independent, energetic, and hospitable publisher, prepared to back such disparate talents as Armitage, Maxwell, Jamie, Duhig, Stainer, Garrett and Herbert . . . these multiple fruits may well have withered on the vine. (6)

However much we might agree with his praise of Bloodaxe, which I would endorse, Forbes's assertion spawns ironies. First, he ignores the acknowledgment on the journal's first page which begins: 'Very many people have helped to make the New Generation possible . . . ,' where by 'people' he means neither the poets nor their parents but 15 'institutions' whose names are set off in a little box. Secondly, the New Generation did not rise; they were created by committee. Finally, whatever their anti-establishment stance in 1994, eight of these poets, some previously published by Bloodaxe, are in the year 2001 published by

Faber, and some have inherited the sort of editing roles once filled by Raine, Morrison, and Motion. One of the most independent poets in England, Carol Ann Duffy, who has maintained the same virtuous, small-scale publisher Anvil Press throughout her career, was a popular favorite and apparent runner-up to Andrew Motion for the 1999 appointment to the English Poet Laureateship. Many journalists and critics expressed regret that this lively and inventive poet was passed over for the poetically staid Motion; far more than commented on the irony of her 'standing' for this monarchial position. Even with the efforts to widen the poetic franchise and to limit peerages in the poetic establishment, the success of poetic boosterism in England says more about the important role of poetry within English culture and about the very idea of English culture, than it does about the quality of poetry being written. The persistence of what is called, accurately or not, the English, Hardyesque line of ironic, elegiac poetry, of which the official success of Larkin's biographer Andrew Motion may be symptomatic evidence, may account for the relative marginalization, or at least undervaluation, over the century of such independent British poets as David Jones, Basil Bunting, Charles Tomlinson, Tony Harrison, Douglas Dunn, Peter Reading, Tom Raworth, Roy Fisher, and J. H. Prynne. Likewise, overemphasis of the poet's public role within English culture may contribute to the not fully realized promise of gifted poets closer to the English mainstream such as Auden, Hill, Raine, Fenton,and perhaps even Hughes.

Consequently, like the overhyping of the New Generation, the prediction of Morrison and Motion nearly two decades ago sounds hollow:

> In 'How to Read' (1928) Ezra Pound claimed that 'the language is now in the keeping of the Irish.' But just as Auden and others rescued the reputation of English poetry in the 1930s, so in the 1970s and 80s a new generation of poets has started to do the same.          (16)

If we measure the success of English and Irish poets in relation to the relative size of those populations, it now seems as if the Irish poets have been more successful in tapping into the artesian sources of poetry and of renewing poetic language. Thomas Kinsella, who is comparable to Hill in many respects, seems now the greater poet, as the astute critic David Wheatley has noted:

> A poet like Thomas Kinsella . . . has shown that it is possible to address public themes without sacrificing any of the modernist high seriousness to which Hill plainly aspires. But Kinsella also possesses what

Hill so singularly fails to display in *Canaan* – a sense of humour. This is a shame, because Hill at his best is a gifted writer and a powerful antidote to all that is facile and complacent in English verse.   (10)

Seamus Heaney, still in mid-flight, now seems likely to outdistance Hughes. Muldoon and Mahon have been declared models for English poets;[36] Carson and McGuckian, in quite different modes, are both traditional and totally revisionary in ways that make most English poetry seem placid. Montague, Ní Chuilleanáin, and Ní Dhomhnaill, if properly read by English readers, would earn their place among the most treasured poets. Conor O'Callaghan, who has developed his formal skills by studying Auden and James Fenton, as well as Muldoon, may be as good as any young poet in Britain. Perhaps among major Irish poets only Eavan Boland, who is published by Carcanet, and Faber poets Heaney and Muldoon, have been properly read and appreciated in England. Derek Mahon and Michael Longley, who have had English publishers and a large English following, maintain their readership in spite of their sometimes criticized shift toward longer lines and radical imaginative swervings.

The bases for these judgments concerning the relative worth of English and Irish poets, secondary to the reading of individual poems and certainly not fully illustrated in this study, would not be available to many English readers. Paradoxically, this is true mostly because of the success of publishers within the Republic of Ireland. Whereas Salmon, Dedalus, and New Writers presses have published regional poets or some competent poets who have no special appeal to British readers, the Gallery Press, situated near Oldcastle in County Meath, has developed one of the fullest and most illustrative poetry lists in the British Isles. Especially after the death of Liam Miller in 1987 and the closing of Dolmen Press, major poets such as Derek Mahon, John Montague, Ciaran Carson, Medbh McGuckian, and Nuala Ní Dhomhnaill have gravitated to Gallery where their books receive expert editing from Peter Fallon and good production. Because Gallery's priority has been successful distribution within its own island, and then within North America, Gallery books have not always been widely available within Britain. Partly as a consequence of this limited distribution, as well as of the relative disregard of poetry from the Republic by *Poetry Review* and other journals, poetry from below the border in Ireland has often been underread and undervalued. It might be said, then, that the exchange between English and Irish poetry has diminished although it has hardly stopped.

## Heaney and English poetry: a postscript

In 1998, several weeks prior to the death of Ted Hughes, which had been foreseeable by his friends, Seamus Heaney published in the *New Yorker*, and later revised, a poetic response to Hughes's *Birthday Letters*, poems to Sylvia Plath which themselves had been published earlier in that year to a clamor of divergent critical views. One aspect of *Birthday Letters'* controversy was Hughes's management of intimacy, his disclosure of some secrets about himself and Plath and his masking of others. In his poem 'On First Looking into Ted Hughes's "Birthday Letters,"' Heaney avoids intruding on these intimate spaces by referring to Hughes very indirectly, as *oneself* and *one* or through kennings, and by translating Hughes's places of grief into his own: 'a bridge I had passed under,' 'a listening post,' and 'railway lines / Shining in silence,' all suggestive of Heaney poems. In its revised form, this poem, now entitled 'On His Work in the English Tongue,' brings the poem further from Hughes, shifting his name from the title to the dedication, and closer to Heaney: 'Over the railway lines at Anahorish –.'[37]

In fact, as both titles suggest, Heaney's poem is about translation, 'On First Looking Into . . .' not Chapman's Homer but the origin of the English literary tradition and the initial work on the English syllabus, which Heaney himself had just translated. The revised title suggests, consistent with the quotation from Wordsworth earlier, that all poetry translates from a primary language of the 'soul on its lonely path.' Responding to the deep grief of the *Birthday Letters*, Heaney would lead Hughes, who was not past 'understanding or telling / or forgiveness. / But often past oneself,' to *Beowulf* and the solace of Hughes's own tradition.

To leave no doubt that he refers to the English tradition, rather than merely *Beowulf*, Heaney relates Hughes's suffering to the First World War poets and the soul-sickening effects of the Great War on England which had become one of Hughes's major themes:

> Passive suffering: who said it was disallowed
> As a theme for poetry? Already in 'Beowulf'
> The dumbfounding of woe, the stunt and stress
> Of hurt-in-hiding is the best of it –

We know that Arnold spoke so of 'passive suffering' when he withdrew 'Empedocles Upon Etna' from republication and that Yeats echoed him in omitting the War Poets from his *Oxford Book of Modern Verse*. So, we recognize that Heaney is disagreeing with Yeats and extending the tradition of melancholy to which Hughes belongs. At the same time, Heaney's own alliteration and his adaptation of 'heart in hiding' from Hopkins, the Irish poet's first guide to the ancient core of English, makes this poem and the translation it celebrates an act of appropriation.

The lines above introduce Heaney's summary of an episode from *Beowulf*:

> As when King Hrethel's son accidentally kills
> His older brother and snaps the grief-trap shut
> On Hrethel himself, wronged father of the son
> Struck down, honor bound to exact
> The death price from his own surviving son –

We cannot know the extent to which the fate of this ruler, who is forced to be judge/executioner and victim of this execution, may be analogous to Hughes's. The most direct reference to the English poet concerns a night on Dartmoor when the Irish poet recalls 'night tremors':

> The power station wailing in its pit
> Under the heath, as if Lear's breaking heart
> And Cordelia's breaking silence called to you,
> Chooser of poem light, ploughshare of fields unsunned.

Perhaps straining to produce these kennings for Hughes, Heaney stumbles into the awkward pun 'poem light' more appropriate to late Auden and Larkin and that tradition of the 'literate English middle-class culture' Hughes opposes, as Heaney argues in the interview with Haffenden, quoted earlier.

Yet, finally, the poem comments on Heaney's place more than Hughes's. As the *Irish Times* reviewer of this translation said, referring to the book's preface: 'Heaney has gradually come to feel that *Beowulf* was part of his "voice-right"; to translate it was to make the strongest possible claim for a native place in the English poetic tradition.'[38]

The translation may claim even more than that. The final section of the poem closes with a restatement concerning the uniqueness of poetry as an expression of the otherwise ineffable:

> Soul has its scruples. Things not to be said.
> Things for keeping, that can keep the small hours' gaze
> Open and steady. Things for the *aye* of God

> And for poetry. Which is, as Milosz says,
> 'A dividend from ourselves,' a tribute paid
> By what we have been true to. A thing allowed.

Heaney returns to his European-Catholic ombudsman Milosz whom he invokes in the essay 'Death or Night?' In this translation that carries Anglo-Saxon into Hiberno-English and Scots-Irish terms such as 'bawn,' 'steadings,' 'hoked,' and 'thole,' Heaney suggests that the native place of English literature may have become Ireland as much as anywhere else. In Heaney's pun, even the yea-saying of God, the theological version of Molly Bloom's great *Yes*, has been translated from standard English into the local affirmation *aye*. Within the economy of modern English and Irish poetry, the greater dividend of which Heaney speaks may arise from and accrue mostly to Irish poets.

# Notes

## Preface

1. See Declan Kiberd, *Inventing Ireland*, Seamus Deane, *Celtic Revivals* and *Strange Country*, Edna Longley, *Poetry in the Wars* and *The Living Stream*, and Peter McDonald, *Mistaken Identities*. Shane Murphy's survey in *Graph* of the last decade's writing on Irish identity suggests that Kiberd, Deane, and Longley have not exhausted the subject.
2. Julia Kristeva, *Étrangers à nous-même* (Paris: Fayard, 1988), 26–7. Passage translated by, and cited in, Cronin, 5.

## Chapter 1   Yeats, Hardy, and Poetic Exchange

1. Timothy Webb, 'Yeats and the English,' in *The Internationalism of Irish Literature and Drama*, ed. Joseph McMinn (Savage, MD: Barnes & Noble, 1992), 232–51, 249–50. See also *The Letters of W. B. Yeats*, ed. Allan Wade (New York: Macmillan (now Palgrave), 1961) 542, 544, 550, 872. Hereafter, this book will be cited as *YL* with page numbers, whereas the *Collected Letters of W. B. Yeats* will be cited as *YCL* with page numbers.
2. In appealing for the Committee's interference on behalf of Moore, Yeats wrote to Edmund Gosse: 'Thomas Hardy has I hear offered help.' The status of Hardy the novelist as a martyr to public prudery would have made him a particularly important ally in such disputes. See *YCL*, 556 and Bridge, 16–17.
3. Paul Turner in *The Life of Thomas Hardy* (Oxford: Blackwell, 1998) calls attention to this echo (164).
4. Yeats's first volume with Dun Emer sets itself apart as antique artifact by appearing in a Celtic typeface, later eschewed by Cuala Press for a more European typeface.
5. In 'the only book review Hardy ever wrote,' according to R. L. Purdy, Hardy praised William Barnes's dialect poetry, quoted from two poems, and cited these lines as 'an almost perfect expression of the Arcadian lover's ecstasy': 'O whistle, gäy birds, up bezide her, / In drong-way, an' woodlands.' Hardy later employed this review from the *New Quarterly Magazine* as preface to an edition of Barnes's poem, which he also selected. *The Poetry of William Barnes* (Edinburgh: Tragara Press, 1979), 11.
6. I will return to the topic of museums in Chapter 3 for a discussion of 'Musée des Beaux Arts.'
7. From the seventeenth century, Celtic enthusiasts such as John Aubrey and John Toland falsely attributed every standing stone to the Druids. See MacKillop, 135, and L. E. Jones, 134.
8. To a more superficial culture of story, song, and folktale, Hardy may have been more indigenous than Yeats was to his Sligo and Galway sources, but that Dorset society was fading faster than its Irish counterpart, and Hardy

was increasingly separated from the class that harbored these stories by his ascension to the upper middle class.

9. Quoted by Stallworthy (227) who, when he writes of Owen's passionate indignation toward 'the children's poet who exhorted them to "play the Game"', extends the group to Newbolt, the author of this phrase.

10. For example, in 'Dead Man's Dump,' Isaac Rosenberg writes, 'The quivering bellied mules, / And the rushing wheels all mixed / With his tortured upturned sight,' and in 'Mental Cases,' Owen writes, 'There still their eyeballs shrink torments / Back into their brains . . .'

11. See especially Seamus Deane, *Celtic Revivals*, Declan Kiberd, *Inventing Ireland*, and David Lloyd, *Anomalous States*.

12. According to James W. McAuley, 'Cuchulain has now been re-claimed by the "Red Hand" Loyalist paramilitaries who have cast him as defender of Ulster.' See 'Cuchullain and an RPG-7: the ideology and politics of the Ulster Defence Association,' in Eamon Hughes (ed.), *Culture and Politics in Northern Ireland 1960–1990* (Milton Keynes: Open University Press, 1991), 45–68, cited in Geraldine Higgins, 'The quotable Yeats: modified in the guts of the living,' *South Carolina Review*, Sept./Oct. 1999, 1–9.

# Chapter 2   The Cultural Value of Poetry

1. Williams, *Culture & Society: 1780–1950*. New York: Columbia University Press, 1958, 1983; Chris Baldick, *The Social Mission of English Criticism: 1848–1932*. Oxford: Clarendon Press, 1983, 1987. More recent comprehensive studies of culture, such as Terry Eagleton's or Lloyd and Thomas's, pay little or no attention to poetry's special role within culture.

2. His position as inspector of schools undoubtedly led Arnold to associate culture and schools more closely than he might have if he were observing culture from, say, the directorship of a national theatre or gallery or of a major publishing firm.

3. In *Culture and Anarchy*, Arnold defines culture as the best that has been thought and said.

4. The *OED* reminds us that *culture*, a cognate of *cult*, meant worship, presumably from a cyclical sense of the rounds of responsibility which the practice of worship shares with other seasonal or cyclical responsibilities.

5. In continuing to describe 'the little shrivelled, meagre, hopping, though loud and troublesome insects of the hour,' Burke aligns the English Jacobins with the hapless Tithonus, who cannot rise effectively to the recurrent dawns of revolution. Whereas the much greater number of non-revolutionary citizens are 'great cattle,' somewhat mysterious in their silence, they are nevertheless, in Burke's analogy, cast as cows, subclassed synecdochically by their stomachs, ruminating, one presumes, over the cud of memory.

6. Perhaps Arnold's most interesting horticultural image appears in 'Stanzas from the Grande Chartreuse' in which the speaker visits the Alpine monastery where Carthusian monks, recluses from the world's conflicts, nurture herbs for the making of liqueur: 'The garden, overgrown yet mild, / See, fragrant herbs are flowering there! / Strong children of the Alpine wild' (lines 55–7). Encumbered with world-weariness, the speaker begs, 'Take me,

cowl'd forms, and fence me round' (93), presumably like the other subjects of the herbalists' culture. The horticultural metaphor persists but, apparently, just below the level of authorial consciousness: whereas the ending – 'We are like children rear'd in shade / Beneath some old-world abbey wall' – maintains consistency with earlier references to these herbal children, appeals from men of the world to 'follow too!' (192) and the response that our 'bent was taken long ago. // Long since we pace this shadow'd nave,' interchange the herbs and the monks in such a confusing way that I can only suppose that *culture* and *horticulture* hung side by side in the dark closet of Arnold's mind from which they were donned by feeling in the dark.

7.  The Burkean poetic phrases are from 'Prayer for My Daughter' and 'The Tower.'

8.  Thomas Weiskel succinctly summarizes the effect of Enlightenment secularism on the creation of the Sublime: 'The emotions traditionally religious were displaced from the Deity and became associated first with the immensity of space and secondarily with the natural phenomena (oceans, mountains) which seemed to approach that immensity' (14).

9.  John Baillie remarked (1747) that 'it is the *Reflections* arising from *Sensations* only which makes her [the Soul] acquainted with Herself'; quoted by Samuel Monk in Weiskel (14).

10. Alasdair MacIntyre, perhaps because he stresses Burke's English allegiances, cannot specify what this 'other than and more than' become.

11. Yeats does not comment on the *visionary* source of this historical tree, that after the wholesale felling of oaks in the eighteenth century for British shipbuilding and smelting, images in the mind's eye of great oaks, like *aislings*, may have arisen from the peasant's deprivation.

12. In characterizing national types in terms of gender, Arnold invokes the ancient Greek distinction between the masculine principle that gives form to matter and the feminine material or mater that needs to be formed and governed.

13. Arnold's contemporary at Oxford, Strangford, became a viscount in 1857. Although, according to the *Cambridge Biographical Dictionary* he 'wrote little more than a few brilliant *Saturday, Pall Mall* and *Quarterly* articles' before posthumous publications edited by his widow, *The Times* obituary of 12 January 1869 recorded that 'Lord Strangford was probably the best philologist and most varied linguist this country has ever produced' and that he was 'completely at home' in all of the languages and dialects of the East, obviously an exaggeration which may arise from the same class deference that seems to move Arnold (Magnusson, White).

14. In the poem 'Rugby Chapel,' Matthew represents his father as both Moses and the Holy Ghost who will revisit and inspire 'the host of mankind' on their exodus: 'Years they have been in the wild!'

15. Arnold does not specifically equate Hellenism and Celticism. However, Arnold argues that 'the children of Taliesin and Ossian have now an opportunity for renewing the famous feat of the Greeks, and conquering their conquerors' (390). Even allowing for a convention of gracious rhetoric, we can still recognize the suggestion that Celticism will become ascendant enough at least to lighten Saxon stolidity, a role later assigned to Hellenism.

16. See Guinn Batten's 'Where All the Ladders Start: Identity, Ideology, and the Ghosts of the Romantic Subject in Yeats and Muldoon,' *Romantic Generations: Essays in Honor of Robert F. Gleckner.* Lewisburg, PA: Bucknell University Press, 2001.

17. More complexly, this passage may also reflect Wilde's troping in 'The Portrait of Mr. W. H.' of Arnold's terms 'Hebraisim' and 'Hellenism' which Wilde interprets, respectively, as 'fear of the Lord' and 'Love' as love is developed in Plato's 'Symposium.' The 'strange influence over men' of this dialogue, Wilde writes, derives from its suggestion of 'sex in soul' and of the relation of 'intellectual enthusiasm and . . . physical passion' (183–4). Although Buck, most ostensibly, would draw on the fluent bumpers of Greek hedonism, his homophobia and frequent mixing of erotic references with talk of friendship suggest that his interest in 'Hellenism' extends beyond the Hippocrene and the blushful hippocras.

18. Beyond the Englishman's prior acquisition of the language, Stephen implies his own succession as keeper of the language. Many readers approaching *A Portrait* do not know either that an Irish language exists or how recent and disruptive was its demise as the majority language in Ireland. For example, in 1892, when Joyce was ten, Douglas Hyde recalls in Co. Mayo addressing questions in Irish to a boy who answered him in English. When Hyde asked him, *Nach labhrann tu Gaedheilg?* (i.e. 'Don't you speak Irish?'), the boy answered, 'And isn't it Irish I'm spaking?' (from Hyde, 'The Necessity for De-Anglicising Ireland,' in Deane, 1991, II, 532).

19. This passage from 'The Nature of Gothic' continues: 'The work of the Gothic heart is fretwork still, and it can neither rest in, nor from, its labour, but must pass on, sleeplessly, until its love of change shall be pacified for ever in the change that must come alike on them that wake and them that sleep' (214), phrasing that also may have haunted Gabriel Conroy's reflections on the dead.

20. . . . as I have argued in *Irish Poetry After Joyce* (1985, rev. 1997).

21. In *Culture and Anarchy*, Arnold takes his reader on this gallop: 'The pursuit of perfection, then, is the pursuit of sweetness and light. He who works for sweetness and light, works to make reason and the will of God prevail. He who works for machinery, he who works for hatred, works only for confusion. Culture looks beyond machinery, culture hates hatred; culture has one great passion, the passion for sweetness and light. It has one even yet greater! – the passion for making them *prevail*' (ACPW, V, 112).

22. In his preface to Hone and Rossi's *Bishop Berkeley*, Yeats cites as worthwhile but inconsistent Dunne's *An Experiment with Time* (1927), which popularized new ideas of relativity (xxi). It seems likely that *The Third Policeman* by Flann O'Brien, who also cites Dunne, derived its cycles from these two books.

23. In 'The Child and the State' lecture to the Irish Literary Society, republished in two parts in *The Irish Statesman* on 5 and 12 December 1925, Yeats said, 'In Gaelic literature we have something that the English-speaking countries have never possessed – a great folk literature. . . . The modern Irish intellect was born more than two hundred years ago when Berkeley defined in three or four sentences the mechanical philosophy of Newton, Locke and Hobbes, the philosophy of England in his day, and I think of England up to our day, and wrote after each, "We Irish do not hold with this", or some like

sentence' (*YUP*, 2, 458). See the related discussion in Chapter 1, 'Translations from the English and Irish past.'

24. In 'The Buried Life,' fate sinks beneath the changing surface of our life the 'genuine self, . . . the unregarded river of our life,' which continues, nevertheless, its horizontal flow.

25. Seamus Deane writes, 'When this cultural factor is intensified to the point where it becomes or gives grounds for the emergence of a racial factor, then Burkean liberalism begins to be transformed into a defence for Irish nationalism, even though this is very far from Arnold's (not to mention Burke's) intention. Arnold, in his efforts to Hellenise England, also helped Irishmen like Yeats and Pearse in their efforts to Celticise Ireland. In defining the deficiency of the English middle-class civilisation, he gave the Irish the cultural distinction which they sought. . . . By the 1880s he had completed the transformation of Burkean liberalism into Irish Revival nationalism' (Kearney, 153).

26. Thomas O. Phillips developed this idea for a thesis at Wake Forest.

27. Ultimately, Arnold does not distinguish among kinds of knowledge or different ways of knowing: 'All learning is scientific which is systematically laid out and followed up to its original sources, and . . . a genuine humanism is scientific' (384).

28. Arnold says 'a sort of touchstone' because strictly speaking the jasper or basalt onto which the softer gold rubs off contains no valuable mineral in itself.

29. At age 87, Hardy wished for a very modest representation in such a fetishized gathering of poems – 'His only ambition . . . was to have some poem or poems in a good anthology like the Golden Treasury' (*LYH*, 263) – which amounts to having one foot in the Palgrave.

30. Visit to the Macmillan Archive in Basingstoke, Hampshire, January of 1994.

31. Joyce's 'feather bed mountain' suggests a heroic erection, coupling under cover, and one of the Dublin Mountains, or, anticipating *Finnegans Wake*, all three.

## Chapter 3    The 1930s: Yeats, Auden, and Others

1. In the 1930s, Clarke published three poems in the *Spectator*, two poems in the *London Mercury*, and one poem each in *Nation* and *Atheneum* and in *The Saturday Review*, although he published reviews regularly in these and other London journals and papers. Kavanagh published a few poems in London journals such as *The Spectator* and *John O'London's Weekly*.

2. *The Bell*, major adversary of censorship and repressive forces in the Catholic Church, was published between 1940 and 1953; in Belfast *Lagan* ran from 1943 to 1947 and *Rann* from 1948 to 1953. The long-running *Dublin Magazine* expired in 1950; *Envoy* in 1951.

3. References to Auden's writing – *Collected Poems*, *The English Auden*, and *Forwords and Afterwords* respectively – will be cited parenthetically as *ACP*, *EA* or *AF&A*, followed by page numbers.

4. The psychiatrist W. H. R. Rivers, who studied the soldier-patients he treated at the Craiglockhart War Hospital in the First World War, speculated on the

relation of 'the feminine passivity' enforced by trench warfare and the high incidence of homosexuality in his patients. See his *Conflict and Dream* (London: Kegan Paul, 1923), and his fictional representation in Pat Barker's *Regeneration* (London: Penguin, 1991), 107–8. In regard to the 1920s, historian C. L. Mowat writes, 'For a time femininity and the maternal instincts were kept under heavy disguise. Women's fashions in the twenties emphasised this spirit of emancipation and the domination of youth. One writer has described the style as the "schoolboy shape." .... Gradually, the cultivation of feminine charms and a more heterosexual standard of taste returned' (212).

5.  Some readers may disparage Auden's reticence to claim his homosexual affiliation. For one example of his social discomfort with his sexual nature, consider this response in 1946 to the American poet Robert Duncan's proposal of an essay on Auden's homosexuality:

> I must ask you not to publish the essay you propose. I'm sure you will realize that the better the essay you write, the more it will be reviewed and talked about, and the more likelihood there will be of it being brought publicly to my attention in a way when to ignore it would be taken as an admission of guilt. As you may know, I earn a good part of my livelihood by teaching, and in that profession one is particularly vulnerable. Further, both as a writer and as a human being, the occasion may always arise, particularly in these times, when it becomes one's duty to take a stand on the unpopular side of some issue. Should that ever occur, your essay would be a very convenient red herring for one's opponents (think of what happened to B. Russell in New York).
>
> (Quoted in Fass, 195; brought to my attention by Devin Johnston)

6.  *Leonardo da Vinci: A Study in Psychosexuality.* New York: Vintage Books, 1947, 26.

7.  The opening of *Speak Memory*, where Nabokov studies a picture of his unmourning mother waving from an upstairs window over his empty pre-natal baby-carriage, sign of his non-existence, could serve as a rich gloss for this complex image.

8.  We could accept James's *banalities*, if we intend the original sense of 'a summons to feudal service' with the secondary meaning of 'banishment.'

9.  The associative net in these lines – *thunderbolt, ruin, stain* – leads to *rain* which suggests a threateningly charged situation followed by discharge.

10. We witness Auden's ambivalence in an essay on Oscar Wilde in which Auden asserts that 'to ninety-nine per cent of practicing homosexuals, ... [the law against homosexuality] makes no difference, so far as their personal liberty is concerned,' after, two pages earlier, asserting that 'the reader also feels his first shivers of pity and fear' when he reads of Wilde's visit to an American prison (*AF&A*, 309, 307).

11. D. W. Harding writes, 'He had always kept himself fit by physical activity.... It was a part of his identity in which he took some pride (liking to remark, for instance, that being able to swim 50 yards under water was a help in reading Swinburne aloud) ...' (199), a remark that makes dubious any assumption that athletic discipline restrains poetic excess.

12. Of Stephen Spender, 'the Shelley of the Poetic Renaissance,' Leavis boasted that he had done him in, with the critic's perfidious bark, we must presume.

13. Q. D. Leavis's phrase, applied to the Auden group, is a code word which echoes, for example, Goldsworth Lowes Dickinson's statement that in the late-Victorian era the public school Charterhouse was 'a hothouse of vice' (quoted in Weeks, 109).

14. In attempting to understand his own sexual nature, Auden relied on contemporary psychological studies that were restrictive in assigning cause for his homosexuality and often unsympathetic.

15. See Tom Nairn's *The Break-Up of Britain*.

16. Later in his autobiography Isherwood complained that this stipend was weakened by Britain's flight from gold and the consequent devaluation of the pound.

17. For example, see Fuller and Rodway.

18. In a 1935 review in *New Verse* of Pound's *Jefferson and/or Mussolini*, a reviewer suggests that many of Auden's contemporaries were reading the economic theories of C. H. Douglas, promoted by Ezra Pound in the pages of *The Criterion*. The reviewer remarks, 'It is time that someone examined and criticised the attraction of Social Credit for middle-aged intellectuals. Social Credit is supported, for example, by Ezra Pound (born 1885), T. S. Eliot (born 1888), Herbert Read (born 1883), Edwin Muir (born 1887), William Carlos Williams (born 1883), Bonamy Dobrée and Hugh MacDiarmid (born, we suppose, round about the same years), 'No. 16 (Aug.–Sept. 1935). The observation, for which Douglas's theories attempt to account, are – stated simply by Pound in a letter to *The Criterion* – 'That every factory and every industry creates in a given period a mass of prices greater than the amount of purchasing power it puts into circulation,' XIII: 50 (Oct. 1933), 128. The gap between prices and purchasing power arises from credit, which banks claim as their own, but which actually arises from inventions, designs, and other intellectual properties that should belong to the community. By Pound's extension, these intellectual properties include past literature as well as other creations. Douglas's notions, as extended by Pound, orient themselves toward the past by acknowledging our indebtedness to the tradition. Caudwell's ideas, in contrast, direct his readers to the future where poetic imagination will be realized collectively.

19. After another half-century's grim history, Paul Muldoon establishes that the ultimate commodities are arms for nations and drugs for individuals because – beyond serving an insatiable need – as, Guinn Batten pointed out to me, his title suggests 'The More A Man Has the More A Man Wants.'

20. Although the Ashmolean was founded in the seventeenth century and the Sloan Museum, which became the British Museum, in the eighteenth, the British Museum did not open to the general public until the nineteenth century, and most major British museums, such as the National Gallery, the Tate, the National Portrait Gallery, the Victoria and Albert, and the Birmingham Museum and Art Gallery, were founded in that same century. The *OED* traces the word *museuming*, indicating a popular practice, to 1838. Ideas concerning museums and therefore the trajectory of my reading of this poem arise from discussions with Guinn Batten about Keats and museums but also from Malraux's seminal study *The Imaginary Museum* and

     Donald Davie's extension of Malraux's work in *The Poet in the Imaginary Museum*.

21.  Of course the paintings referred to in Auden's poem are displayed in Brueghel's homeland, but Auden imports into an English poem references to sixteenth-century North European paintings. Auden may have been attracted to Brueghel because his translations of the ancient Greek and Mideastern narratives into Lowlands, often snowbound, settings are themselves so radically uprooted and displaced that they seem precursors of Modernist literature and art.

22.  Implausibly restrictive of meaning within this one poem, Riffaterre's methodical intertextuality would not permit him to qualify the following statement which he applies acutely to this one poem – 'It would be difficult to find a more distracting and therefore exemplary instance of the indirection of meaning, the figurative parti-pris, and the all-pervasive catachresis that characterize literariness' (10) – in light of Auden's decade-long development of a 'language of indirection' that I have been tracing.

23.  One could argue that with a sympathetic prescience Auden anticipates the trajectory of Yeats's thought. In 'A General Introduction for My Work,' a preface to a complete edition that was cancelled, Yeats compares English and Irish poetries to rivers: 'An Irish preference for a swift current might be mere indolence, yet . . . the English mind is meditative, rich, deliberate; it may remember the Thames valley' (*YE&I*, 523). In Auden's elegy, in lines that seem to allude to Yeats's essay, all poetry flows together

> In the valley of its saying where executives
> Would never want to tamper; it flows south
> From ranches of isolation and the busy griefs,
> Raw towns that we believe and die in; it survives,
> A way of happening, a mouth.

(EA, 242)

     Poetry survives its individual recitations as well as, in Wordsworth's phrase, 'being passed away' into the river's mouth and then the oblivious ocean. Auden, thus, returns poetry to its role in consumption: it is both ingested, into the guts of the living, and expounded through the mouth. In this same portion of Yeats's essay where he discusses finding a rhythm that allows him to blend personal and public statements, Yeats says, 'All that is personal soon rots; it must be packed in ice or salt' (522). Using Shakespearean deaths to illustrate his point, Yeats argues that in those moments of enlarged vision that poetry brings, 'All must be cold . . . cold winds blow across our hands, upon our faces, the thermometer falls, and because of that cold we are hated by journalists and groundlings' (523). As if applying this statement and Shakespeare's chilling of emotion to Yeats's own death, Auden writes, 'The mercury sank in the mouth of the dying day, / O all the instruments agree / The day of his death was a dark cold day.'

24.  MacNeice quotes from *Explorations*, 429, where Yeats also says, 'Berkeley destroyed the new . . . and established for ever the subjectivity of space.

No educated man to-day accepts the objective matter and space of popular science...' (435–6).

25. As mentioned early in this chapter, Shelley speaks of a similar creation out of nothing (or the fear of nothing): 'Thou – that to human thought art nourishment, / Like darkness to a dying flame!' ('Hymn to Intellectual Beauty') and '...what were thou...? If to the human mind's imaginings / Silence and solitude were vacancy?' ('Mont Blanc').

26. In this sense it functions like certain paradoxical passages admired by Auden in Shakespeare's work, where by denying its own efficacy, art deepens its authority. For example, in his under-recognized master work *The Sea and the Mirror*, Auden finds in *The Tempest* the suggestion that art only appears to be a bridge into some Edenic world; Auden's spokes-monster Caliban argues that art, by conveying the illusion that it is a bridge, can obscure the fact that we are 'swaying out on the ultimate wind-whipped cornice that overhangs the unabiding void...' (*ACP*, 340). Earlier in this work, Auden's Alonso suggests that art must reveal the priority of life over art. He offers his son,

> ...the blessing
> Of Alonso, your father, once King
> Of Naples, now ready to welcome
> Death, but rejoicing in a new love,
> A new peace, having heard the solemn
> Music strike and seen the statue move
> To forgive our illusion.

(*ACP*, 322)

Alonso refers to Queen Hermione, at the conclusion of *The Winter's Tale*, who poses as a statue of herself in the presence of her culpable but repentant husband, who believes she has died years earlier, before she assumes her living form. When she abandons her pose and enters her husband's arms, she 'forgives' our illusion that art, rather than the loving sequestration of Paulina, can preserve life or immortalize it. As with Auden's elegy, to the extent that we honor Shakespeare's plays and *The Sea and the Mirror* for conveying this truth about the priority of life over art, to that extent these works of art gain authority.

27. See Chapter 2, 66–8.

28. In a letter dated '1918–19?' Yeats wrote to his agent A. P. Watt, 'You can point out to Macmillan that the Unwin Book brings in more in a year than all the works of mine which he has. The Unwin book was written before I was thirty. I have never met anyone to-day who believed that it contained my best work. I want Sir Frederick Macmillan to do as well for my best work.' Macmillan Archive 54898, British Museum Department of Manuscripts.

29. Ironically, in the 1940s and 1950s, MacNeice came to know more and more of what would basically be his readership through his work with the BBC.

30. Macmillan, with Hardy, Yeats, and Kipling, *New Directions*, with American Modernists, and Farrar, Strauss, Giroux with major contemporary poets edited by Jonathan Galassi also come to mind, just before, say, the 1960s

version of the Oxford University Press and Atheneum, under the editorship of Jon Stallworthy and Harry Ford, respectively.

31.  Interview with Charles Monteith, 11 January 1993; also Charles Monteith, 'Eliot in the Office.'

32.  In a 1925 letter to Sir Frederick Macmillan in which A. E. was promoting his periodical the *Irish Statesman*, A. E. listed 16 contributors, who represented 'all who have won any distinction in literature or science or economics' in Ireland, but excluded the name of Clarke who had published widely in Ireland and been included in many of A. E.'s weekly literary evenings.

33.  Clarke was invited to the Poetry Bookshop in Museum Steet where he observed Eliot 'in the attitude of Mallarmé, on his famous Tuesday nights,' and recognized he was attending a 'weekly meeting of the Criterion Circle which had so powerful an influence,' but he failed to respond to further invitations (*Penny*, 188).

34.  Letter to Olivia Shakespear, 9 May 1932. Yeats asked her to get a copy from the library and advise him on whether or not Clarke should be appointed to the Irish Academy. He added, 'I find it very difficult to see, with impartial eyes, these Irish writers who are as it were part of my propaganda' (*YL*, 795).

35.  In 'The Abbey Theatre Fire,' Clarke says of Yeats, 'So, I forgot / His enmity' (136), on the basis of which lines Kinsella ascribes to Clarke the virtue of 'Magnanimity.' See poem of that title in Kinsella's *Collected Poems* (72).

# Chapter 4   Publishing and Poetry in Ireland and England in the 1960s

1.  For health reasons Kinsella has restricted public readings to, perhaps, two over the last decade. Consequently, this reading, to recognize the acquisition of Kinsella's papers by the Special Collections of Woodruff Library, seemed momentous to audience and poet alike (23 October 1997).

2.  The Dolmen Archive, Wake Forest University, Z. Smith Reynolds Library, Rare Books; cited as the Wake Forest Archive.

3.  See, for examples, Bedient and Kenner.

4.  Although these women represent the Triple Goddess, most frequently Hecate, and the Jungian feminine principle, Kinsella skillfully tethers them to actual people in his childhood. If he deletes Mrs Delaney's identity, he gives her a name appropriate both to children's nomenclature and to myth or fairy tale. His comment to Miller – in response to a reviewer who suggested that he did not understand the implications of his goddess figures – confirms his intention to retain some independence from the White Goddess: 'I don't understand the implications of my material! After fifteen years avoiding the facile feckology of Mother Goddess and Mithraic cult...' (Wake Forest Archive, 10/12/69).

5.  See Rosenberg and *New Larousse*.

6.  'I was more than content. Primary Irish publication is what I want.' Letter to me, 11 July 2000.

7.  Edward Blishen, 'Interview with Thomas Kinsella' for 'The World of Books,' BBC, 36: 73, 13 September 1973. Typescript in the Dolmen Archive, Box 84 (10).

8. The deadly accuracy of Kinsella's 'Butcher's Dozen' (1972), his satire against the Widgery Tribunal's whitewashing of the murder of Derry citizens by the British Army, was confirmed by a governmental enquiry into that injustice this past year. The adverse reaction in 1972 of Donald Davie and other English critics may have completed Kinsella's estrangement from his English readership.

9. As the Miller–Montague correspondence reveals, their relationship was confessional; Montague became the godfather of Tim O'Keeffe, Jr.

10. Seamus Deane, 'Poetry and Song 1800–1890,' preface in *The Field Day Anthology of Irish Writing*, 3 vols, vol. 2, 1–9, 2.

11. Phone conversation with John Montague between Ballydehob, Cork, and Winston-Salem on 29 August 1998.

12. At this time he was drawing a salary of £60 a month from Bord Fáilte.

13. Yet, in a letter dated 16 April 1961, Montague refers to this publication by its earlier Yeatsian title *The Tower*. Rare Books, Z. Smith Reynolds Library, Wake Forest University, hereafter called the Wake Forest Archive.

14. 3 November 1961; 6 December 1961; Letter from Montague to O'Keeffe, from the Timothy O'Keeffe Papers, Department of Special Collections, McFarlin Library, The University of Tulsa, hereafter cited as the Tulsa Archive.

15. 7 January 1961, 27 February 1961, and 5 February 1962, Wake Forest Archive. Eventually, Montague became the editor of *The Dolmen Miscellany*.

16. Wake Forest Archive: undated postcard, late summer of 1962; Montague to Miller, 10 March 1963.

17. Montague to O'Keeffe: letter dated 16 June 1963, Tulsa Archive.

18. Montague to Miller, 18 November and 24 November 1965, Wake Forest Archive.

19. Hardbound notebook entitled *Minute Book*, page 67, Wake Forest Archive. See also Neil Corcoran, *Seamus Heaney* (London: Faber & Faber, 1986), 23.

20. Phone conversation, 29 August 1998; letter 28 November 1966, Wake Forest Archive.

21. Montague to O'Keeffe, 5 July 1965: Tulsa Archive.

22. 7 and 15 July 1966, Tulsa Archive.

23. January 1969, Tulsa Archive.

24. Dolmen Editions, 9 May 1966, 9, 10.

25. Montague to O'Keeffe, 18 January 1967, Tulsa Archive; *Times Literary Supplement*, 5 and 19 January 1967 (pages 10 and 47). Montague had heard that the reviewer, who called the *Tribute* 'scrappy and disappointing,' was Anthony Cronin.

26. Special Collections, Library, Southern Illinois University, hereafter called the Southern Illinois Archive; Montague to Miller, 20 October 1965, Wake Forest Archive.

27. Guinn Batten has helped me with this supposition. See her *The Orphaned Imagination* (Durham, NC: Duke University Press, 1998), especially her discussion on pages 234–6.

28. Promotional copy for this tour, which emphasized sectarian distinctions, was written by Michael Longley who conceived of and organized the tour, as he did tours that featured Simmons/Muldoon and Mahon/Heaney ('Blackthorn & Bonsai,' a talk delivered to the Arts Council in Dublin).

29. In 'Reading the Renaissance: John Derricke's *Image of Irelande*... (c. 1579) and The Dolmen Press (1966–72),' David Gardiner examines closely the use in this tour both of the Derricke woodcuts and the Elizabethan identities of 'planter' and 'Gael.' See *Nua Studies in Contemporary Writing* (I: 2 (Autumn 1998), 47–57).

30. Roy Fuller says that in 1988, membership stood at 1800. Jonathan Barker (ed.), *Thirty Years of the Poetry Book Society, 1956–1986*, with preface by Blake Morrison (London: Hutchinson, 1988), 185.

31. See letters of 7 April 1960, 16 April, 19, 22, 28 June, 5 and 10 July; see also 17 January 1961, Tulsa Archive.

32. 2 July 1963, Wake ForestArchive.

33. In letters dated October 1966 and 27 October 1966, he reminds O'Keeffe of the early submission date. Over the spring of 1967, in three or four letters to O'Keeffe, he expresses his anxiety about the Choice.

34. Montague to Miller, dated 'Over Easter, 1967,' Wake Forest Archive.

35. Letter dated 'Over Easter' with no clear year; Miller's answer dated 5 July 1967, Wake Forest Archive.

36. *Poetry Book Society Bulletin* (Spring 1984) with write-ups about the Choice: Tom Disch and *The Dead Kingdom* among five recommendations. Indisputably one of the world's great jockeys, Richards never won the English Derby.

37. 'Index to the Poetry Book Society Bulletin Choices, Recommendations, Special Commendations, and Translations,' *Bulletin of Bibliography*, 53: 3 (Sept. 1996), 219–26.

38. Also noticeably missing from the list of Choices before 1994 are Medbh McGuckian, Eiléan Ní Chuilleanáin, Ciaran Carson, Michael Hartnett, and Brendan Kennelly.

39. Blake Morrison, 'Preface,' *Thirty Years of the Poetry Book Society, 1956–1986*, ed. Jonathan Barker (London: Hutchinson, 1988), 9–10.

40. Montague to O'Keeffe, 15 July 1966, Tulsa Archive.

41. Quoted by Steven E. Smith, in 'Index to the *Poetry Book Society Bulletin*,' *Bulletin of Bibliography*, 51: 3 (Sept. 1994), 273–93.

42. The lukewarm British reception of English poets who have been 'Americanized,' such as Charles Tomlinson or Basil Bunting, would lend credence to my assumption.

43. No date, from Angelsea Street before returning to Paris, probably the summer of 1967, Tulsa Archive.

44. In dating the events of Montague's life, I found Thomas Dillon Redshaw and Mark Waelder's 'Biographical Notes' invaluable. See *The Figure in the Cave & Other Essays*, ed. Antoinette Quinn (Syracuse, NY: Syracuse University Press, 1989), 221–6.

45. This account of the Roundhouse reading is based exclusively on Montague's recollections: telephone conversation, 29 August 1998. From this point, Montague's relationship with OUP continued to deteriorate. On 6 October 1976, anticipating co-publishing a revised edition of *Poisoned Lands* with Oxford, Liam Miller rejected OUP's counter-offer as being below Dolmen's basic costs for the book. Writing to Carol Buckroyd, he continued, 'I am amazed at the poor performance of *A Slow Dance* in the bookshops, as I have heard from a couple of people who failed to get this title at your

London Bookshop. The notices the book received should have generated better sales in your area' (Wake Forest Archive).

46. Letter to the author from Simon Armitage, dated 5 October 1998, confirming Montague's omission from the *Penguin Book of Poetry: From Britain & Ireland Since 1945*.

47. In July of 1955, Larkin wrote to his intimate friend from Belfast Patsy Murphy who was living with her husband Richard in Galway: 'I'm passing through an anti English phase at present – they are miles uglier and noisier and vulgarer than the Irish. . . .' He then follows with a satirical catalogue of the English suburbs familiar to readers of his last two volumes (248).

48. Quoted in Larkin's *Required Writing*, 132.

49. Quoted in Ian Hamilton, *A Poetry Chronicle* (London: Faber & Faber, 1973), 128–9.

50. More recently, the film *Brassed Off* (1996) plays so heavily on the underdog miners keeping open the post-Scargill mines that the economic unfeasibility of mining and its inhumanity as a way of life are never considered.

51. See Helen and Baron Duckham, *Great Pit Disasters: 1700 to the Present* (Newton Abbot: David & Charles, 1973).

52. The 'Evangeline stanza' is distinguished by its hurdy-gurdy mixture of trochees and alliteration.

53. This assertion is based on a conversation with Hill at Washington University in St Louis (March 1999) and correspondence with Kinsella in June of that same year.

54. Hughes returns to this pun – 'The moorlines cast off ropes . . .' – in 'There Come Days to the Hills' in *Remains of Elmet* (1979).

55. Hughes quotes Hopkins on 'reversed rhythm': 'putting the stress where, to judge by the rest of the measure, the slack should be, and the slack where the stress, and this is done freely at the beginning of a line and, in the course of a line, after a pause' (*HWP*, 341).

56. In 'The Wanderings of Oisin,' Yeats's hero willfully mounts his horse and rides into the Otherworld, but Hughes's poet waits for the horses to bring the underworld to him. In this sense the two poets embody the willfulness and the wise passivity that Heaney ascribes to Yeats and Wordsworth respectively. In this regard, Plath's assertive will contrasts even more sharply with Hughes's Eastern passivity. In 'Ariel,' which begins like 'The Horses' – 'Stasis in Darkness. / The the substanceless blue / Pour of tor and distances' – she would ride her horse like 'the arrow, / The dew that flies / Suicidal, at one with the drive / Into the red / / Eye, the cauldron of morning.' In a remarkably complex and convincing analysis of 'Sylvia Plath: The Evolution of "Sheep in Fog,"' Hughes shows how a poem that sets off toward the wise passivity of 'The Horses' nevertheless keeps veering toward an abortive drive – Phaeton's or Icarus's – into the sun. See *Winter Pollen*, 191–211.

## Chapter 5   Towards the Present of English and Irish Poetry

1. Yeats said, 'There have been other translators but they had a formal eighteenth century style that took what Dr. Hyde would call the "sap and pleasure" out of simple thought and emotion.' Quoted from Yeats's preface

to a Dun Emer limited edition in Ó hAodha's preface (vi) and cited in Cronin (135).

2. Ó Searcaigh has been translated by Seamus Heaney, Gabriel Fitzmaurice, McCarthy, Joan McBreen, Sarah Berkeley, John F. Deane, Peter Sirr, Muldoon, and Montague; Davitt by Montague, Hartnett, Muldoon, Mary O'Malley, Kennelly, Greg Delanty, and others.

3. Ní Dhomhnaill provides poetic 'cribs' of her poetry, approximate English translations, which she offers to her translators. These cribs are accessible in the Boston College library's special collection where Ní Dhomhnaill's papers reside. I consulted photocopies kindly provided by the poet herself.

4. The poem reads acrostically, 'Is this a *New Yorker* poem or what?' I mentioned this in a *Colby Review* essay in 1992, 202–15. In 'My Two Lughs' Muldoon describes a key as 'teeny-weeny' rather than small, and thereby refers us to 'The Key' in *Madoc* and to a sequence of teasing clues throughout the volume.

5. In his *Commentary*, Jeffares offers only a single sentence: 'The poem was written in a spirit of mockery' (420).

6. Muldoon's line reads 'comelier than golden candlesticks at Mother Mary's feet' which approximates Yeats's 'purer than a tall candle before the Holy Rood / Is Cathleen, the daughter of Houlihan,' whereas fair Úna is like 'a candlestick of gold on a queenly table' (Kinsella's translation of 'Úna Bhán' by Tomás Mac Coisdealbhaigh. I have depended heavily on the highly informed commentary of Eiléan Ní Chuilleanáin and Maureen Murphy, which I solicited through telephone and fax. I have interpreted freely their readings of 'First Communion' so they are not responsible for my conclusions.

7. See my essay, 'The Go-Between of Recent Irish Poetry,' in *Cultural Contexts and Literary Idioms in Contemporary Irish Literature*, ed. Michael Kennealy (Colin Smythe/Barnes & Noble, 1988), 172–85.

8. Paul Muldoon, *The Annals of Chile* (London: Faber & Faber; New York: Farrar, Straus, Giroux, 1995), 13–28.

9. Kendall, 217.

10. Muldoon's characterization of *pied* literature as being virtually 'unintelligible without a supporting apparatus' (Clarendon, 84) seems quite close to Shields's characterization of *údar*. Hugh Shields, *Narrative Singing in Ireland* (Cork: Irish Academic Press, 1993), 83.

11. *Irish Literary Supplement*, reprinted in Curtis (ed.), *As the Poet Said . . .*, 85.

12. Walter George Strickland, *A Dictionary of Irish Artists*, 2 vols (Shannon: Irish University Press, 1969), vol. 1, 415–20.

13. In eighteenth-century Britain and Ireland this widespread taste for scenic ruins and the divorce of these ruins from their historical causes may have been influenced by a similar practice, which validated the Grand Tour of Catholic countries, of making Roman ruins, rather than Romish art, the ostensible focus of an esthetic tourism. Certainly the place of Latin and the Classics in the university curriculum would have also attracted British tourists to Roman ruins.

14. W. J. T. Mitchell, *Picture Theory: Essays on Verbal and Visual Representation* (Chicago: University of Chicago Press, 1994), 31.

15. In her informative study *Women Creating Women* (Syracuse, NY: Syracuse University Press, 1996), Patricia Haberstroh quotes from Padraic Colum's introduction to Strong's *Songs of Living* (1961) where he says this ancient

figure of the sphere-woman appears in Strong's poetry in her three guises 'bringing "her knowledgeableness out in measured sayings"' (31).

16. In the most penetrating study to date of Ní Chuilleanáin's poetry, John Kerrigan writes that 'a scepticism about verse which frames the poet against an authenticating place can be found as early as *Acts and Monuments* [Ní Chuilleanáin's first publication], '"The modern Irish poet is not a man in the foreground, silhouetted against a place", she insists' (86).

17. Shields, 68.

18. *The Brazen Serpent*, 23.

19. Luce Irigaray, *Speculum of the Other Woman*, trans Gillian C. Gill (Ithaca, NY: Cornell University Press, 1985; orig. French 1974).

20. Ellis Waterhouse, *Italian Baroque Painting* (London: Phaidon Press, 1962), 105; Charles McCorquodale, *The Baroque Painters of Italy* (Oxford: Phaidon, 1979), 12.

21. Gould, 109.

22. Waterhouse, 69.

23. Kevin Ray, 'Interview with Eiléan Ní Chuilleanáin,' *Éire-Ireland*, 31: 2 (Spring/Summer 1996), 62–73. Of course when we take up the topic of bodies and architectural space, we enter a realm very familiar to readers of Medbh McGuckian who may be the most radically innovative poet in the 'British Isles.'

24. Seamus Deane (ed.), *Field Day Anthology* (Derry: Field Day, 1991), I, 876.

25. To Lady Elizabeth Pelham: 'Man can embody truth but he cannot know it.' (*YCL*, 922).

26. Sean O'Brien, *The Deregulated Muse* (Newcastle: Bloodaxe, 1998), 241.

27. Michael Hofmann, dust jacket.

28. Quoted in David Kennedy, *New Relations* (Mid Glamorgan, Wales: Seren Books, 1996), 61.

29. *Moon Country*, 107. Whereas Muldoon and Ní Dhomhnaill can trace their white deer to the Finnian cycle, Armitage can evoke only Wordsworth's white doe which brings with it a different regional association.

30. Seamus Heaney, 'An Open Letter,' in *Ireland's Field Day* (Notre Dame, IN: University of Notre Dame Press, 1986), 19–30, 25–6.

31. Many fellow poets and other readers were deeply moved by this poem which appeared in the *TLS* just before Christmas of 1977. Apparently Hughes wrote to Larkin praising the poem; Larkin responded, 27 March 1979: 'Thanks for your kind words about "Aubade". Since writing it I stopped being afraid of death for a few months, but it is beginning to creep back now.' Special Collections, Woodruff Library, Emory University.

32. Johnston, 'Q. & A. with Blake Morrison' (An Interview), *Irish Literary Supplement*, 8: 2 (Fall 1989), 18–19.

33. Seamus Heaney, *Opened Ground: Selected Poems 1966–96* (London: Faber & Faber; New York: Farrar, Straus & Giroux, 1998).

34. This figure is extrapolated from Mumby's reported number of titles of 'Poetry and Drama' at the ratio of 7 to 2, roughly the ratio of poetry to plays reported by BookTrack for more recent years. See Ian Norrie, *Mumby's Publishing and Bookselling in the Twentieth Century*.

35. Figures were supplied by Colin Randall of the Bookseller, who photocopied them from BookTrack's *Book Sales Yearbook*, 1st edition.

36.  Muldoon is frequently touted as the exemplary poet, and in the preface to *The New Poetry* Mahon, with Ashbery, Auden, and Bishop, was proclaimed one of the four 'presences of the anthology' (28).
37.  Letter from Heaney to author, 1 September 2000.
38.  Bernard O'Donoghue, 'The Master's Voice-Right,' *Irish Times*, 9 October 1999, Weekend, 8.

# Works Cited

Ackroyd, Peter. *T. S. Eliot: A Life*. New York: Simon & Schuster, 1984.

Allen, Walter. *As I Walked Down New Grub Street: Memories of A Writing Life*. Chicago: University of Chicago Press, 1981.

Arac, Jonathan. *Commissioned Spirits*. New Brunswick, NJ: Rutgers University Press, 1979.

Armitage, Simon. *CloudCuckooLand*. London: Faber & Faber, 1997.

——. *The Dead Sea Poems*. London: Faber & Faber, 1995.

Armitage, Simon and Glyn Maxwell. *Moon Country*. London: Faber & Faber, 1996.

Arnold, Matthew. *Culture and Anarchy. The Complete Prose Works of Matthew Arnold*, ed. R. H. Super, vols V and IX. Ann Arbor: University of Michigan Press, 1965 and 1973 (cited as *ACPW* with volume and page number).

——. *Lectures and Essays in Criticism*, ed. R. H. Super, vol. III. Ann Arbor: University of Michigan Press, 1962.

——. *Philistinism in England and America*, vol. VIII. Ann Arbor: University of Michigan Press, 1974.

Auden, W. H. *Collected Poems*, ed. Edward Mendelson. London: Faber & Faber, 1976.

——. *The English Auden: Poems, Essays and Dramatic Writings, 1927–1939*, ed. Edward Mendelson. London: Faber & Faber, 1977.

——. *Forewords and Afterwords*, selected by Edward Mendelson. New York: Vintage Books, 1989.

——. 'Yeats As An Example,' *Kenyon Review*, X: 2 (Spring 1948), 187–95.

—— and Louis MacNeice. *Letters from Iceland*. London: Faber & Faber, 1937.

Baldick, Chris. *The Social Mission of English Criticism: 1848–1932*. Oxford: Clarendon Press, 1983, 1987.

Barker, Pat. *Regeneration*. London: Penguin/Plume, 1993.

Barnes, William. *The Poetry of William Barnes*, ed. Thomas Hardy. Reprinted Edinburgh: Tragara Press, 1979.

Bearden, Romare and Carl Holty. *The Painter's Mind: A Study of the Relation of Structure and Space in Painting*. New York: Crown Publishing, 1969.

Bedient, Calvin. *Eight Contemporary Poets*. London: Oxford University Press, 1974.

——. 'Review of *Notes from the Land of the Dead and Other Poems*,' *New York Times Book Review*, 16 June 1974, 7.

Benstock, Bernard. 'The Assassin and the Censor: Political and Literary Tensions,' *Clio*, 11: 3 (Spring 1982), 219–38.

Bergonzi, Bernard. *Reading the Thirties: Texts and Contexts*. Pittsburgh: University of Pittsburgh Press, 1978.

Betjeman, John. *Collected Poems*, ed. the Earl of Birkenhead. London: John Murray, 1958.

——. *Summoned by Bells*. London: John Murray, 1960.

Blamires, Harry (ed.). *Twentieth-Century Literature in English*. London: Methuen, 1983.

*Book Sales Yearbook*, 1st edn. London: BookTrack, 1999.

Bridge, Ursula (ed.). *W. B. Yeats and T. Sturge Moore: Their Correspondence 1901–1937*. New York: Oxford University Press, 1953.

Brodzki, Bella. 'History, Cultural Memory, and the Tasks of Translation in T. Obinkaram Echewa '*I Saw the Sky Catch Fire*,' *PMLA*, 114: 2 (March 1999), 207–20.

Burke, Edmund. *Letters, Speeches and Tracts on Irish Affairs*, collected and arranged by Matthew Arnold. London: Macmillan, 1881.

——. *A Philosophical Enquiry into the Origin of Our Ideas of the Sublime and Beautiful*, ed. Adam Phillips, World's Classics Edition. Oxford: Oxford University Press, 1990.

——. *Reflections on the Revolution in France*, ed. Conor Cruise O'Brien. London: Penguin Classics, 1968.

Butler, Lance St John. *Thomas Hardy After Fifty Years*. Totowa, NJ: Rowman & Littlefield, 1977.

Carpenter, Humphrey. *W. H. Auden: A Biography*. London: Allen & Unwin, 1981.

Carson, Ciaran. *Fishing for Amber: A Long Story*. London: Granta Books, 1999.

——. *The Twelfth of Never*. Oldcastle: Gallery Press; Winston-Salem, NC: Wake Forest University Press, 1998.

Chesterton, G. K. *The Victorian Age in Literature*. London: Oxford University Press, 1966.

Christopher Caudwell, *Illusion and Reality: A Study of the Sources of Poetry* (New York: International Publishers, 1937; sixth printing, 1970).

Clarke, Austin. *A Penny in the Clouds: More Memories of Ireland and England* London: Routledge & Kegan Paul, 1968.

——. *Selected Poems*, ed. Hugh Maxton. Dublin: Lilliput Press; Winston-Salem, NC: Wake Forest University Press, 1991.

Corcoran, Neil. *English Poetry since 1940*. London: Longman, 1993.

Cronin, Michael. *Translating Ireland: Translations, Languages, Cultures*. Cork: Cork University Press, 1996.

Cunningham, Valentine. *British Writers of the Thirties*. Oxford: Oxford University Press, 1988.

Curtis, Tony (ed.), *As the Poet Said . . .* , from Dennis O'Driscoll's *Poetry Ireland Review* Column. Dublin: Poetry Ireland, 1997.

Davie, Donald. *Articulate Energy: An Inquiry into the Syntax of English Poetry*. London: Routledge & Kegan Paul, 1971.

——. 'Donald Davie on Critics and Essayists,' *Poetry Review*, 85: 3 (Autumn 1995), 38–40.

——. *Kenneth Allott and the Thirties*, The Kenneth Allott Lectures, University of Liverpool, No. 2, 17 January 1980. Liverpool: University of Liverpool Press, 1980, 16 pages.

——. *The Poet in the Imaginary Museum: Essays of Two Decades*, ed. Barry Alpert. New York: Persea Books, 1977.

——. *The Shires*. Oxford: Oxford University Press, 1975.

——. *Thomas Hardy and British Poetry*. New York: Oxford University Press, 1972.

Day Lewis, Cecil. *A Hope for Poetry*, 2nd edn. Oxford: Basil Blackwell, 1935.

Deane, Seamus, *Celtic Revivals*. London: Faber & Faber; Winston-Salem, NC: Wake Forest University Press, 1985.

—— (General Editor). *The Field Day Anthology of Irish Writing*, 3 vols. Derry: Field Day Publications, 1991.

——. *A Short History of Irish Literature*. London: Hutchinson, 1986.

——. *Strange Country: Modernity and Nationhood in Irish Writing since 1790*, The Clarendon Lectures in English Literature of 1995. Oxford: Clarendon Press, 1997.

Dollimore, Jonathan. *Sexual Dissidence: Augustine to Wilde, Freud to Foucault*. Oxford: Clarendon Press, 1991.

Duckham, Helen and Baron. *Great Pit Disasters: Great Britain 1700 to the Present*. Newtown Abbot: David & Charles, 1973.

Dunne, J. W. *An Experiment with Time*. New York: Macmillan, 1927.

Eagleton, Terry. *The Idea of Culture*. Oxford: Blackwell, 2000.

Eliot, T. S. *Notes towards the Definition of Culture*. New York: Harcourt, Brace & Co. 1949.

——. *Selected Prose of T. S. Eliot*, ed. Frank Kermode. New York: Harcourt, Brace, Jovanovich, 1975.

Ellmann, Richard. *Eminent Domain: Yeats Among Wilde, Joyce, Pound, Eliot, and Auden*. New York: Oxford University Press, 1967.

——. *Oscar Wilde*. New York: Vintage Books, 1988.

Farnan, Dorothy J. *Auden in Love*. New York: Simon & Schuster, 1984.

Fass, Ekbert. *Young Robert Duncan: Portrait of the Poet as Homosexual in Society*. Santa Barbara, CA: Black Sparrow Press, 1983.

Forbes, Peter. 'Talking About the New Generation,' *Poetry Review*, 84: 1 (Spring 1994), 4–6.

Forster, E. M. *Howard's End*, ed. Alistair Duckworth. Boston: Bedford Books, 1910, 1997.

Foster, Roy. *W. B. Yeats, A Life: I. The Apprentice Mage*. Oxford and New York: Oxford University Press, 1997.

Freud, Sigmund. *Leonardo de Vinci: A Study in Psycho sexuality*. New York: Vintage Books, 1947.

Fuller, John. *W. H. Auden: A Commentary*. Princeton, NJ: Princeton University Press, 1998.

Fussell, Paul. *The Great War and Modern Memory*. New York: Oxford University Press, 1975.

Gerber, Helmut and W. Eugene Davis (eds). *Thomas Hardy: An Annotated Bibliography*, 2 vols. DeKalb: Northern Illinois University Press, 1973.

Gervais, David. *Literary Englands: Versions of 'Englishness' in Modern Writing*. Cambridge: Cambridge University Press, 1993.

Gordon, Lindall. *Eliot's New Life*. New York: Farrar, Strauss, Giroux, 1988.

Gould, Cecil. *The Paintings of Correggio*. Ithaca, NY: Cornell University Press, 1976.

Gould, Warwick. '"Playing at Treason with Miss Maud Gonne": Yeats and His Publishers in 1900,' *Modernist Writers and the Marketplace*, eds Ian Willison, Warwick Gould and Warren Chernaik. London: Macmillan (now Palgrave), 1996.

Goux, Jean-Joseph. *Symbolic Economies: After Marx and Freud*, trans. Jennifer Curtiss Gage. Ithaca, NY: Cornell University Press, 1990.

Grigson, Geoffrey. 'The Danger of Taste,' *New Verse*, 1: 4 (July 1933), 1–2.

——. *Recollections: Mainly of Writers and Artists*. London: Hogarth Press/Chatto & Windus, 1984.

Gross, John (ed.). *The Modern Movement: A TLS Companion.* London: Harper/ Collins, 1992.

Haberstroh, Patricia. *Women Creating Women.* Syracuse, NY: Syracuse University Press, 1996.

Haffenden, John (ed.). *Viewpoints: Poets in Conversation.* London: Faber & Faber, 1981.

—— (ed.). *W. H. Auden: The Critical Heritage.* London: Routledge & Kegan Paul, 1983.

Hamilton, Ian. *A Poetry Chronicle: Essays and Review.* London: Faber & Faber, 1973.

Hand, Timothy. *Thomas Hardy,* Writers in Their Time Series. New York: St. Martin's Press (now Palgrave), 1995.

Harding, D. W. 'No Compromise,' in *The Leavises,* ed. Denys Thompson, Cambridge: Cambridge University Press, 1984, 187–200.

Hardy, Florence Emily. *The Early Life of Thomas Hardy, 1840–1891.* London: Macmillan, 1928; *The Later Years of Thomas Hardy, 1892–1928.* London: Macmillan, 1930; reprinted together as *The Life of Thomas Hardy.* London: Studio Editions, 1994.

Hardy, Thomas. *The Complete Poems,* ed. James Gibson. The New Wessex Edition. London: Macmillan (now Palgrave), 1976.

——. *The Collected Letters of Thomas Hardy,* eds Richard Little Purdy and Michael Millgate, vol. III, 1902–08, Oxford: Clarendon Press, 1982, vol. IV, 1909–1913, Oxford: Clarendon Press, 1984.

——. *Tess of the d'Urbervilles,* New Wessex Edition. London: Macmillan, 1975.

——. *Wessex Poems.* London: Harper & Brothers, 1898; reprinted in facsimile edition, Oxford: Woodstock Books, 1994.

Harvey, David. *The Condition of Postmodernity: An Enquiry into the Origins of Cultural Change.* Oxford: Basil Blackwell, 1989.

Heaney, Seamus (trans.). *Beowulf.* London: Faber & Faber, 1999.

——. 'On First Looking into Ted Hughes's "Birthday Letters,"' *New Yorker,* 74 (5 October 1998), 64–5.

——. *The Government of the Tongue: The 1986 T. S. Eliot Memorial Lecture and Other Critical Writings.* London: Faber & Faber; New York: Farrar, Straus, Giroux, 1988.

——. 'An Open Letter,' *Ireland's Field Day.* Notre Dame, IN: University of Notre Dame Press, 1986, 19–30.

——. *Opened Ground: Selected Poems 1966–96.* London: Faber & Faber; New York: Farrar, Straus, Giroux, 1998.

——. *Preoccupations: Selected Prose, 1968–1978.* London: Faber & Faber; New York: Farrar, Straus, Giroux, 1980.

——. *The Redress of Poetry.* London: Faber & Faber; New York: Farrar, Straus, Giroux, 1995.

——. *Station Island.* London: Faber & Faber, 1984; New York: Farrar, Straus, Giroux, 1985.

Hertz, Neil. *The End of the Line: Essays on Psychoanalysis and the Sublime.* New York: Columbia University Press, 1985.

Hill, Geoffrey. 'Dividing Legacies,' *Agenda,* 34: 2 (Summer 1996), 9–28.

——. *King Log.* London: André Deutsch, 1968.

——. *New and Collected Poems.* Boston: Houghton, Mifflin, 1994.

Hone, J. M. and M. M. Rossi. *Bishop Berkeley: His Life, Writings, and Philosophy*, with an introduction by W. B. Yeats. London: Faber & Faber, 1931.

Hughes, Ted. *Crow*. London: Faber & Faber, 1970; New York: Harper & Row, 1971.

——. *Rain Charm for the Duchy and Other Laureate Poems*. London: Faber & Faber, 1992.

——. *Shakespeare and the Goddess of Complete Being*. London: Faber & Faber, New York: Farrar, Straus, Giroux, 1992.

——. *Winter Pollen: Occasional Prose*, ed. William Scammell. London: Faber & Faber, 1994; New York: Picador, 1995.

——. *Wolfwatching*. London: Faber & Faber, 1989.

Hulse, Michael, David Kennedy and David Morley (eds). *The New Poetry*. Newcastle upon Tyne: Bloodaxe Books, 1993.

Hynes, Samuel. *The Auden Generation: Literature and Politics in England in the 1930s*. Princeton, NJ: Princeton University Press, 1976.

——. 'The Voice of Exile: Auden in 1940,' *Sewanee Review*, 90: 1 (January–March 1982), 31–52.

Irigaray, Luce. *Speculum of the Other Woman*, trans Gillian C. Gill. Ithaca, NY: Cornell University Press, 1985; orig. French 1974.

Isherwood, Christopher. *Christopher and His Kind*. New York: Farrar, Straus, Giroux, 1976.

James, Clive. *At the Pillars of Hercules*. London: Faber & Faber, 1979.

Jameson, Fredric. *The Ideologies of Theory, Essays 1971–86*, vol. 2: *Syntax of History*, Theory and History of Literature Series 49. Minneapolis: University of Minnesota Press, 1988.

——. *Nationalism, Colonialism and Literature: Modernism and Imperialism*, Field Day Pamphlet No. 14. Derry: Field Day Theatre Company, 1988.

Jay, Martin. 'Scopic Regimes of Modernity,' in *Vision and Visuality*, ed. Hal Foster. Seattle, WA: Bay Press, 1988, 3–23.

Jeffares, A. Norman. *A New Commentary on the Poems of W. B. Yeats*. Stanford, CA: Stanford University Press, 1984.

—— (ed.). *W. B. Yeats: The Critical Heritage*. London: Routledge & Kegan Paul, 1977.

Jenkinson, Biddy. 'A Letter to An Editor,' *Irish University Review*, 4: 21 (1991), 34.

John, Brian. *Reading the Ground: The Poetry of Thomas Kinsella*. Washington, DC: Catholic University of America, 1996.

Johnston, Dillon. 'The Go-Between of Recent Irish Poetry,' in *Cultural Contexts and Literary Idioms in Contemporary Irish Literature*, ed. Michael Kennealy. Gerrards Cross: Colin Smythe; New York: Barnes & Noble, 1988, 172–85.

——. *Irish Poetry After Joyce*, rev. edn. Syracuse, NY: Syracuse University Press, 1997.

——. '"Our bodies' eyes and writing hands"; Secrecy and Sensuality in Ní Chuilleanáin's Baroque Art,' in *Gender and Sexuality in Modern Ireland*, eds. Anthony Bradley and Maryann Valiulis (Amherst: University of Massachusetts Press, 1997), 187–211.

——. *'Poetic Discoveries and Inventions of America,'* *Colby Review*, special edition edited by Eamon Grennan, XXVIII: 4 (December 1992), 202–15.

——. 'Q. & A. with Blake Morrison' (An Interview), *Irish Literary Supplement*, 8: 2 (Fall 1989), 18–19.

Jones, David. *In Parenthesis*. London: Faber & Faber, 1937, 1963.

Jones, L. E. *Druid Shaman Priest*. Middlesex: Hisarlik Press, 1998.

Joyce, James. *A Portrait of the Artist As A Young Man*, ed. Seamus Deane. London: Penguin, 1992.

——. *Ulysses*, ed. Hans Gabler. New York: Random House, 1986.

Kearney, Richard (ed.). *The Irish Mind: Exploring Intellectual Traditions*. Dublin: Wolfhound Press, 1985.

Kelleher, John V. 'Matthew Arnold and the Celtic Revival,' in *Perspectives of Criticism*, ed. Harry Levin. Cambridge, MA: Harvard University Press, 1950.

Kendall, Tim. *Paul Muldoon*. London: Faber & Faber, 1996.

Kennedy, David. *New Relations*. Mid Glamorgan, Wales: Seren Books, 1996.

Kenner, Hugh. *The Pound Era*. Berkeley: University of California Press, 1971.

——. 'Thomas Kinsella: An Anecdote and Some Reflections,' in *The Genres of Irish Revival*, ed. Ronald Schleifer. Dublin: Wolfhound Press, 1980, 179–87.

Kerrigan, John. 'Hidden Ireland: Eiléan Ní Chuilleanáin and Munster Poetry,' *Critical Quarterly*, 40: 4 (Winter 1998), 76–100.

Kershaw, Nora (trans.). *Anglo-Saxon and Norse Poems*. Cambridge: Cambridge University Press, 1922.

Kiberd, Declan. *Inventing Ireland: The Literature of the Modern Nation*. London: Jonathan Cape, 1995.

——. *Synge and the Irish Language*. 2nd edn. Dublin: Gill & Macmillan, 1993.

Kinsella, Thomas. *Collected Poems 1956–1994*. Oxford: Oxford University Press, 1996.

——. 'The Irish Writer,' in *The Field Day Anthology of Irish Writing*, gen. ed. Seamus Deane, vol. III. Derry: Field Day, 1991, 625–9.

Langbaum, Robert. *The Poetry of Experience*. New York: W. W. Norton, 1963.

Laplanche, Jean and J.-B. Pontalis. *The Language of Psycho-Analysis*, trans. Donald Nicholson-Smith. New York: W. W. Norton, 1973.

Larkin, Philip. *Collected Poems*, ed. and intro. Anthony Thwaite. London: Faber & Faber Marvell Press, 1988.

——. *Required Writing: Miscellaneous Pieces 1955–1982*. London: Faber & Faber, 1983.

——. *Selected Letters: 1940–1985*, ed. Anthony Thwaite. London: Faber & Faber, 1992.

Leach, Edmund. *Social Anthropology*. Oxford: Oxford University Press, 1982 (cited in *PMLA*, 114).

Leavis, F. R. *For Continuity*. Freeport, NY: Books for Libraries Press, 1968; 1933.

——. *Letters in Criticism*, ed. John Tasker. London: Chatto & Windus, 1974.

——. *New Bearings in English Poetry*, new edn. London: Chatto & Windus, 1950; 1932.

——. Review of *Another Time*, in *Scrutiny*, IX: 1 (June 1940), 200.

—— and Q. D. Leavis. *Lectures in America*. New York: Pantheon, 1967.

Leavis, Q. D. 'The Background of Twentieth Century Letters,' *Scrutiny*, 8: 1 (June 1939), 72–7.

Lee, J. J. *Ireland 1912–1985: Politics and Society*. Cambridge: Cambridge University Press, 1989.

Lloyd, David. *Anomalous State: Irish Writing and the Post-Colonial Moment*. Durham, NC: Duke University Press, 1993.

——. *Nationalism and Minor Literature: James Clarence Mangan and the Emergence of Irish Cultural Nationalism*. Berkeley: University of California Press, 1987.

—— and Paul Thomas. *Culture and the State*. New York and London: Routledge, 1998.

Longley, Edna. *The Living Stream: Literature and Revisionism in Ireland*. Newcastle upon Tyne: Bloodaxe Books, 1994.

——. *Louis MacNeice: A Study*. London: Faber & Faber, 1988.

——. *Poetry in the Wars*. Newcastle upon Tyne: Bloodaxe Books, 1986.

Longley, Michael. *Selected Poems*. London: Jonathan Cape; Winston-Salem, NC: Wake Forest University Press, 1999.

——. *The Weather in Japan*. London: Jonathan Cape, 1999; Winston-Salem, NC: Wake Forest University Press, 2000.

Lucas, John. *Modern English Poetry from Hardy to Hughes*. Totowa, NJ: Barnes & Noble, 1986.

Lucy, Sean. 'Metre and Movement in Anglo-Irish Verse,' *Irish University Review*, 8: 2 (Autumn 1978), 151–77.

McAuley, James W. 'Cuchullain and an RPG-7: the Ideology and Politics of the Ulster Defence Association,' in *Culture and Politics in Northern Ireland 1960–1990*, ed. Eamon Hughes. Milton Keynes: Open University Press, 1991, 45–68.

McCorquodale, Charles. *The Baroque Painters of Italy*. Oxford: Phaidon, 1979.

McDonald, Peter. *Louis MacNeice: The Poet in His Contexts*. Oxford: Clarendon Press, 1991.

——. *Mistaken Identities: Poetry in Northern Ireland*. Oxford: Clarendon Press, 1997.

——. 'Seamus Heaney as a Critic,' *Poetry in Contemporary Irish Literature*, ed. Michael Kenneally, Studies in Contemporary Irish Literature No. 2. Gerrards Cross: Colin Smythe, 1995, 175–89.

McGann, Jerome. *Black Riders: The Visible Language of Modernism*. Princeton, NJ: Princeton University Press, 1993.

MacIntyre, Alasdair. 'Poetry as Political Philosophy: Notes on Burke and Yeats,' in *On Modern Poetry: Essays Presented to Donald Davie*, eds Vereen Bell and Laurence Lerner. Nashville, TN: Vanderbilt University Press, 1988.

MacKillop, James. *Dictionary of Celtic Mythology*. Oxford: Oxford University Press, 1998.

MacNeice, Louis. *The Collected Poems of Louis MacNeice*, ed. E. R. Dodds. London: Faber & Faber, 1966.

——. *Modern Poetry*. New York: Haskell House, 1969, 1938.

——. *The Poetry of W. B. Yeats*. New York: Oxford University Press, 1941.

——. *The Poetry of W. B. Yeats*, foreword by Richard Ellmann. London: Faber & Faber, 1967.

——. *Selected Poems*, ed. Michael Longley. Winston-Salem, NC: Wake Forest University Press; London: Faber & Faber, 1990.

Magnusson, Magnus (Gen. Ed.). *Cambridge Biographical Dictionary*. Cambridge: Cambridge University Press, 1990.

Mahon, Derek. *Selected Poems*. Oldcastle: Gallery Press; Oxford: Oxford University Press; New York: Viking, 1991.

Malraux, André. *Museum Without Walls*, trans. Stuart Gilbert and Francis Price. Garden City, NJ: Doubleday, 1967.

Martin, Augustine. 'Donald Davie and Ireland,' in *Donald Davie and the Responsibilities of Literature*, ed. George Dekker. Manchester: Carcanet, 1983, 49–63.

Meisel, Perry. *The Myth of the Modern: A Study in British Literature and Criticism after 1850*. New Haven, CT: Yale University Press, 1987.

Mendelson, Edward. *Early Auden.* New York: Viking Press, 1981.

Miller, J. Hillis. 'History As Repetition in Thomas Hardy's Poetry: The Example of "Wessex Heights,"' Stratford-upon-Avon Studies No. IX (London, 1972), 223–54; reprinted in *Thomas Hardy Critical Assessments*, ed. G. Clarke, vol. II. Mountfield, East Sussex: Helm, 1993.

Miller, Liam. *Dolmen XXV: An Illustrated Bibliography of the Dolmen Press 1951–1976.* Portlaoise: Dolmen Press, 1976.

Mitchell, W. J. T. *Picture Theory: Essays on Verbal and Visual Representation.* Chicago: University of Chicago Press, 1994.

Montague, John. *Collected Poems.* Oldcastle: Gallery Press; Winston-Salem, NC: Wake Forest University Press, 1995.

Monteith, Charles. 'Eliot in the Office,' *Grand Street*, 9: 3 (Spring 1990), 90–100.

Morgan, Charles. *The House of Macmillan, 1843–1943.* New York: Macmillan (now Palgrave), 1944.

Morrison, Blake and Andrew Motion. *The Penguin Book of Contemporary British Poetry.* London: Penguin, 1982.

Motion, Andrew. *Philip Larkin: A Writer's Life.* London: Faber & Faber, 1993.

Mowat, Charles Loch. *Britain Between the Wars, 1918–1940.* London: Methuen, 1955.

Muldoon, Paul. *The Annals of Chile.* London: Faber & Faber, 1994; New York: Farrar, Straus, Giroux, 1995.

——. 'Getting Round: Notes Towards an *Ars Poetica*,' The F.W. Bateson Memorial Lecture, Oxford University, 1998, in *Essays in Criticism*, XLVIII: 2 (April 1998), 107–28.

——. *Quoof.* Winston-Salem, NC: Wake Forest University Press, 1983.

——. *To Ireland, I.* The Clarendon Lectures in English Literature 1998. Oxford: Oxford University Press, 2000.

Murphy, Shane. 'Clearing Rooms,' *Graph*, 2nd Series: 2 (1996), 102–15.

Nairn, Tom. *The Break-Up of Britain: Crisis and Neo-Nationalism.* London: New Left Books, 1977.

*New Larousse Encyclopedia of Mythology*, intro. Robert Graves, trans. Richard Aldington and Delano Ames. New York: Hamlyn, 1968.

Newbolt, Henry. *The Later Life and Letters of Sir Henry Newbolt*, ed. Margaret Newbolt. London: Faber & Faber, 1942.

——. *A New Study of English Poetry.* London: Constable, 1917; New York: E. P. Dutton, 1919.

——. *Selected Poems of Henry Newbolt*, ed. Patric Dickinson. London: Hodder & Stoughton, 1981.

Ní Chuilleanáin, Eiléan. 'Acts and Monuments of an Unelected Nation: The *Cailleach* Writes about the Renaissance,' *Southern Review*, 31: 3 (July 1995), 570–80.

——. *The Brazen Serpent.* Oldcastle: Gallery Press, 1994; Winston-Salem, NC: Wake Forest University Press, 1995.

——. *The Magdalene Sermon.* Oldcastle: Gallery Press, 1989.

——. *The Magdalene Sermon and Earlier Poems.* Winston-Salem, NC: Wake Forest University Press, 1991.

Ní Dhomhnaill, Nuala. *The Astrakhan Cloak*, trans. Paul Muldoon. Oldcastle: Gallery Press, 1992; Winston-Salem, NC: Wake Forest University Press, 1993.

Norrie, Ian. *Mumby's Publishing and Bookselling in the Twentieth Century.* London: Bell & Human, 1982.

Nowell-Smith, Simon (ed.). *Letters to Macmillan*. London: Macmillan (now Palgrave), 1967.

O'Brien, Conor Cruise. *The Great Melody: A Thematic Biography and Commented Anthology of Edmund Burke*. Chicago: University of Chicago Press, 1992.

O'Brien, Sean. *The Deregulated Muse*. Newcastle upon Tyre: Bloodaxe, 1998.

O'Donoghue, Bernard. 'The Master's Voice-Right,' *Irish Times*, 9 October, Weekend, 8.

——. 'The Translators' Voice: Irish Poetry before Yeats,' *Princeton University Library Chronicle*, LIX: 3 (Spring 1998), 299–320.

Osborne, Charles. *W. H. Auden: The Life of A Poet*. New York: Harcourt Brace Jovanovich, 1979.

Owen, Wilfred. *The Poems of Wilfred Owen*, ed. Jon Stallworthy. New York and Oxford: W. W. Norton, 1986.

Palgrave, Francis Turner. *The Golden Treasury of the Best Songs and Lyrical Poems in the English Language*. London: Oxford University Press, 1951.

Parry, Benita. 'Problems in Current Theories of Colonial Discourse,' *Oxford Literary Review*, 9: 1–2 (1987), 27–58.

Paulin, Tom. *Ireland and the English Crisis*. Newcastle upon Tyne: Bloodaxe, 1984.

——. *Thomas Hardy: The Poetry of Perception*, 2nd edn. London: Macmillan (now Palgrave), 1986.

Perse, Saint-John. 'Andre Gide: 1909,' *Sewanee Review*, LX: 4 (October–December, 1952), 593–604.

Philip, Neil. *The Penguin Book of English Folktales*. London: Penguin, 1992.

Ray, Kevin. 'Interview with Eiléan Ní Chuilleanáin,' *Éire-Ireland*, 31: 2 (Spring/Summer 1996), 62–73.

Richards, I. A. *Science and Poetry*, 2nd edn. London: Keegan Paul, Trench, Trubner, 1935.

Ricks, Christopher. *The Force of Poetry*. Oxford: Clarendon, 1985.

Riffaterre, Michael. 'Textuality: W. H. Auden's "Musée des Beaux Arts,"' in *Textual Analysis: Some Readers Reading*, ed. Mary Ann Caws. New York: Modern Language Association, 1986, 1–13.

Rivers, W. H. R. *Conflict and Dream*. London: Kegan Paul, 1923.

Roche, Anthony. 'A Reading of *Autumn Journal*: The Question of Louis MacNeice's Irishness,' *Text and Context*, 3 (1988).

Rodgers, W. R. (ed.). *Irish Literary Portraits*. New York: Taplinger, 1973.

Rodway, Allan. *A Preface to Auden*. London: Longman, 1984.

Rosenberg, Carolyn. *Let Our Gaze Blaze: The Recent Poetry of Thomas Kinsella*. PhD dissertation, Kent State University, 1980.

Ruskin, John. *The Works of John Ruskin*, eds E. T. Cook and Alexander Wederburn. London: George Allen, 1904, vol. 10.

Sagar, Keith. *The Art of Ted Hughes*. 2nd edition. London: Cambridge University Press, 1978.

Said, Edward. *Culture and Imperialism*. New York: Knopf, 1993.

Sedgwick, Eve Kosofsky. *Tendencies*. Durham, NC: Duke University Press, 1993.

Shell, Marc. *Money, Language, and Thought*. Baltimore, MD: Johns Hopkins University Press, 1982, 1993.

Shields, Hugh. *Narrative Singing in Ireland. Lays, Ballads, Come-All-Yes and Other Songs*. Blackrock: Irish Academic Press, 1993.

Simmel, Georg. *On Individuality and Social Forms*, ed. Donald N. Levine. Chicago: University of Chicago Press, 1971.

Sinfield, Alan. *Society and Literature, 1945–1970*. New York: Holmes & Meier, 1973.

——. *The Wilde Century: Effeminacy, Oscar Wilde and the Queer Moment*. New York: Columbia University Press, 1994.

Spender, Stephen. *The Thirties and After: Poetry, Politics, People, 1933–1970*. New York: Random House, 1978.

Stallworthy, Jon. *Wilfred Owen*. London: Oxford University Press/Chatto & Windus, 1974.

Steiner, George. *On Difficulty and Other Essays*. New York: Oxford University Press, 1978.

Stocking, George W. *Victorian Anthropology*. New York: Free Press, 1987.

Stuart, Robert, 'Ted Hughes,' in *British Poetry Since 1970: A Critical Survey*, eds Peter Jones and Michael Schmidt. Manchester: Carcanet, 1980, 75–84.

Swarbrick, Andrew. *Out of Reach: The Poetry of Philip Larkin*. New York: St. Martin's Press (now Palgrave), 1995.

*The Táin*, trans. Thomas Kinsella with drawings by Louis Le Brocquy. Oxford: Oxford University Press, 1970.

*The Teaching of English in England: Being the Report of the Departmental Committee Appointed by the President of the Board of Education to Inquire into the Position of English in the Educational System of England* (London: HMSO, 1921).

Tolley, A. T. *The Poetry of the Thirties*. London: Gollancz, 1975.

Torchiana, Donald T. *W. B. Yeats and Georgian Ireland*. Evanston, IL: Northwestern University Press, 1966.

Turner, Paul. *The Life of Thomas Hardy*. Oxford: Blackwell, 1998.

Waterhouse, Ellis. *Italian Baroque Painting*. London: Phaidon Press, 1962.

Webb, Timothy. 'Yeats and the English,' in *The Internationalism of Irish Literature and Drama*, ed. Joseph McMinn. Savage, MD: Barnes & Noble, 1992, 232–41.

Weeks, Jeffrey. *Sex, Politics and Society: The Regulation of Sexuality Since 1800*, 2nd edn, Themes in British Social History Series. London: Longman, 1989.

Weiskel, Thomas. *The Romantic Sublime*. Baltimore, MD: Johns Hopkins University Press, 1976, 1986.

Whalen, Terry. *Philip Larkin and English Poetry*. Vancouver: University of British Columbia Press, 1986.

Wheatley, David. 'An Estranged Spirit,' *Brangle* (Belfast), 2 (1997), 8–11.

Whitaker, Thomas R. *Swan and Shadow: Yeats's Dialogue with History*. Chapel Hill: University of North Carolina Press, 1964.

White, Geoffrey H. (ed.). *The Complete Peerage*, vol. XII. London: St Catherine Press, 1953.

Whitehead, Frank. 'F. R. Leavis and the Schools,' in *The Leavises: Recollections and Impressions*, ed. Denys Thompson. Cambridge: Cambridge University Press, 1984, 140–52.

Widdowson, Peter (ed.). *Re-reading English*. London: Methuen, 1982.

Wilde, Oscar. *The Artist as Critic: Critical Writings of Oscar Wilde*, ed. Richard Ellmann. Chicago: University of Chicago Press, 1969.

Williams, Merryn. *Thomas Hardy and Rural England*. New York: Columbia University Press, 1972.

Williams, Raymond. *The Country and the City*. New York: Oxford University Press, 1973.

——. *Culture and Society: 1780–1950*. New York: Columbia University Press, 1958, 1983.

Wordsworth, William. *Selected Prose*, ed. John O. Hayden. London: Penguin Books, 1988.

Yeats. W. B. *Autobiographies: Memories and Reflections*. London: Bracken Books, 1955.

——. *Collected Letters of W. B. Yeats*, Vol. III, eds John Kelly and Ronald Schuchard. Oxford: Clarendon, 1994.

——. *Essays and Introductions* New York: Macmillan (now Palgrave), 1961.

——. *Explorations*, selected by Mrs W. B. Yeats. New York: Macmillan (now Palgrave), 1962.

——. *The Letters of W. B. Yeats*, ed. Allan Wade. New York: Macmillan (now Palgrave), 1955.

—— (ed.). *The Oxford Book of Modern Verse, 1892–1935*. Oxford: Oxford University Press, 1936.

——. *The Poems of W. B. Yeats*, ed. Richard J. Finneran. New York: Macmillan (now Palgrave), 1983.

——. *Uncollected Prose, 1: First Reviews and Articles, 1886–1896*, collected and edited by John P Frayne. New York: Columbia University Press, 1970.

——. *Uncollected Prose, 2: Reviews, Articles and other Miscellaneous Prose, 1897–1939*, collected and edited by John P. Frayne and Colton Johnson. New York: Columbia University Press, 1976.

——. *A Vision*. London: Macmillan (now Palgrave), 1937; reissued with revisions, New York: Collier Books, 1966.

# Index

Yeats, William Butler, xi, xii, xiii, xv,
1, 2, 3, 9, 14, 19–24, 26, 47, 48,
49–52, 53–64, 66, 69, 71, 73, 76,
78, 81, 96, 99, 101, 122, 124, 125,
128, 149, 156, 159, 161, 162, 190,
195, 206–7, 209n, 211n, 212n,
216n, 218n, 221n
Merrion Square, 3; Woburn
Building, 3; ambivalence, 112;
and 1923 Nobel Prize, 24; and
A. E., 124; and Arnold, 39–43;
and Auden, 108–12; and
Berkeley, 49–50, 216n; and
Cuchulain, 52; and
*dinnseanchas*, 18; and Dublin
Lockout, 4; and Emma Hardy,
5; and First World War poets,
25; and the Irish language, 21;
and Irish otherworld 162; and
the mask, 48; and modernism,
21, 55; and Parnell, 52; and
Thomas Hardy, 1; and
translation, 22; and Vico, 110;
and Wilde, 49, 87; annual
pension, 2; antipathy to
Catholic Church, 2; Byzantium
poems, 67; de-Anglicize
Ireland, 55; in England, 3;
interest in ethnology, 21;
interest in philology, 21; Irish
homes, 3; Leavis' criticism,
65–71, 94; Macmillan's
rejection of, 62; New Irish
Library, 62; Nietzschean
influence, 38; *Poetry* (Chicago),
3; pre-Raphaelites, 162; reaction
to Wyndham Act, 35; reading
Burke's *Letters, Speeches and
Tracts on Irish Affairs*, 38;
relation to Burke and Arnold,
34; relation to Burke, 36; Sligo,
3, 21; speech to Irish Literary
Society, 36; Thoor Ballylee, 3
'1919', 112
'All Things Can Tempt Me', 176
'Among School Children', 20, 67
'At the Abbey Theatre', 4
'Blood and the Moon', 38
'The Cap and Bells', 63

'The Child and the State', 212n
'Circus Animals' Desertion', 8, 71
'The Cold Heaven', 22, 196
'The Dawn', 19, 109
'Dialogue of Self and Soul', 156
'Easter, 1916', 112
'The Fisherman', 18, 19, 109
'High Talk', 7, 71–2
'Hound Voice', 174
'In Memory of Major Robert
Gregory', 112
'Lapis Lazuli', 51, 95, 111
'The Man and the Echo', 111, 196
'Meditations in Time of Civil
War', 112
'A Memory of Youth', 165
'On Those That Hated *The Playboy
of the Western World*, 1907', 3,
52–3
'A Prayer for my Daughter',
36, 211n
'Red Hanrahan's Song about
Ireland', 174
'Ribh Considers Christian Love
Insufficient', 38
'The Rose of Battle', 51
'The Tower', 110
'The Wanderings of Oisin', 162,
221n
'Sailing to Byzantium', 67–8, 111
'The Secret Rose', 63
'September, 1913', 4
'The Seven Sages', 36
'The Song of the Old Mother', 63
'The Song of Wandering Aengus',
19, 63
'The Spirit Medium', 8
'Supernatural Songs', 125
'The Three Beggars', 19, 109
'To a Friend Whose Work has Come
to Nothing', 19, 109
'To a Wealthy Man', 4
'Under Ben Bulben', 110
'Upon a House Shaken by the Land
Agitation', 35
*Collected Works in Verse and Prose*, 24
*Explorations*, 216n
*Fairy and Folk Tales of the Irish
Peasantry*, 22